Racing Post Floor 7, The Podium, South Bank Tower Estate, 30 Stamford Street, London, SE1 9LS. 0203 034 8900

Editor Nick Pulford
Art editor David Dew
Cover design Duncan Olner
Chief photographers Edward Whitaker, Patrick McCann
Other photography Alain Barr, Mark Cranham, Getty, John Grossick, Caroline Norris
Picture artworking Stefan Searle
Feature writers Mark Boylan, Scott Burton, David Carr, Steve Dennis, Andrew Dietz, Richard Forristal, Jonathan Harding, David Jennings, Lee Mottershead, Julian Muscat, Lewis Porteous, Nick Pulford, John Randall, Alan Sweetman, Sam Walker

Archant Dialogue
Advertising Sales
Gary Millone, 01603 772463, gary.millone@archantdialogue.co.uk
Advertising Production Manager
Kay Brown, 01603 772522, kay.brown@archantdialogue.co.uk
Prospect House, Rouen Road, Norwich NR1 1RE. 01603 772554
archantdialogue.co.uk

Distribution/availability
01933 304858 help@racingpost.com

Published by Pitch Publishing on behalf of Racing Post, A2 Yeoman Gate, Yeoman Way, Worthing, Sussex, BN13 3QZ

A CIP catalogue record is available for this book from the British Library.

ISBN 9781785318337

Printed in Great Britain by Pureprint Group

racingpost.com/shop

WELCOME to the tenth edition of the Racing Post Annual. It is a milestone we are proud to reach, although for some time this year, along with so many aspects of our lives big and small, it was thrown into doubt.

With British and Irish racing in lockdown for 11 weeks, it was unclear how much action there would be to fill our 224 pages. Thankfully, for those who love this great sport, racing's return at the start of June was one of the success stories in a world turned upside down by the coronavirus pandemic.

It has to be acknowledged, of course, that there are more serious things than sport. Never has the old adage of racing as a mere triviality, coined by the Timeform sage Phil Bull, seemed so apposite than in this most dreadful year. Yet it is also true that racing is an important business, supporting many thousands of livelihoods, and it plays a vital part in the lives of millions as a form of entertainment and escapism. That, too, has been brought home to us in clear terms this year.

And so to the racing. There was plenty of it, both before and after lockdown, and one of the central themes – as we show on the front cover – was the sense of things carrying on just as before with the repeat big-race successes of Al Boum Photo, Enable, Stradivarius, Battaash and Magical.

There were plenty of new stars, including Love, Ghaiyyath and Mohaather, and we also salute the people for whom this will be a memorable year in a sporting sense – among them Barry Geraghty, Paul Townend, Hollie Doyle, Tom Marquand, Donnacha O'Brien, Brian Hughes and Jim Crowley.

Their achievements helped to raise our spirits in this immensely challenging year and we hope you enjoy reading about them again in these pages.

Above all, we wish all our readers the best of health.

Nick Pulford

Nick Pulford
Editor

CONTENTS

BIG STORIES

88

84

188

136

196
OXTED

120

The Lady and The Champ

Enable and Frankie Dettori had one last fling in 2020, making history in the King George but falling short again in the Arc

By Lee Mottershead

ON AN autumn day in Paris, the world capital of love, there were two lovers. As one held the other, it was obvious a parting was taking place before our eyes. It was not a final goodbye, for granted good health and fair fortune, Frankie Dettori will still have many a moment to share with his darling Enable. Here, however, it felt as though something between them was ending. What a something it had been.

No horse in history has ever amassed a finer record in the Prix de l'Arc de Triomphe. Not, however, in this particular Arc. The story of this season, just like the story of the previous season, had ultimately ended in defeat. Her first attempt to make history had so narrowly failed. This second effort played out altogether differently, the loss more comprehensive than any she had ever experienced.

An extraordinary piece of history would not be hers, yet many a record had already been broken. There are still eight dual winners of the Arc but none also managed a second-place finish in the sport's supreme championship. Nor, indeed, had any horse except Enable secured Arc glory on two different racecourses. For all that she did on four October afternoons the evergreen mare sits atop this great French monument. In what proved to be her swansong campaign, there was a further mountain Enable climbed higher than any horse who had gone before.

▸▸ *Continues page 6*

ENABLE

It was the dream of a third success at Longchamp, not a 'three-peat' in the King George VI and Queen Elizabeth Stakes, that had so sportingly led Khalid Abdullah to allow his most precious mare to race for one more year. For three to truly have become the magic number, that greatest of all destiny dates had to be met with success.

It was not, nowhere near in fact, yet by once again placing her name on the honour roll of Britain's Arc equivalent, Enable ensured Abdullah's bravery had been vindicated. On her return to Paris, Enable was unable to claim the maillot jaune. That will always be a cause for regret, but at Ascot in July she was victorious on the most important of summer stages.

****

THE farewell tour had begun at Sandown. The expectation, or certainly the hope, had been that Royal Ascot would be graced by Enable for the first time, but it came and went with Nathaniel's now six-year-old daughter passing the time in her box at John Gosden's Clarehaven Stables.

In this strangest of seasons, it was feared Covid-19 could cause the royal meeting's abandonment. Gosden was adamant it would have been wrong to prepare his yard's number-one resident for a target that failed to materialise. The two races for which Enable was being considered, the Prince of Wales's Stakes and Hardwicke Stakes, both did take place and were won by horses trained by Gosden. So far, so good.

It was in the Coral-Eclipse that we first got to reacquaint ourselves with Enable, although it was an eerie sort of welcome. None of Enable's four races in 2020 were staged in front of paying customers. At Sandown that was a particular shame because had fans been permitted entry, they would have seen more of Enable than they had ever seen before.

Speaking after her retirement was announced, Dettori's able deputy Rab Havlin recalled riding Enable on the day in November 2016 when she stormed home at Newcastle on what proved to be her only juvenile outing. "She was just a big, plain old thing," said Havlin, evidently not much of a romantic. At Sandown on what was

'She's the horse I've loved the most'

Frankie Dettori rode Enable in every one of her 14 Group 1 starts, emerging victorious in 11 of them, and he paid this emotional tribute on her retirement

It's been an amazing journey for the last three and a half, four years. The Arc this year unfortunately didn't work out. It was the worst performance of her career, so I'm not surprised at the decision. She owes nobody anything, she's been an absolutely super mare.

I did have a cry last night when I was told but more of joy than sadness because of all the great memories she gave me. She's the horse I've loved the most in all my career, she really touched my heart. I'm pleased she bows out of the sport in one piece.

It's very easy to say but she has got by far the best CV of any great horse I've ridden. Her longevity and the performances over the last four years have been incredible. When I rode Golden Horn I thought, "Oh God, I'll never get another horse like him", and then she turns up and she fills in the gap.

Because she's been around for so long I've got very attached to her. I was tearful last night and of course it's emotional but today I went to see her and I'll always remember her for the good stuff.

Enable's trophy cabinet

King George 🏆🏆🏆
Arc 🏆🏆
Yorkshire Oaks 🏆🏆
Eclipse 🏆
Oaks 🏆
Irish Oaks 🏆
Breeders' Cup Turf 🏆
Starts 19
Wins 15
Prize-money £10,724,320
Racing Post Rating 129

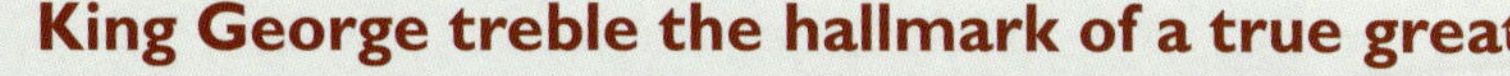

King George treble the hallmark of a true great

Enable's unique three King Georges and record-equalling two Arcs, plus her Group 1 and prize-money records and long winning streak, have earned her an exalted place in racing history.

Her victory in this year's King George VI and Queen Elizabeth Stakes, admittedly against only two rivals, made her the only three-time winner of that Ascot prize. Previously, only Dahlia and Swain had won it twice.

Few of the world's great races have been won three times by the same mare and only Winx has surpassed her in that respect, being the first four-time winner of the Cox Plate (2015-18), Australia's premier weight-for-age race.

The other historic female triple winners have been Kincsem (Grosser Preis von Baden 1877-79), Hyeres (Grand Steeple-Chase de Paris 1964-66), Makybe Diva (Melbourne Cup 2003-05) and Goldikova (Breeders' Cup Mile 2008-10).

In 2017 Enable became unique among fillies and mares in winning Europe's top two weight-for-age races, the King George and the Arc, in the same season. Only six colts have achieved that double.

She is one of only three fillies or mares to win the Arc twice, along with Corrida and Treve, and one of eight dual winners in all. She also became the sole Arc winner to follow up at the Breeders' Cup when landing the Turf in 2018.

Enable scored 11 Group/Grade 1 victories, beating Frankel's record of ten by a horse trained in Britain. The world record is 25 by Winx (2015-19) and the record for a Flat horse trained in Europe is 14 by Goldikova (2008-11).

In her five-season career she earned £10,724,320 in prize-money, at one point beating Highland Reel's record for a horse trained in Europe before herself being surpassed by Thunder Snow, whose second Dubai World Cup win took him past £12 million.

By winning 12 consecutive races up to her defeat in the 2019 Arc, she became only the third filly or mare trained in Britain or Ireland since 1900 to compile such a long winning streak. The others were Pretty Polly (15 including the fillies' Triple Crown in 1904) and Sweet Wall (13, notably the 1928 Irish Cambridgeshire).

Enable achieved her highest Racing Post Rating of 129 in her first Arc. The highest-rated filly or mare trained in Britain since RPRs were introduced in 1988 is still Bosra Sham (130); the top in Europe are Goldikova and Treve (both 131); and the best anywhere in the world is Australian star Black Caviar (133). The overall greatest is Frankel (143).

JOHN RANDALL

Biggest prize-money earners on the Flat trained in Britain and Ireland

Thunder Snow **£12,671,799**
ENABLE **£10,724,320**
Highland Reel **£7,513,355**
Benbatl **£5,829,203**
So You Think **£5,058,956**
Found **£5,058,029**
Red Cadeaux **£4,998,408**
Postponed **£4,995,979**
St Nicholas Abbey **£4,954,590**
Monterosso **£4,780,239**

** Figures correct at time of Enable's retirement*

▲ Queen of the King George: Enable scores her historic third win in the Ascot showpiece (main picture) for a delighted Frankie Dettori (inset top left); her wins in 2017 (inset top right) and 2019 (inset bottom right); below left, Arc triumphs in 2017 and 2018; below, the Racing Post front page the day after Arc defeat in her final race

RACING POST
No fairytale in Paris
Sottsass lands Arc but Dettori leads outpouring of love for Enable

for the first time Eclipse Sunday, she was bigger, not simply through age but because at this more mature stage of her racing life it was taking a little longer for her to reach full fitness.

Like Havlin, Gosden can do straight talking. He had said Enable would need the run prior to her triumph in the 2019 Eclipse. This time he stressed she really would need the run, having been slow to blossom and trim down. Mindful not to embarrass the sport's leading lady, he declined to publicly reveal her weight but did offer a figure on her fitness – and 85 per cent was never going to be sufficient if Godolphin's front-running galloper Ghaiyyath performed to his best. With Enable two and a quarter lengths behind him at the line, that's what Ghaiyyath did.

****

COME King George day there were not even two and a quarter opponents to face Enable. Twelve months earlier she had duelled with Crystal Ocean up Ascot's home straight in a finish that evoked memories of Grundy and Bustino. There had been 11 runners on that occasion, including raiders from France and Japan. This time there were only three runners representing two countries and two trainers. There should at least have been a quartet, but Anthony Van Dyck's defection left Aidan O'Brien with just Japan and Sovereign. They were not enough.

Such was the manner in which Enable gained her third King George, one that moved her past dual champions Dahlia and Swain, it is highly improbable Ballydoyle could have fielded any challenger to trouble the 4-9 favourite. This was her 11th Group 1 triumph.

Against Enable's name were now three King Georges, two Arcs, two Yorkshire Oaks, an Eclipse, Oaks, Irish Oaks and a Breeders' Cup Turf. She would not add to that top-flight tally but the final success at the highest level was achieved in style.

"What a mare she has been," said commentator Simon Holt as Enable approached the stalls. What a mare she had been and what a mare she still was. It could not have been easier. With the two-furlong pole passed and Sovereign almost caught, Dettori savoured a long look over his left

▸▸ *Continues page 8*

shoulder and saw Ryan Moore flat out and going nowhere fast on Japan. Enable was still cruising.

"I couldn't believe it," said Dettori, before comparing the empty grandstands with the near emptiness behind him. "Look, first of all there is nobody here. Then I thought: 'Where is he?' I was surprised he was so far back and off the bridle because he's a good tool. It's great. She was like a hot knife through butter today."

She was also drenched. On this day, as on so many days when Enable raced, the heavens had opened. Unsurprisingly, the weather did nothing to diminish her adoring jockey's enthusiasm.

"The girl is back!" screamed Dettori as he made his way to the now obligatory post-race Zoom conference. "Good for the sport – and good for my wallet," he gleefully pointed out and then showed further delight when reminded he had equalled Lester Piggott's record of seven King George triumphs.

"Seven King Georges!" he shouted. "Can you imagine? I remember when the Queen gave me the trophy after one of my early ones. I was talking to her and said that it was my third or fourth King George. She turned around to me and said: 'Well, Lester won seven.' She put me straight back in my box. Well, now I've done it!"

★★★★

HE HAD and so had she. The next time she did it, and for the final time in Britain, was at Kempton, where a September Stakes penalty kick was preferred by Gosden over what would inevitably have been a much more arduous encounter with Love in the Yorkshire Oaks. Heavy ground at Longchamp eventually meant a showdown with the season's dominant three-year-old filly never happened. There was no semblance of a showdown about the Kempton race. Enable had been quoted by bookmakers at 1-5 in the morning. As off time approached, the only bookmaker in the racecourse ring was offering 1-16. They were fair odds. As expected, it was all so simple.

It was also the final time Gosden would see the most celebrated horse he has ever trained race in the flesh,

Continues page 10

End of the affair: Enable and Frankie Dettori go to post before the Arc

L. DETTORI
8
QATAR

not because he was peeved Enable tried to kick him when saddling up, but because quarantine rules meant a trainer who went to Longchamp would not have been able to attend the following week's opening leg of the Tattersalls October Yearling Sale. When he spoke at Kempton, Gosden knew he would have to watch the Arc from home.

"Very likely, very possible," he admitted. "I don't want to get emotional about it because we have to build up to the Arc. We can have a drink after that, one of sorrow or one of joy, we'll see."

It would be one of sorrow. France Galop had been poised to allow a crowd of 5,000 into Longchamp. That would have created some sort of meaningful atmosphere. Instead, with Covid cases rising in Paris, only 1,000 spectators, none of them paying fans, were permitted admittance to a racecourse that should have been buzzing with British and Irish visitors. Everyone wore masks. Almost everyone hoped Enable would win. We were left disappointed.

Rain had pummelled Paris through the week, causing Love to be scratched by O'Brien. That still left him with four runners, but they disappeared at around the time on Saturday evening when restaurant diners were embarking on their creme brulees and iles flottantes. The Ballydoyle horses had tested positive to a prohibited substance as a result of contaminated feed. Only 11 horses were left in the 99th Arc, one being staged on the centenary of the contest's birth. It seemed as though fate was smiling on Enable from above. Down below, however, the ground was horribly heavy.

The most brilliant performance of her career had come when winning her first Arc on a soft surface at Chantilly, yet deep mud had been cited as a reason for her loss in 2019. Local punters were unconcerned and backed her into odds-on favouritism but there was a nervousness about Dettori as he kicked his heels just minutes before his 32nd Arc ride. A paddock fist pump with Abdullah's racing manager Teddy Grimthorpe sent him on his way and on to Enable's back for the last time.

High standards

Consistency and longevity were Enable's defining features, so reducing her career to a conversation about her one or two best performances will never do her justice.

She actually measures up well on her peak RPRs. While clearly not up to Frankel (143) standards, her peak RPR of 129 in her first Arc ranked her among the best middle-distance performers in the world in recent years.

The difficulty when comparing fillies and mares to colts is that the weight allowance females carry when racing against males is never added into the end-of-year standings. This means mares have trouble winning world titles using a ratings-based system.

If you take the view that the sex allowance should be factored in – to better reflect performances on the track – then the extra 3lb added to Enable would see her ranked as the best middle-distance performer in the world across the last five years.

Consistency may be Enable's defining feature and a more telling view of her career comes from looking at the lowest ratings she achieved during her prolonged spell at the top.

For example, between winning the Oaks in 2017 and this year's September Stakes she went 15 races spanning more than three years without producing a single RPR below 121, which is outstanding.

Her averages are also exceptional. Her median RPR across all races in 2019 (125.5) ranked best in the world and in 2018 she also had the best median in the world (124, joint with Cracksman).

That remarkable consistency over time is a rarity and her longevity is particularly notable when considering that high starting point, as most three-year-old Arc winners fail to run anywhere near their Longchamp figure again as older horses. For instance, Treve's peak RPR dropped 5lb from three to four, while Danedream dropped 4lb.

Enable earned her best figure in that 2017 Arc but she was never far off that level for the next three seasons, including hitting a mark of 128 in 2019. Essentially she quickly ascended to a high level and stayed there unflinchingly for four full seasons.

SAM WALKER

▲ Thanks for the memories: Frankie Dettori with Enable after the Irish Oaks in 2017; left, Enable in the pre-parade ring at Ascot before the 2019 King George

★★★★

WE STILL hoped and believed history was about to be made in front of our small, privileged brethren. And we were still hoping and believing when Enable turned for home apparently full of running. The two Longchamp commentators referred to her as la reine – the queen – and it felt as though her coronation was coming. But no. As soon as Dettori asked a question two furlongs from home, Enable was beaten. Outsider Chachnak even tried to take a bite out of the regal flank. At no point did Dettori touch her with the whip. To have done so in the circumstances would have seemed almost disrespectful. Sottsass won the Arc. Enable finished sixth.

Dettori revealed he had wanted to make the running but the horse beneath him had been unable to do so. When the final call was made, the answer was similarly negative.

"When I pressed the button nothing was there," Dettori said. "She couldn't pick her legs up in the ground, a bit like in the final furlong last year. It wasn't to be. I'm not emotional at the moment but I will be when I see her again. I'm still a bit angry because things didn't go my way – but we tried."

There had certainly been no anger directed towards Enable when he rode her back into the paddock. Before dismounting he leaned forward and kissed her repeatedly down the neck. He then remained with her, passing on a few sweet nothings, lingering for a cuddle, an arm around her shoulder. Dettori has said so many beautiful words to express how he feels about Enable. This time no words were needed. You just had to look at the two of them.

"He knows her and she knows him," said Grimthorpe after the lovers had parted. Then, in a vignette that summed up the ruthlessness of sport, a security official ordered groom Imran Shahwani to take Enable away. She was standing on a patch of grass Sottsass would have to cross before entering the winner's circle.

"Okay, okay, let's go, let's go," he said to Shahwani, shooing them from the scene. Enable was taken away. Eight days later, she was retired. Dettori had been told the news the previous evening. He admitted there were tears, but more of joy than sadness.

"She really touched my heart," he said, as sincere then as he had been on the afternoon when it all ended. Dettori and Enable will always have Paris but so much more besides. A little sadness, yes, but an abundance of joy.

IN THE PICTURE

One Master strikes again in Foret for historic hat-trick

ENABLE may have come up short again in her bid for a historic third Prix de l'Arc de Triomphe, but on the same afternoon at Longchamp there was still a unique hat-trick for a British-trained six-year-old mare.

Less than two hours after Enable's defeat, One Master took to the track for her own shot at history in the Group 1 Prix de la Foret and she completed the fabulous feat in thrilling style for trainer William Haggas.

One Master rarely wins by far and it was a close call again in a tremendous battle with the favourite Earthlight, who stepped up the pace in front under Mickael Barzalona early in the home straight. Pierre-Charles Boudot, One Master's regular Longchamp partner, was alert to the move but Earthlight proved extremely difficult to pass.

Finally, in the last 75 yards, One Master edged in front to become the first three-time winner in the Foret's 162-year history. The winning distance was a neck from Earthlight, with the running-on Safe Voyage a short head behind in third. One Master's first two Foret victories came by similarly small margins, a short head in 2018 and half a length in 2019.

"I love her," said Boudot, who has ridden her to all three Foret wins and celebrated wildly after this latest last-gasp triumph. "When I asked her she was very strong in the last furlong. Hopefully we'll be able to come back for four in a row."

Haggas, who trains One Master for owners Gretchen and Roy Jackson, had handed the ride back to Boudot after Tom Marquand had partnered the mare in three consecutive races, starting with a Glorious Goodwood success in the Group 3 Oak Tree Stakes. The margin that day? A short head.

The trainer was frank in his reasoning for the jockey switch. "Tom will learn how to ride that track [Longchamp] in time but Pierre-Charles has done nothing but good things on her," he said.

After Boudot and One Master had completed the three-peat in the seven-furlong contest, Haggas said: "We're really proud of her. She's a fantastic filly and she seems to come good over this track and trip. She's particularly good on soft ground and was given another brilliant ride by Pierre-Charles. She wants to win.

"It's very sad the big filly [Enable] didn't manage to win three Arcs, but this was a good feat in itself to win three Forets, as it's never been done before. These six-year-olds have had a remarkable year. If you look after them when they're young, they'll look after you when they're older."

Picture: EDWARD WHITAKER (RACINGPOST.COM/PHOTOS)

8

BACK WITH A BANG

Sottsass stepped up from Arc defeat in 2019 to claim the prize 12 months later

By Scott Burton

THE applause breaks in gentle waves over Longchamp's fabled enclosure to begin with but, as the vanquished heroine Enable returns to be unsaddled, cheers ring out. Even after an Arc featuring fewer runners than expected, the paddock is a maze of people, some connected in one way or another to one of the 12 returning horses, with at least as many media personnel frantically dashing between groups to grab first reactions.

Jean-Claude Rouget is staring at a replay as Sottsass is led in gentle warm-down circles and I manage to catch a couple of sentences with him before the pandemonium sets in as Waldgeist and a triumphant Pierre-Charles Boudot enter the arena.

"He's run a great race," says a seemingly distracted Rouget. "We'll just have to come back and win it at four."

The scene described is, of course, from straight after the 2019 Qatar Prix de l'Arc de Triomphe. Rouget's could have been a throwaway line designed to satisfy a quote-hungry journalist so that he could go back to private thoughts of what might have been. There were certainly plenty of times in the intervening 12 months when there appeared little substance to the thought that Sottsass could build on that third-placed effort.

After the chaos of a Covid-19 spring he took top billing on a starry opening card at Longchamp on May 11 but ran a lifeless fourth in the Prix d'Harcourt behind Shaman, Way To Paris and Simona. After a few days of rumination Rouget declared that we would all see a different horse in the Prix Ganay, a race subsequently moved to Chantilly as Paris racetracks were forced to reclose their doors. The son of Siyouni reversed the form with the three from the Harcourt but the official French handicapper rated him 6lb below his run in the Arc on 117.

After a summer break the decision was made to swerve the Juddmonte International in favour of a home tie in Deauville's Group 3 Prix Gontaut-Biron, where a rusty Sottsass was arguably set up to fail against Skalleti, in receipt of 6lb and on poached terrain that Andre Fabre would later compare unfavourably to Chantilly forest after wild boar had been on the rampage.

After that neck defeat Rouget continued to confound predictions by taking the bold choice of the Irish Champion Stakes rather than a confidence booster in the Prix Foy. From the outside it was hard to take confidence from Sottsass's fourth place behind Magical at Leopardstown. It was another defeat and seemingly another dent in the theory that Sottsass was the leading hope in the Arc for France, but his connections thought differently.

★★★★

SITTING in the socially distanced press centre an hour and a half after he and Sottsass had powered to that yearned-for Arc success, jockey Cristian Demuro did not try to rewrite history. "I won't lie, before the Irish Champion Stakes I expected to ride Raabihah [in the Arc]," said Demuro, who had just become the first Italian not named Dettori to win Europe's greatest race since Enrico Camici aboard Molvedo in 1961.

"This horse didn't feel like the same horse as last year, he didn't have the same appetite or the same fitness. But shortly after the Irish Champion Stakes Monsieur Rouget told me he felt the horse was coming back. I told him if he was sure I trusted him and I'd ride Sottsass. The race in Ireland really helped him because he hadn't been made to run at that pace all year in France. He really needed it and then when I worked on him I could feel he was back."

For Demuro it had been a whirlwind 15-month ride with Sottsass, as well as a traumatic few weeks following the death of his father, Giovanni Battista.

Now 28, Demuro had first struck up a relationship with Rouget as retained jockey to leading owner Gerard Augustin-Normand. He only came in for the ride aboard Sottsass in the Prix du Jockey Club in June 2019 when the Aga Khan's decision to run Zarkallani – just a week after breaking his maiden – took Christophe Soumillon out of the equation.

By the end of the year Augustin-Normand had taken his horses housed with Rouget elsewhere, while Demuro stayed. No official contract was signed. Just a handshake and an understanding that he was now the trainer's number one.

By the start of Arc week confidence was growing within the Rouget camp. Yet that closed circle managed to keep the secret of riding arrangements right up until Sottsass and Demuro stepped out on to the Deauville track for a final breeze five days before their rendezvous with destiny. Maxime Guyon had been smuggled onsite to partner Raabihah a few minutes later.

★★★★

AMONG those kept constantly abreast of developments was Peter Brant, the owner of Sottsass and a man obliged by the coronavirus to watch from his home in Connecticut as the days and hours ticked down to a race that had intrigued and beguiled him since he visited Longchamp in 1971 to watch the victory of Mill Reef, another American-owned colt.

His ownership of Sottsass goes back to a few weeks in the summer of 2017, during which his agent Michel Zerolo acquired leading Prix de Diane hopeful Sistercharlie, who would ultimately run a luckless second at Chantilly. While Sistercharlie was quickly shipped to the States to join Chad Brown

▸▸ *Continues page 16*

for what would turn into a stellar career, Brant and Zerolo had already seen enough to return to the source and they purchased her Siyouni half-brother from the Ecurie des Monceaux draft at the Arqana August Yearling Sale. Brant named the colt after Ettore Sottsass, a nod to one of his other great passions in life, the world of modern art, design and architecture.

In the days leading up to the 2020 Arc, Brant had also been convinced by Rouget that, after a season where the spark in Sottsass had gone missing, the real version was ready to show up at Longchamp.

Speaking 48 hours after watching his two-tone green silks triumph, Brant recalled the transformative effect on Sottsass of the run behind Magical and Ghaiyyath in the Irish Champion. "I was very confident as one of my trainers in Ireland [Ger Lyons] saddled the horse for me at Leopardstown and he said Sottsass would run very well in the Arc and that was like a prep race for him," he said.

"What does a power of good is to run against really good horses. Between Magical and Ghaiyyath, those are the best horses in the world along with Sottsass. He needed a race like that before the Arc. They weren't focused to that day but on the Arc de Triomphe. That's what Jean-Claude is an expert at doing. He has a race in mind that he thinks a horse has the ability to win and he focuses on that."

Confidence is one thing. But having been in that sun-dappled Longchamp paddock 12 months earlier to see Sottsass walking round, how did the horseman in Brant cope with relying on television coverage from more than 3,000 miles away? "I was with my wife in our bedroom watching it. We were so excited the house almost came down. It was phenomenal. It's been a lifetime dream to win that race, which I consider one of the greatest in the world."

★★★★

ROUGET had suggested a contributing factor to the defeat of Sottsass in 2019 was the timing of Demuro's bid to beat Enable and Dettori, with both Italians having started racing a fraction early and then succumbed to the late thrust of Waldgeist. This year, on even deeper ground, the trainer expected Sottsass to be ridden more patiently.

But with Rouget watching the same big screen in the paddock he had studied so intently 12 months earlier, it immediately became apparent that plan A had gone out the window, as Demuro quickly moved past his compatriot and settled Sottsass on the shoulder of the leader, Persian King.

Turning into the straight the six-metre gap of the open stretch cutaway rail tempted Demuro to his right but he took the tiniest of pulls on the reins, before angling Sottsass to the left of Persian King and launching his bid for glory.

Reviewing the race for the media, Demuro said the surprising start to the race had only increased belief that this was to be his and the gallant chestnut's day. Asked by moderator Liz Price when he thought he would win, Demuro's face was wreathed in a smile. "I think it was won at the start because I didn't feel we were going that fast," he said. "I saw Enable wasn't leading and when I realised we weren't going that fast I felt confident he could outsprint them in the straight. It was a big help and I knew his turn of foot would kill off the others."

If the words of Rouget in 2019 were a good place to start this remarkable tale, the 67-year-old also provides a fitting ending.

For several years he has repeated to French-based journalists his conviction that the races restricted to three-year-olds – the Poules d'Essai, the Jockey Club and the Diane – are the prizes he covets most. To the amazement of the foreign writers and broadcasters who made the trip to the Arc, he doubled down on the notion.

▲ Green day: Sottsass and Cristian Demuro win the Arc from In Swoop, Persian King and Gold Trip; below from top, Demuro goes for home and celebrates victory; trainer Jean-Claude Rouget greets his Arc winner; and Sottsass is paraded in triumph

"This is a very difficult race to win and an event like no other," Rouget said. "I've always loved the spring Classics because in many ways they are less complicated to prepare. So many good horses are beaten in the Arc because they're over the top or because of the ground. Again you've seen Enable couldn't do it.

"I continue to say I love the Classics but of course it's great to win today and I'm very happy. This has been the plan all year and we have been beaten a few times along the way. It's not an easy thing to do – you have to work spring, summer and autumn to the same objective – and it's not an easy thing to explain to owners that you need to let some races go in order to be in top form for this one day."

It had become a modern article of faith that, for the colts, it was a case of first time or never in the Arc. Waldgeist chipped away at that belief in 2019, stepping up from fourth the year before, and Sottsass undermined it further. A dazzling winner of the Prix du Jockey Club, he had given it his best shot in 2019 but come up short. For most of 2020 he seemed destined to play a supporting role to an emerging three-year-old or, more likely, one of the brilliant fillies and mares who have lit up the European scene in recent seasons.

But Rouget knew his horse. And now he, and Demuro, and Brant, have their Arc.

THE BIGGER PICTURE

Star trails over the Millennium grandstand on the Rowley Mile in Newmarket in May

EDWARD WHITAKER (RACINGPOST.COM/PHOTOS)

THE JOCKEY CLUB
UPPORTING BRITISH RACING
SINCE 1750

The CUPS KING

Stradivarius left more marks in the record books with Ascot and Goodwood triumphs in another superlative season in staying races

By Steve Dennis

THERE'S many a good tune played on an old fiddle, and on a Stradivarius they sound all the sweeter. No-one minds hearing the old songs over and over again and this year there was an added comfort in their repetition; in a world turned upside down, even the smallest familiarity will breed content. Stradivarius, the little swaggering sensation of a stayer, was perfect for the job.

We had become used to seeing Stradivarius dominate his rivals in the long-distance division, with his status upon which the season would centre.

This year, though, normality was mixed with novelty, the reasons being three-fold. Firstly, the redrawing of the racing schedule owing to the Covid-19 pandemic meant the loss of the Yorkshire Cup, in which the six-year-old had begun his campaign on a winning note for the previous two seasons. Then there was the cancellation of the £1 million bonus for winning four major staying races that Stradivarius had scooped in 2018 and 2019, the sponsor Weatherbys Hamilton being twice bitten, thrice shy.

Thirdly, and as a consequence of

roll of honour groaning under the weight of two Gold Cups at Ascot, three Goodwood Cups, two Yorkshire Cups, two Lonsdale Cups, a Doncaster Cup and a Long Distance Cup (and quite possibly a partridge in a pear tree). He was the undisputed Cups King of British racing. In 2020 we expected something similar from a horse so consistently good it is almost unnerving, and a third Gold Cup, to match the great Sagaro, was the pivot to legendary

the first two, this allowed for a different shape to Stradivarius's campaign, fuelled in no small part by owner Bjorn Nielsen's desire to test his paragon over a shorter trip in the Prix de l'Arc de Triomphe. Unfortunately, Gold Cup winners have not had a successful record in the Paris showpiece since Levmoss beat Park Top in 1969, and Stradivarius could manage only an undistinguished seventh at Longchamp on desperate ground in a race run to suit speedier types.

Stradivarius did at least show he might have that particular string to his bow when third in the Coronation Cup on his seasonal debut behind Ghaiyyath, emerging with plenty of credit considering the race was merely serving as a top-level sharpener for Royal Ascot. After that it was full steam ahead for the assault on the history books, but as far as Stradivarius is concerned full steam ahead is simply the way he lives his life.

"He's a six-year-old entire, so he's quite noisy," said trainer John Gosden, who wears his affection for the pony-sized powerhouse high on his well-tailored sleeve. With upwards of 200 horses in the yard it must take something special to stand out from the crowd, and Stradivarius has no shortage of that attribute.

"He likes shouting and saying hello to all the other horses. He has an amazing personality and is one of the all-time great characters to be around. He really enjoys life. He's very involved in everything and nosy as well. He's been tremendous fun to train and we're all very fond of him."

It helps, naturally, that Stradivarius is a superstar and not a 68-rated maiden, but Gosden – a man of the racing world, from Venezuela to Los Angeles to Manton to the 'Gaza Strip' of Newmarket – has the air of an indulgent father towards his playboy son. Big bill at the casino? Wrote off the Ferrari? Expensive mistress to maintain? Don't worry, old sport, here's a cheque, that'll cover it. Just keep winning those races. Just bring home that Gold Cup again.

★★★★

THE greatest obstacle in the way of that third Gold Cup was not a rival – he was odds-on in a field of eight, with his presumed main challenger Kew Gardens an absentee – but the weather. Soft ground doesn't play to the strengths of a stayer with such an uncharacteristic turn of foot, but the Last of the Domestic Playboys – Gosden had yet to let him stray any closer to the fleshpots of the Riviera than Goodwood – wasn't afraid to get his feet wet.

Staying races run on soft ground are prone to wide winning

▸▸ *Continues page 26*

margins, so when Stradivarius cruised up to the front-running Nayef Road a quarter of a mile out the possibility was there, but it was still surprising, exhilarating to see him clear away without exertion, skipping over the mud, winning by an eye-widening ten lengths, taking his third Gold Cup with the same ease and panache as Sagaro had done 43 years earlier.

Let no-one doubt the magnitude of the achievement. The inaugural Gold Cup was run in 1807, and in more than two centuries only two horses had won it more than twice, the other being four-time hero Yeats, who we will get to later. Now Stradivarius became the third, and he had done it with something else on his mind, like that playboy son counting cards at the blackjack table while trying to remember some showgirl's telephone number.

"He was having a little shout and playing up beforehand," Gosden said. "When he smelled my aftershave as I was saddling him up he got quite coltish, so I've obviously overdone that or something. He thinks life is a bit of fun and when you win races like that I suppose it is."

It certainly is. The pleasure of training Stradivarius must make the hard work of keeping a six-year-old entire at his peak mentally and physically far less onerous for John 'splash it on all over' Gosden, although his task should not be underestimated.

Simply getting a good horse to a big race is difficult enough, let alone doing it regularly and successfully over the course of three and a half seasons. Many entires lose the thread of competition and become as sex-obsessed as any horny teenager, and indeed Stradivarius did enter the paddock at Longchamp before the Arc in what is usually and prudishly called an 'excited state', which may indicate that the playboy is now ready to devote himself full-time to the bedroom.

Comparisons with former greats are both odious and unnecessary, and often descend into a futile argument between quantity and quality. Is Stradivarius better than Ardross, Le Moss or Sagaro, the crowned princes of the most recent (and possibly last) golden age of stayers? Is he better than Yeats, who has a statue in the Ascot parade ring for winning four Gold Cups, although those races were not of a particularly high standard?

Yeats was a slogger where Stradivarius is a quickener, but to insist that one is better than the other (Racing Post Ratings have Yeats 1lb ahead) is to miss the point. Next season Stradivarius may emulate Yeats in quantity, but that won't answer the question of 'better than'.

★★★★

SIX weeks after Ascot, Stradivarius outstripped Double Trigger (who also has a statue, at Doncaster) by winning his fourth Goodwood Cup, although this victory was in the balance until he thrust his white face in front in the long shadow of the post.

It was in the balance beforehand, when Irish Derby winner Santiago was reckoned a truly dangerous rival in receipt of 15lb weight-for-age. It was in the balance two furlongs out, when the Cups King was caught up in the usual Goodwood trouble in running and Frankie Dettori looked frantic as he angled this way and that for daylight, his mount's head tilted to one side as though he were helping in the search.

▲ Team work: Frankie Dettori partners Stradivarius on the Limekilns round gallop in Newmarket in September; previous page, victory in the Gold Cup at Royal Ascot for the third time

For the first time in a long time the little playboy looked in trouble, the creditors crowding round him, all the mistresses made aware of each other and comparing notes, yet where there's a will to win there's a way out and Stradivarius found it, drifting outside Santiago and old rival Nayef Road and once again producing that change of gear that true stayers should not be able to produce. The path opened before him like a fresh line of credit and he embraced it with vigour.

A furlong out he was getting there,

▸▸ *Continues page 28*

Roll of honour

Goodwood Cup 🏆🏆🏆🏆
Gold Cup 🏆🏆🏆
Yorkshire Cup 🏆🏆
Lonsdale Cup 🏆🏆
Doncaster Cup 🏆
Long Distance Cup 🏆
Starts 26
Wins 16
Prize-money £2,874,029
Racing Post Rating 125

100 yards out he was there, Dettori able to ease down in the final strides, the winning margin a length. "What a stayer this horse is, Stradivarius creates history," called Racing TV commentator Ian Bartlett.

Stradivarius doesn't so much create history as bend it to his will. Dettori, enjoying surely the most roseate and prolonged sunset to any riding career, offered an insight into the steely core of resolution that underpins his exuberant personality. Stradivarius's, that is, not Dettori's.

"If you want to sprint with Stradivarius you've got to be pretty good," he said. "I don't remember a stayer with a turn of foot like his. He's got too many gears. He's all heart."

He showed those gears again in the Group 2 Prix Foy, his Arc prep, when quickening better off a funereal pace than anything except last year's Derby winner Anthony Van Dyck, who held him off by a short neck. The performance entitled him to respect in the big race itself, but his chance expired in the Bois de Boulogne mud, extinguished by a dawdling gallop.

That was not the real Stradivarius, the one we expected to see, the one who knew all the old tunes and played them so well, and neither was the one who trailed in a dismal second-last on the cloying ground at Ascot in the Long Distance Cup, running the worst race of his life four months after running the best race of his life. It didn't matter. Everyone had got what they most needed in midsummer, thanks to the familiar brilliance of a stayer whose like comes along but rarely in a racing lifetime.

Next year he will be seven, a year older than Sagaro, a year younger than Yeats when they won their last Gold Cups. They say age is just a number; another number is four, a fourth Gold Cup, a tempting proposition for owner Nielsen. But four wins or no, Stradivarius has left an indelible mark on those closest to him and on the sport itself.

"To be able to say one day when I'm sitting on my rocking chair that I rode the horse who won three Gold Cups is amazing," Dettori said after Ascot.

Dettori is not yet ready for his rocking chair. Neither, hopefully, is Stradivarius, for the old songs are the best.

▲ Cup winners: Frankie Dettori and Stradivarius on their way to the gallops; left from top, easy does it at Royal Ascot and Dettori lifts a third Gold Cup; a hard-earned fourth Goodwood Cup, celebrated by Dettori and Bjorn Nielsen

馬

WINNING FORMULA

Willie Mullins followed a tried and tested short-haul route to a second Cheltenham Gold Cup triumph with Al Boum Photo

By Steve Dennis

IT TAKES two, as the old song goes. Many horses win one Cheltenham Gold Cup, but to win two is to be instantly installed into the pantheon. That's where Al Boum Photo now sits, alongside jumping greats Kauto Star, L'Escargot and Easter Hero.

Only seven horses before him – the others being five-timer Golden Miller and hat-trick heroes Cottage Rake, Arkle and Best Mate – have ever won more than one Gold Cup, so Al Boum Photo has now run himself into the realm of the extraordinary. Whisper it, but some Gold Cup winners are less than brilliant, fortunate that everything fell into place on the day that matters most. After all, anything can happen once. To be above this sort of faint praise, to remove doubt, it takes two.

Sometimes, mind, it just takes one. That is the schedule that primes Al Boum Photo so efficiently for Gold Cup glory, one run at Tramore on New Year's Day and then straight to Cheltenham, a campaign of brief authority that works so well it would be folly to meddle with it.

It's a workload that makes the campaigning of Best Mate – the last horse to win the Gold Cup in consecutive years – look positively hectic, although back then his trainer Henrietta Knight was routinely taken to task for keeping her horse in cotton wool, for denying his public the opportunity to connect with him. Nearly 20 years have passed since Best Mate's era and now the Al Boum Photo method is commonplace, the lure and allure of the Cheltenham Festival being so all-consuming that few other opportunities are considered worth considering.

After all, it took his trainer Willie Mullins so frustratingly long to win the Gold Cup – he had trained the runner-up six times before Al Boum Photo broke the sequence in 2019 – that it is understandable the wily master of Closutton charted an identical course for a second year. Trainers are notoriously creatures of habit in any case, disinclined to tinker with a winning system, and the old ungrammatical saw about things not being broke comes readily to mind.

"Last season just worked out well for Al Boum Photo, going from Tramore to Cheltenham," said Mullins, as the countdown to the big day ticked on. "I didn't even enter him for the Dublin Racing Festival this year, just in case I was tempted to run him. When something works, we go back, we do it again and hope for the best."

★★★★

MULLINS did it again. He waited, with a steely resolution, until New Year's Day, until all 11 of Al Boum Photo's eventual Magners Gold Cup rivals had staked a claim to the crown. Clan Des Obeaux strolled away with the King George, Lostintranslation turned back Bristol De Mai in a compelling Betfair Chase, Delta Work outfought Monalee in the

» *Continues page 34*

Savills Chase with Kemboy and Presenting Percy behind, Elegant Escape ran third in the Ladbrokes Trophy under top weight, Santini scrambled home at Sandown before having his wind done, Chris's Dream hacked up by nine and a half lengths in the Troytown Chase. Even stablemate Real Steel had a Grade 2 at Down Royal to his name.

Mullins waited, and then, like a high roller arriving late at the World Series of Poker, sat down at the table, pushed all his chips into the middle and showed his hand. He had the ace up his sleeve all along.

This year, the role of the Grade 2 Savills New Year's Day Chase at little Tramore was not to demonstrate Al Boum Photo's credentials for the Gold Cup but merely to illustrate that he was still around, had finally emerged, blinking against the light, from hibernation.

The trip was not right, his three rivals were well overmatched, it almost stretched the definition of the word 'race'. It should have been a cakewalk and it was, six lengths the winning margin, exactly the same as the year before, exactly the same colours worn by the runner-up. Boy, when Mullins goes back and does something again, he really ticks all the boxes.

And then he knew. "I was more nervous there than when I was watching the Gold Cup. I couldn't be happier with how the day worked out," he said afterwards, his breath in clouds around that familiar brown trilby. After not quite six minutes' work, the Gold Cup winner was perfectly primed for another Gold Cup.

The usual pressure was off Mullins' shoulders, given that he had broken that soul-destroying streak of second places in the race everyone wants to win. There was instead the unusual pressure of bringing back the reigning champion, especially considering the terrible record of reigning champions in the Gold Cup, but in Al Boum Photo he knew he had a horse with the right stuff.

Looking back, Florida Pearl didn't quite stay, Hedgehunter stayed too slowly, Sir Des Champs met a good horse who ran the race of his life, On His Own wasn't really good enough, Djakadam (twice) was an enigma even

Bletchley Park couldn't unravel with any certainty. Al Boum Photo is different. He stays the Gold Cup distance, but is not a one-dimensional stayer. He has the speed to win at 2m5f, he jumps well in the main, he is tactically versatile, he is essentially straightforward. He is simply the real deal. And Mullins knew now how the key fitted the lock.

★★★★

COME Gold Cup day, though, the simple seemed more complicated. Al Boum Photo was in the right place, sure, but his people were still looking at the map. In the build-up to the big meeting all the major players ramble on unconvincingly about how one winner is all they're worried about, but for the likes of Mullins and jockey Paul Townend one winner at the festival is an unmitigated disaster. And by Friday, the meeting had been no better than a slightly mitigated disaster for both.

No winner for either man on day one was bad enough but it was turned into a calamity by Benie Des Dieux's odds-on defeat in the Mares' Hurdle, where Townend and Robbie Power on stablemate Stormy Ireland contrived to open the door to victory for Honeysuckle and Rachael Blackmore. Amid the torrent of criticism were these stinging words from Ruby Walsh, Townend's predecessor as stable jockey: "Paul Townend should have choked Robbie Power in and closed the door on Honeysuckle . . . it's the basics of race-riding." Mullins kept his counsel but admitted later: "I self-medicated a lot that night!"

The hangover did not clear quickly. Their Queen Mother Champion Chase star Chacun Pour Soi was a non-runner on day two, although something small was salvaged from the wreckage as dusk fell when Ferny Hollow won the Champion Bumper. Day three went to press with one more winner for Townend and two for Mullins. Now Al Boum Photo was not just wanted but needed.

The eight-year-old had played a redemptive role in the career of his rider once before. After the ludicrous 'brain fade' of Punchestown in 2018, when Townend pulled him round the final fence because of something he thought he had heard, Al Boum

▸▸ *Continues page 36*

Multiple Gold Cup winners

Al Boum Photo became the eighth to win more than one Cheltenham Gold Cup since the race's inception in 1924 and the first trained in Ireland since L'Escargot half a century ago. Ireland's other multiple winners are Cottage Rake and Arkle

Easter Hero
1929, 1930

Golden Miller 1932, 1933, 1934, 1935, 1936

Cottage Rake
1948, 1949, 1950

Arkle
1964, 1965, 1966

L'Escargot
1970, 1971

Best Mate
2002, 2003, 2004

Kauto Star
2007, 2009

Al Boum Photo
2019, 2020

Photo restored Townend's reputation as a safe pair of hands with victory in the Gold Cup. Here, now, with the man on top suffering from a rare shortage of success at his first festival as stable jockey to Mullins, could he do it again?

As another old song goes, he had a little help from his friends. Townend won two of the first three races; Mullins won them all. Confidence was high again. The cake was on the table. The cream had been slathered thickly on. Now for the cherry on top.

Unusually for a Gold Cup, the pace was merely steady, something that might have militated against the strong stayers Lostintranslation and Santini but not the more malleable favourite. Townend let his partner find his feet and did not ask him to move forward until there were six to jump, whereupon the picture changed swiftly.

All that tactical speed in Al Boum Photo's locker came in handy now. Aware that the race was there for the taking for the first man to make a move, Townend sent his mount on four out, changing the dynamic and putting his main rivals on the back foot for a crucial few strides. Turning in, Al Boum Photo lay between Santini on the rail and Lostintranslation on the outer, and the race lay between them.

An impeccable jump at the last gave Al Boum Photo the advantage and he never looked like ceding it. His speed took him ahead and his stamina kept him going strongly enough to withstand the late and unavailing surge of Santini. A neck was enough for that second Gold Cup, that golden ticket to exalted status. Perhaps it wasn't as visually eyecatching a performance as the year before, but that was not worth quibbling over. The feat itself, and the way that feat had been engineered, was what counted.

★★★★

MULLINS' minimalist approach and Townend's tactical tour de force had done it again. In the giddy aftermath, both these vital aspects of the great day were held, gleaming, to the light.

"I thought I would never feel anything like the feeling I had here last year, but I think this is even better," said Townend, the trophy for leading rider at the meeting in his saddlebag. "It's a credit to Willie. To go to Tramore two years in a row and come here with one run, the man is a genius."

The genius beamed. "I suppose the light campaign paid off. When you win you're right. Paul's plan came together and I'm delighted for him. Paul does his own thing and he probably rides better under a little bit of pressure."

History is made by the victors as well as written by them, and Townend put his own spin on the question on everyone's lips – the mathematical problem of turning two into three next spring. An evocation of the last horse to solve that problem seemed apt.

"After Best Mate had won his first Gold Cup, Henrietta Knight came to my father Tim's yard to look at a horse," Townend said. "She bought the horse and later sent me a photo of Best Mate that was signed by herself, Terry [Biddlecombe] and Jim [Culloty].

"I still have the photo. I was only 11 and it was a massive thing for me at the time, that she had taken the time out of her schedule to send me something. The photo took pride of place in my bedroom for many a year, and she did remind me at Cheltenham that Best Mate won three. It would be something special to match that."

Wouldn't it? 'Same again, Willie' is not just the cry you'll hear at his local pub, the Lord Bagenal, it's the mantra for the season ahead. The old one-two – Tramore and Cheltenham – might yet add up to three.

▲ Golden day: Al Boum Photo (right) jumps the last alongside Lostintranslation; bottom from left, the pair start up the run-in together but Al Boum Photo comes home in front; Paul Townend gives thanks and holds the trophy with Willie Mullins; below, the Racing Post front page the following day, reflecting Al Boum Photo's victory and the growing awareness that racing's shutdown was imminent

RACING POST

The last hurrah

As sports across the world grind to a halt, Townend and Al Boum Photo join the greats with epic Gold Cup victory roared home by 70,000

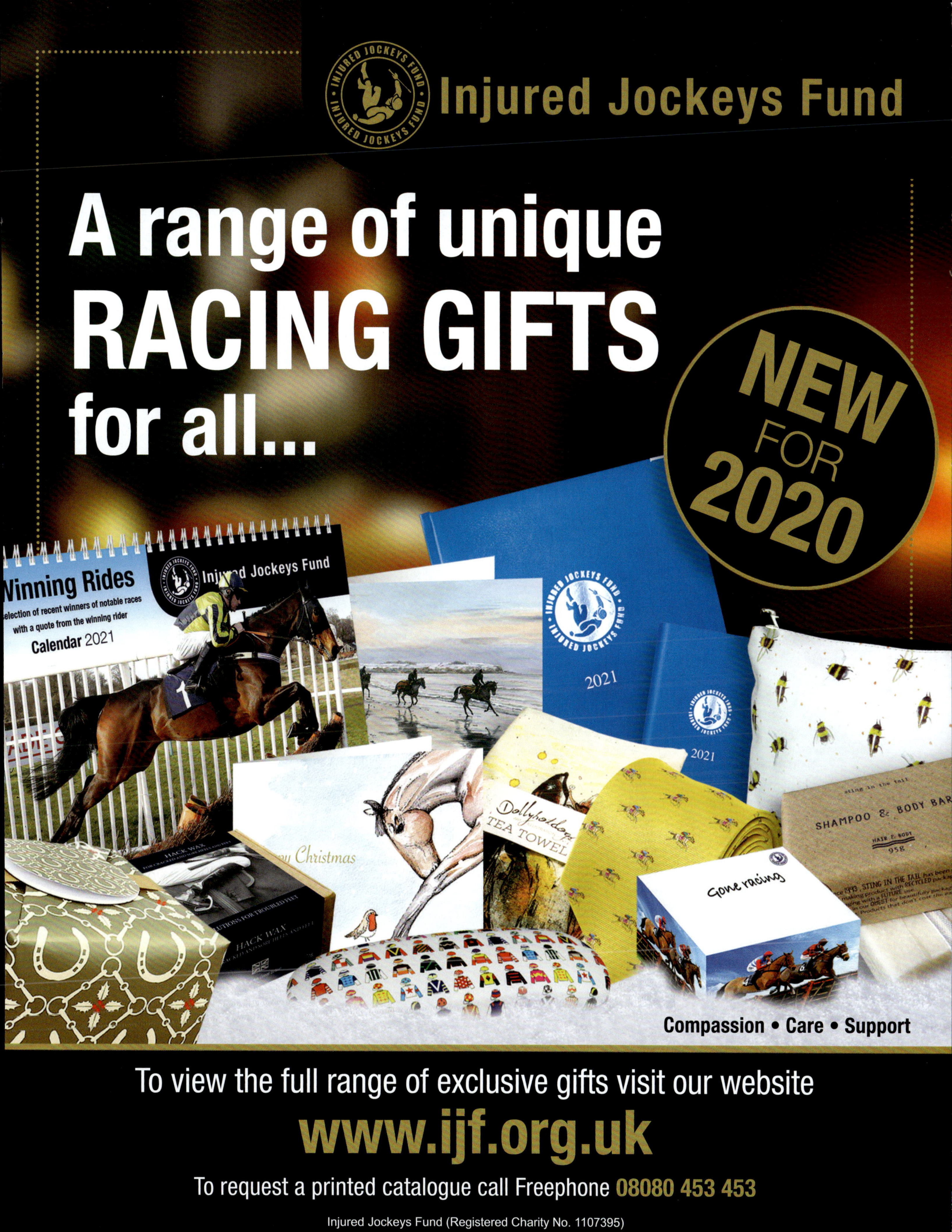
Injured Jockeys Fund
A range of unique
RACING GIFTS
for all...
NEW FOR 2020
Winning Rides
Calendar 2021
Injured Jockeys Fund
2021
2021
SHAMPOO & BODY BAR
Gone racing
TEA TOWEL
Compassion • Care • Support
To view the full range of exclusive gifts visit our website
www.ijf.org.uk
To request a printed catalogue call Freephone 08080 453 453
Injured Jockeys Fund (Registered Charity No. 1107395)

Paul Townend faced tough questions in his first year as number one for Willie Mullins but came up with the winning answers

FINAL PROOF

By Nick Pulford

LATE on Gold Cup afternoon, symbolism hung heavy in the Cheltenham air as Ruby Walsh presented the leading jockey award at the festival to Paul Townend. This was not just the passing over of a trophy named in honour of Walsh, winner of the award a record 11 times in his glittering career; it also represented affirmation of Townend's successful transition from Walsh's long-time understudy to become the undisputed number one for Willie Mullins.

Back-to-back Gold Cup triumphs on Al Boum Photo had demonstrated Townend's class and coolness in the big-race cauldron, but being first jockey for Mullins is about more than that. It is about delivering that kind of excellence day after day, hour after hour, race after race. The pressure is relentless, the demands on body and mind are unremitting. Townend had risen to that challenge and proved himself the worthy successor to Walsh.

When things go wrong, as they had for Townend and Mullins on the Tuesday of festival week, the glare of the spotlight is blinding. Fingers will be pointed and hard questions will be asked, and above all it is the stable jockey's job to come up with the answers. The horses are all prepared and there is not much more Mullins can do; success on raceday depends on how well his chosen jockey stands up to the pressure.

Townend's answer later in festival week was emphatic, particularly on Gold Cup day. With Al Boum Photo as the final leg, he rode a magnificent treble for Mullins that wrested the Ruby Walsh Trophy from Barry Geraghty's hands. They finished level on five winners but Townend's strength in depth gave him the clear edge on placed rides. He had Ruby's trophy in his hands.

★★★★

THAT fabulous Gold Cup day started with a lucky winner when Burning Victory was left to come home in front by Goshen's final-flight fall in the Triumph Hurdle, but there was no doubt Townend deserved his second

▸▸ *Continues page 40*

success of the day on Monkfish in the Albert Bartlett Novices' Hurdle. The betting was tight between four highly rated contenders – 4-1 favourite Thyme Hill for Philip Hobbs, Paul Nolan's Latest Exhibition at 9-2 and the Mullins-trained Monkfish and Gordon Elliott's Fury Road both on 5-1 – and the race was just as close with the quartet locked together going to the final hurdle. Townend just had Monkfish's head in front over the last but already it had been quite a battle to get into that position, with his mount having run quite freely and made a bad mistake down the far side on the final circuit. It was about to get even tougher.

Shortly after the last Townend was passed on his outside by Fury Road under a determined Davy Russell and by Latest Exhibition, the mount of Bryan Cooper, on the inner next to the rail. Thyme Hill in fourth could give no more but Townend and Monkfish were not finished yet and gradually, stride by stride up that punishing hill, they fought back with every ounce of strength they could muster. Near the line Monkfish's head poked back in front to snatch victory by a neck from Latest Exhibition, with Fury Road just a nose behind in third and Thyme Hill a close fourth.

"Wowee. What a race, what a fantastic race," said Rich Ricci, the winning owner. "It could be the best race of the festival in terms of quality – the four that were supposed to win all fought out the finish and hopefully they develop into Gold Cup horses."

Townend's ride was also of the highest quality, the kind habitually produced by Walsh at the festival, and he was given due praise by Mullins. "I don't think the race went according to plan for Paul – he [Monkfish] was just doing a little too much for him but he found himself there. When they passed him after jumping the last I thought we were set for third, but Paul really drove him up the hill. It was a fantastic ride. I'm delighted for Paul to get a winner in that fashion."

Reflecting later in the day on Townend's achievements, Mullins added: "It's fantastic to have a guy like him riding for you. He had a tough job taking over from Ruby Walsh but I think today proved he was well up to it. This was a huge week for him, coming here as the first jockey and not the understudy for the first year. It was a fair bit of pressure, but he has stamped his authority on Cheltenham and I'm really happy for him. He was able to handle the pressure."

It was telling that Townend was able to shrug off his high-profile defeat aboard Benie Des Dieux on day one to deliver with several of his most fancied rides. As well as 100-30 favourite Al Boum Photo in the Gold Cup, he scored on 2-1 shot Min in the Ryanair Chase and Monkfish at 5-1 in the Albert Bartlett. All five of his festival winners came in Grade 1 contests, with Ferny Hollow setting the ball rolling in the Champion Bumper on the Wednesday.

Walsh was full of praise for his former understudy. "By the end of the week I thought he had taken himself to another level," he said on a Paddy Power podcast. "He's a very hard-working guy. Very unassuming and very dedicated. When the pressure was on, he rose to the top. By Friday evening he had cemented himself as one of the best riders around."

****

CHELTENHAM may be the most important week in the jump racing calendar, but it is only one part of the demands placed on the stable jockey by Mullins and his string of 180 horses. There are plenty of big prizes to be won at home too, and countless hot favourites to be ridden, plus the vital task of bringing on the young horses with schooling and the right kind of introduction to racing. Townend is well versed in the Mullins way through a long apprenticeship since joining the yard at the age of 15, but the 2019-20 season was his first without Walsh, the master craftsman, at his side. Once again he rose to the challenge.

▲ Job well done: from top, Paul Townend celebrating on Burning Victory; getting up to score on Monkfish; another success in the bag with Min; driving for the line on Ferny Hollow; previous page, a second golden moment with Al Boum Photo

For the second season running, and the third in all, Townend was Ireland's champion jump jockey and some of his performances were sublime. Above all, he had the consistency, which seems such a prosaic virtue yet is so vital when riding for a top stable. Then came his crowning moment at Cheltenham.

While Townend was denied more success, which would surely have followed at Fairyhouse and the Punchestown festival but for their cancellation amid the Covid-19 shutdown, he could reflect on a job well done in his first season as Mullins' stable jockey. From the cream of Cheltenham to the bread and butter days in Ireland, he had more than proved himself a worthy number one.

MOLENKONING IS THE WORLDS LEADING MANUFACTURER OF HORSE WALKERS & REHABILITATION EQUIPMENT
Walkers · Fences · Roofs · Lunge Pens · Horsepower Plates · Solariums
Horse Walker Plug & Play - All you need is a regular 16 amp outlet to operate
Horse Walker with Round Fence | Key Features
- As standard 10, 12, 15, 16, 18 and 20 meters but larger diameter models are also available on request.
- Our Round Fence offers industry-leading strength, ensuring your horses exercise safely and securely.
- Manufactured to allow enough width for the exercising horses to turn round, you can preset the walker to change direction to distribute pressure on the horses body.
- The Molenkoning Safeguard Pusher Gate is our best seller; inclusive of flexible, safe & long-lasting 2000mm long dividers with 14 PVC rods they encourage your horses to walk successfully and comfortably.
MK
WWW.MOLENKONING.COM
UNITED KINGDOM
T: 01490 413 152
E: sales_uk@molenkoning.com
W: www.molenkoning.com

THE BIGGER PICTURE

Un De Sceaux leads Defi Du Seuil on the first circuit in the Grade 1 Clarence House Chase at Ascot in January. The positions are reversed at the end as the Philip Hobbs-trained Defi Du Seuil wins by two and three-quarter lengths

EDWARD WHITAKER (RACINGPOST.COM/PHOTOS)

MATCHBOOK

Barry Geraghty set the seal on his brilliant career with five winners at the Cheltenham Festival, led by Epatante in the Champion Hurdle

BLAZE OF GLORY

By Richard Forristal

MAYBE the moment that most aptly illustrates Barry Geraghty's trademark capacity to keep his head while all about him are losing theirs is the one just after the 2020 County Handicap Hurdle. Normally you would look to one of the multitude of examples of Geraghty's cool big-race prowess to demonstrate his defining characteristic, but hindsight would suggest his restraint at around 2.20pm on the Friday of Cheltenham matched any of his composed on-track turns.

He had just executed another superlative ride on JP McManus's gambled-on Saint Roi, easing his Willie Mullins-trained mount to a bloodless triumph with the sort of sublime calm that he was synonymous with throughout his career. It was Geraghty's final ride of the week. He retired to the festival clubhouse atop the jockeys' table with a near 50 per cent strike-rate of five wins from 11 rides.

His haul included a fourth Champion Hurdle on Epatante, a mesmerising last-gasp salvage job on Champ in the RSA Chase and three of the week's most illustrious handicaps, Saint Roi and the Coral Cup winner Dame De Compagnie both landing sizeable touches.

In between, he brought the house down on Sire Du Berlais when shading an enthralling cat-and-mouse joust with Davy Russell on The Storyteller in the Pertemps Handicap Hurdle. Each of his five victories was in the McManus silks. At that point in time, as he dismounted Saint Roi, he was the darling of the Cotswolds. It doesn't get much better.

Geraghty absolutely bossed the week and, although chinned for the festival riders' award by Paul Townend's late surge, he had reasserted his status as jump racing's marquee jockey in spectacular fashion. He was also 40 years of age, and we are now aware that he and his wife Paula knew then he would never ride at the festival again.

The world was in turmoil as the Covid-19 calamity closed in, and the impending sense of doom surrounding the inevitable shutdown of racing was palpable. None of us knew how much more would be squeezed out of the jumps season, but we realised the prospects of Aintree going ahead were receding apace.

It was teed up for Geraghty to go out on the grandest of stages with all the fanfare that his glorious career deserved. Instead, he took a pull and decided to soak it all up.

A bit like in the epic 2004 Tingle Creek Chase – when he took a nonchalant glance over his shoulder aboard Moscow Flyer as they tanked to the Pond fence and saw Azertyuiop and Well Chief seemingly poised in his slipstream – there was something satisfying in the knowledge that, despite the frenzy erupting around him, he knew his fate was in his own hands.

It was something to savour and he would not be rushed.

"To sign off on the week by winning the County Hurdle, I was going to pull the plug on it there and then," he explained subsequently. "But then I was thinking that Aintree or Punchestown or Fairyhouse could go ahead, so I had to wait. But that was good, because it left me with the time to reflect. I came to realise it was the right thing to do and that I was completely happy with my decision. I was able to appreciate it then."

▲ Family man: Barry Geraghty at home with his wife Paula and children Siofra, Rian and Orla
◀ Barry and Paula after Epatante's Champion Hurdle

★★★★

THAT Geraghty would mastermind such a glorious swansong in the Cotswolds was as it should be. Nowhere has his class been so consistently manifest as it has been around Prestbury Park each March for the past two decades.

He went into this year's gala as the festival's leading active rider, an enormous yield of 38 wins topped in the all-time record books only by Ruby Walsh. That rarefied status was enhanced by the end of play, his final tally of 43 leaving him a dozen clear of Sir Anthony McCoy, with another gap back to Pat Taaffe on 25. Titans of the sport left trailing.

▸▸ *Continues page 46*

"It was tough last year, but it makes these days all the sweeter," he reflected of his return from injury after Epatante's smooth Champion Hurdle triumph. "It is a battle, but age is just a number – 40 is the new 30. There's no better buzz in the world than going for the last hurdle at Cheltenham, meeting it good and long, the lights are green and we're going – that's what I live for.

"Once the horses were there, and JP was very supportive, I was always coming back. I just want to enjoy it and embrace it, because when it's going right, there is nothing better."

How that rang true in the days that followed. When Geraghty was right, there really were few better. In his pomp, he rode with the sort of swagger that was similarly evident in his demeanour, epitomised by an old-fashioned charisma and a touch of mischief that never compromised his professionalism. He was a joy to watch.

In the end, one of jump racing's most decorated galacticos made the announcement of his retirement late on a Saturday night, July 11, surrounded by family and friends at his home in County Meath.

From his seminal 2003 Grand National victory aboard Jimmy Mangan's Monty's Pass, to his two Gold Cups, four Champion Hurdles, two Stayers' Hurdles and five Champion Chases, plus an Irish Grand National, he had done it all, his roll of honour eventually comprising 121 Grade 1s. There was nothing left to achieve.

"I've fulfilled all my dreams," he told the Racing Post. "As a kid growing up, you're dreaming of Grand Nationals and Gold Cups and Champion Hurdles, so to get the chance to ride in them, let alone win them, was brilliant."

Notwithstanding the Covid-19 interruption, Geraghty went out on his own terms. Moreover, if his spellbinding week in the Cotswolds is anything to go by, he did so at the very top of his game. "I knew this was the lap of honour," he admitted subsequently. It was some lap.

Did he fill an unforgiving minute with sixty seconds' worth of distance run, Kipling might wonder? Too right he did. His was the earth.

Life at the top: Barry Geraghty's career highlights

Born September 16, 1979

First winner Stagalier (trainer Noel Meade), maiden hurdle, Down Royal, January 29, 1997

First Graded winner Cockney Lad (1997 Lismullen Hurdle)

First winner in Britain Miss Orchestra (1998 Midlands Grand National)

First Grade 1 winner Alexander Banquet (1999 Drinmore Novice Chase)

Grand National winner Monty's Pass (2003)

Cheltenham Gold Cup winners Kicking King (2005), Bobs Worth (2013)

Champion Hurdle winners Punjabi (2009), Jezki (2014), Buveur D'Air (2018), Epatante (2020)

Queen Mother Champion Chase winners Moscow Flyer (2003, 2005), Big Zeb (2010), Finian's Rainbow (2012), Sprinter Sacre (2013)

Stayers'/World Hurdle winners Iris's Gift (2004), More Of That (2014)

Ryanair Chase winner Riverside Theatre (2012)

Triumph Hurdle winners Spectroscope (2003), Zaynar (2009), Soldatino (2010), Peace And Co (2015), Ivanovich Gorbatov (2016)

Other Cheltenham Festival Grade 1 winners Moscow Flyer (2002 Arkle), Star De Mohaison (2006 Royal & SunAlliance Chase), Cork All Star (2007 Champion Bumper), Forpadydeplasterer (2009 Arkle), Bobs Worth (2011 Albert Bartlett Hurdle, 2012 RSA Chase), Sprinter Sacre (2012 Arkle), Simonsig (2012 Neptune Investment Novices' Hurdle, 2013 Arkle), O'Faolains Boy (2014 RSA), Defi Du Seuil (2019 JLT Chase), Champ (2020 RSA)

King George VI Chase winners Kicking King (2004, 2005)

Irish Gold Cup (Leopardstown) winner Alexander Banquet (2002)

Punchestown Gold Cup winners Moscow Express (2001), Florida Pearl (2002), Kicking King (2005), China Rock (2012), Carlingford Lough (2016)

BARRY GERAGHTY was a true giant of the sport, and only three jump jockeys have ever won more races in their careers, *writes John Randall.*

He scored 1,920 victories in Ireland (1,252) and Britain (668) combined. Among jump jockeys, only Sir Anthony McCoy (4,348), Richard Johnson (3,749 at the time of Geraghty's retirement) and Ruby Walsh (2,756) have won more. Based on wins in Ireland alone, he ranks fourth behind Walsh, Davy Russell and Paul Carberry.

Geraghty was champion jockey in Ireland only twice and not since 2003-04, because Walsh won 12 titles thanks to Willie Mullins' horses. Yet he won just about every chase and hurdle race worth winning. They included the Cheltenham Gold Cup on Kicking King and Bobs Worth and the Grand National on Monty's Pass – a victory that made him Ireland's Sports Person of the Year in 2003.

The Meath man's 43 victories at the Cheltenham Festival rank him second to Walsh (59) in the all-time list at the meeting; Moscow Flyer and Bobs Worth contributed three each. He broke the jockeys' record for the most wins in the Triumph Hurdle (five) and equalled it in the Queen Mother Champion Chase (five) and Champion Hurdle (four). At the time his five wins in 2003 equalled the record for one Cheltenham Festival, but the record is now seven by Walsh.

The best horse he rode was Sprinter Sacre (RPR 190) – one of the two greatest steeplechasers since Arkle, along with Kauto Star. Geraghty's dual Champion Chase winner Moscow Flyer (RPR 182) was also a great champion. Iris's Gift (RPR 176) put up the best hurdling performance by any of Geraghty's mounts when dethroning Baracouda at Cheltenham in the 2004 Stayers' Hurdle.

Punchestown Champion Chase winners Moscow Flyer (2004), Big Zeb (2011), Sprinter Sacre (2013)

Martell Cup winner Florida Pearl (2002)

Melling Chase winners Moscow Flyer (2004, 2005), Finian's Rainbow (2012), Sprinter Sacre (2013)

Tingle Creek Chase winners Moscow Flyer (2003, 2004), Sprinter Sacre (2012), Defi Du Seuil (2019)

Irish Grand National winner Shutthefrontdoor (2014)

Hennessy Gold Cup winners Bobs Worth (2012), Triolo D'Alene (2013)

bet365 Gold Cup winner Hadrian's Approach (2014)

Irish Champion Hurdle (Leopardstown) winner Macs Joy (2005)

Punchestown Champion Hurdle winners Moscow Flyer (2001), Macs Joy (2006), Punjabi (2008)

Aintree Hurdle winners Oscar Whisky (2011, 2012), Buveur D'Air (2017)

1,000th win over jumps (Ireland/Britain combined) Duc De Regniere, Kempton, November 2, 2009

Main retainer JP McManus 2015-20

Champion jump jockey in Ireland 1999-2000, 2003-04

Leading jockey at Cheltenham Festival 2003, 2012

Most wins in an Irish season 110 (2003-04)

Most wins in a British season 78 (2009-10)

Most wins in a season (Ireland/Britain combined) 123 in 2003-04 (Ireland 110, Britain 13)

Compiled by John Randall

◀ Iris's Gift: the best hurdler Geraghty rode

WINNING PUNCH

Champ finally lived up to his name in a dramatic fight up the hill in the RSA Chase

By Steve Dennis

THERE is a deal of trouble in naming a horse Champ. Admittedly, with all the French imports populating the game one could simply pretend he was named after a particularly nice field, but hubris will always dog his footsteps, waiting for its chance.

That chance seemed to have come in the RSA Insurance Novices' Chase at Cheltenham, when he was nearly ten lengths adrift in third place jumping the final fence, but it was testament to Champ's stoutness of heart and stamina that he shrugged off the perils of nominative determinism and drew victory from the half-clamped jaws of defeat with a flourish. With a name like that he'll always have something to prove, but now he's proving it.

As Minella Indo and Allaho jumped the last the cameras closed in on them, for the race was between the two. A few strides later the view widened and there was Champ, looking weary under Barry Geraghty, booked for third place. Then the eye panned back to Minella Indo and Allaho, duelling for the mastery. Was it an optical illusion or were they beginning to slow down? Ask a spectator.

"I thought we had come an honourable third and that was it, and had actually turned to see what was happening up the front – I don't know where he came from," said Champ's trainer Nicky Henderson, who watched from his usual spot on a manhole cover on the grandstand lawn. "Suddenly Champ came into my sights. I thought 'what's he doing here and how has he got here?'"

The Cheltenham hill has seen as many fortunes change as has the roulette room at the Casino de Monte Carlo – The Dikler outstaying Pendil, Dawn Run "beginning to get up", Might Bite throwing the race away and then retrieving it, to name but three of the most memorable. Of their like was the last-gasp success of Wichita Lineman under an indomitable AP McCoy, and Champ's performance was cut from the same green-and-gold cloth.

Perhaps that should have been expected, given that the wide appreciation is that Champ was named by owner JP McManus for McCoy's nickname; something to do with 20 titles, apparently. Yet it was also unexpected, not least because Henderson had spent much of the pre-Cheltenham festivities bemoaning the fact that his star staying novice was short of experience.

"We wanted to give him another race but there was nowhere to go," he said. "We had that fall, and it was a horrible fall. We would never have been looking for another race if he hadn't come down at Cheltenham, and that upset plans a bit."

★★★★

HENDERSON is not a man who dismisses upset plans with a boyish laugh and a few hummed bars of Que Sera Sera. For most of the year he is as affable a companion as you could wish for, but for the month leading up to that week in mid-March he becomes as edgy as a David Lynch feature, his nerves so taut you could pluck him like a harp. Cheltenham consumes him, and Champ's preparation gnawed greedily at his vitals.

The horrible fall came at Cheltenham on New Year's Day, when the eight-year-old basically failed to take off at the second last while seemingly on track to maintain his unbeaten record over fences. In his earlier victories Champ had looked good but not awe-inspiring, the hype and the hope fuelling his progress rather than anything concrete. He didn't look the most natural of jumpers, a conclusion underlined by that Cheltenham fall. Practice would probably make perfect, and no trainer wants to approach a major objective with a horse coming back from a fall.

It seems, though, that Champ's southpaw tendencies are pronounced, so the Reynoldstown at right-handed Ascot was overlooked. Kelso was reckoned eminently suitable, but the mid-February meeting was blown away by Storm Ciara. Henderson had run out of time and options.

But what you can't do in public you are at liberty to do in private, and Champ made it to Cheltenham on the back of an intensive programme in the indoor school at Seven Barrows. He even jumped half a dozen poles the day before the RSA, so with his homework given full marks he turned up for the big exam with his confidence restored. Any confidence felt by his connections had evaporated, however, by the time the principals turned for home, with Champ toiling in their wake.

"He was on the back foot all the way, it was hard work on that ground," Geraghty said. "Between the last two, he was struggling, but the two in front didn't jump the last that well."

It's a long way home from the last fence at Cheltenham. If he'd been a horse Geraghty might have pricked his ears at the signal that the leaders were beginning to falter, but it was a different part of his anatomy that told him all was not lost. "We landed over the last and I was smelling money again," he said.

Ah, the sweet smell of success. Geraghty and Champ filled their lungs and set off up the hill. Halfway up it was plain that Minella Indo and Allaho were tiring, and where once Champ had been treading water he now appeared to be walking on it. Geraghty drove him spellbindingly

▸▸ *Continues page 52*

◂ Out of nowhere: Champ is a distant third as he jumps the last fence in the RSA Insurance Novices' Chase; above, on the run-in he chases, catches and finally overhauls Minella Indo and Allaho; overleaf, Barry Geraghty celebrates his amazing victory and is greeted in the winner's enclosure by Nicky Henderson

forward, the impossible looking more likely with every stride, and Champ surged between the leading pair, threading the needle, sewing it up with room to spare. In the end he won going away. Champ the Wonder Horse, as all Sunday-serial viewers of a certain age will remember fondly.

★★★★

EVERY winner of the RSA is immediately pitched high in the betting for the following year's Gold Cup and Champ was put up there with the big guns, behind only dual winner Al Boum Photo and his stablemate Santini, a giant beast of a chaser who was beaten just a neck in the main event later in the week.

Santini – whose defeat of Bristol De Mai in the Cotswold Chase in January marked him as an admirably thorough stayer – is a similar stamp to his stablemate and might well be the classier of the two, although brilliance is often an overrated quality in the Gold Cup, in which tenacity and tirelessness and sheer guts are more valuable.

Minella Rocco and Anibale Fly – two dogged plodders who keep going when the flashier types falter, both coincidentally owned by McManus – have been placed in recent renewals of the Gold Cup and perhaps Champ is another in their mould, especially as the New course rewards stamina more than the built-for-speed Old course over which the RSA is run.

The plan (and we know Henderson doesn't like his plans to be upset) was to send him to the Henrietta Knight academy for some schooling before beginning his 2020-21 campaign – "He obviously has an amazing engine, but I'm still not sure whether he jumps like a Gold Cup horse," she said – and if the extra tuition bears fruit there's no doubt Champ could be a real contender for the steeplechasing crown.

Champ by name; yes, we know. Anything else? "He has an attitude to die for," Henderson said. The RSA Chase was the point where Champ truly began to live up to his name. Next year, you know, he might finish the job.

IN THE PICTURE

OBE for Henderson – and more honours on the racecourse

NICKY HENDERSON received an OBE for services to racing from the Prince of Wales at Buckingham Palace in March. The legendary jumps trainer, who is based at Seven Barrows in Lambourn and has been training since 1978, was among those recognised in the New Year Honours List alongside his good friend and rival Paul Nicholls.

"I'm delighted and honoured to receive this award on behalf of my family, Seven Barrows and racing," Henderson said. "It's very nice and an honour to represent racing. I've been very lucky to be involved in a fantastic game for 40-odd years."

Henderson, 69, has sent out more than 3,000 winners and last season he was champion trainer for the sixth time. He had four winners at the Cheltenham Festival, including a record eighth Champion Hurdle with Epatante, and now has 68 in total at the festival, second only to Willie Mullins.

Nicholls, 58, outranks Henderson for trainers' championships with 11 titles and is third on the festival list with 46 winners. Last season he won an 11th King George VI Chase with Clan Des Obeaux and moved alongside Henderson (and Tom Dreaper) with a joint-record sixth success in the Queen Mother Champion Chase when Politologue led home Dynamite Dollars in a one-two for his yard.

On the announcement of the honour, Nicholls said: "I must have impressed the Queen when she visited us in the spring to see the horses. I received a lovely letter a few weeks back, asking me if I would accept an OBE, and I definitely wasn't going to say no. It was a complete shock and it's a great honour."

Nicholls, a former jump jockey who trains at Ditcheat in Somerset, added: "Dad was in the police force and we had no connection with horses whatsoever. We had no money and at one point lived in what was, in effect, a police council house. Mum and Dad built things up from there and they have supported me all the way, making a lot of sacrifices in order to help me."

The 2020 New Year Honours List also included an MBE for Afghan war veteran Captain Guy Disney, who in 2017 became the first jockey to ride a winner under rules in Britain with a prosthetic leg, former Down Royal general manager Mike Todd and David Muir, RSPCA racing consultant. Leading owner Graham Wylie was knighted for his services to business and charity and the Queen's jumps racing adviser Sir Michael Oswald was given the Grand Cross of the (Royal) Victorian Order.

Picture: EDWARD WHITAKER (RACINGPOST.COM/PHOTOS)

Toe to toe: Magical (left) comes out on top against Ghaiyyath in a thrilling battle for the Irish Champion Stakes at Leopardstown in September; opposite page, Magical in the winner's enclosure with groom Leigh O'Brien

CLASH OF THE TITANS

Ghaiyyath beat Magical in world-topping style, then the mare turned the tables in an epic duel

By Steve Dennis

THERE'S one every year. Sometimes we know it at the time, sometimes we see it only through the prism of hindsight, but every year there's a race that stands out from the common throng, becomes another milestone on memory lane. When Magical moved alongside Ghaiyyath in the Irish Champion Stakes, eyeball to eyeball, toe to toe, Coolmore against Godolphin, we had the race by which to remember 2020.

The great Leopardstown contest has previous in this regard. In 2001 Fantastic Light gloriously outmuscled Galileo thanks to a virtuoso Frankie Dettori ride and a spot of team tactics; two years later a race broke out amid the fighting and High Chaparral pipped Falbrav; two years ago Roaring Lion ran down Saxon Warrior to win in the last gasp. Unforgettable stuff, and Magical's duel with Ghaiyyath fits deservedly into the canon.

Let's leave them there, locked in combat on a sunny September afternoon, two furlongs to run and the race to win. For this was the third meeting of the pair, this pair who pulled the strings of the ten-furlong division this season to the virtual exclusion of all others. Two titans together, yet on their first encounter in the 2019 Prix de l'Arc de Triomphe they were merely also-rans, nothing more than extras in a crowd scene.

Magical finished fifth, fading quickly after a brief appearance in the lead, which she had wrested from a weakening Ghaiyyath (tenth) after that horse had set the pace in his habitual fashion. It would not be unfair to describe Ghaiyyath as one-dimensional, albeit thrillingly so, as this powerful individual must make the running, revels in it, becomes a blunt instrument of great beauty as he leaves his pursuers bobbing like rowing boats in his speedboat's wake.

It didn't work at Longchamp, but it soon became the trademark of 2020, the only sound in William Buick's ears the ticking of the clock in his head as beneath him Ghaiyyath dictated an irresistible pace. Buoyed by an easy win in Dubai, the five-year-old then ran his rivals into the ground in the Group 1 Coronation Cup (this year run at Newmarket) over a mile and a half, breaking the track record.

His best performances had hitherto come at that distance, but if he could pull off the same trick, the catch-me-if-you-can, at the faster pace of ten-furlong competition the world seemed his. He could, and it was, judging on his display in the Coral-Eclipse at Sandown when he beat the mighty Enable pointless, although the mare was widely known to be in need of the outing and was not, in any case, a natural at a mile and a quarter, her Eclipse victory of 2018 being her only success at that trip.

Ghaiyyath looked unstoppable; who could stop him? Now, as moody and magnificent as the great warrior Achilles in his tent, he would wait – his preference for time between his races being well documented – for York and the Juddmonte International.

★★★★

SO, THEN, what of Magical? After the Arc, after a long spell of playing second fiddle to Enable's virtuoso brilliance, after winning the Champion Stakes at Ascot, she was retired to the breeding paddocks and a date with No Nay Never. She had been a wonderful racemare, now it was time to be a broodmare. Valentine's Day, as amusingly as it sounds, falls around the start of the covering season – not so much hearts and flowers as, well, y'know, this is a family publication – but in the Racing Post of February 13 there came news that No Nay Never had been stood up at the last minute.

"Magical is still with us in Ballydoyle," Aidan O'Brien said. "The lads [the Coolmore partners] are considering letting her race on this year."

The lads don't often get it wrong. A week before Ghaiyyath's demolition of the Eclipse field, Magical returned to action in the Group 1 Pretty Polly Stakes at the Curragh and made all, winning with ease. "Something just happened with her over the winter," O'Brien said. "She got stronger. She transformed. That's why the lads brought her back. Usually you see that sort of improvement from three to four, but she made it from four to five. The power really came into her body."

A month later, she produced an identical performance in the Group 1 Tattersalls Gold Cup, and was now on course for the Juddmonte herself. Magical and Ghaiyyath, the two titans, like two strands of DNA winding their way through the Flat season and giving it intoxicating life, would come together again.

Achilles came out of his tent at York and put his rivals to the sword without mercy, making all, making it look easy, making it look definitive. In the course of two minutes Ghaiyyath became a phenomenon, was elevated to the status of 'best horse in the world' by earning a Racing Post Rating of 131 and an official rating of 130, compatible in recent years with Golden Horn and Cracksman.

A closer look at his four rivals

▸▸ *Continues page 58*

offers little clarity in that regard – Rose Of Kildare was outclassed, Kameko a patent non-stayer, third-placed Lord North reminded of his subordinate place in the bigger picture after he had won only a garden-variety renewal of the Prince of Wales's Stakes at Royal Ascot – except for Magical, who stayed on grimly for the runner-up spot, beaten three lengths, without ever laying a glove on Ghaiyyath. If Ghaiyyath could do that to six-time Group 1 winner Magical . . . – the thesaurus (generally close at hand) was quickly ransacked for superlatives.

"He's the best I've ridden, without a doubt," Buick said. "He can do things that other horses don't do. He gives you confidence. His comfort zone is different from other horses."

Trainer Charlie Appleby settled for "relentless and exceptional", chief Racing Post writer Lee Mottershead coined him as the 'brute in blue', alliteratively and literally. Even John Gosden, trainer of Lord North, paid his dues with what were prescient words: "The winner is great. If you let him bowl along in front you'll never see him again."

****

THE score, for those keeping count, and there weren't many, was 1-1 between Ghaiyyath and Magical, although statistics can be made to prove anything. Few outside Ballydoyle considered that if the two met again in the Irish Champion Stakes it would resemble a decider. Look, hadn't Ghaiyyath just decided everything?

The trouble, though, with being tactically transparent is that everyone knows what you're going to do. Ghaiyyath would lead, that was Ghaiyyath. And if everyone knows what move you'll make, there is scope to counteract it. After all, as everyone knows, even Achilles had his heel.

"We feel we haven't really seen the very best of Magical yet," said O'Brien, coaxed into clairvoyance by the onset of the Irish Champion Stakes, which the mare had won comfortably the previous year. "Some day, when everything falls right, she'll be at the height of her powers. It could come one of these days."

▲ On top of the world: Ghaiyyath and William Buick after his signature performance in the Juddmonte International
▼ Ghaiyyath leaves Magical (right) trailing three lengths behind as he earns a Racing Post Rating of 131

One of these days. Let's go back to where we came in, two horses locked in combat on a sunny September afternoon, two furlongs to run and the race to win. Two horses locked in combat? How did we get here? Surely . . .

Ghaiyyath was sent off at 8-13 to add another ten-furlong jewel to his crown. He would lead. Everyone knew it. He did lead. There he goes. And Magical went with him.

Magical – ridden by Seamie Heffernan in the second-choice white cap after Ryan Moore had chosen to partner her increasingly disappointing stablemate Japan – was at his heels the whole way. Ghaiyyath set his own fractions but Magical sat there like his shadow, something that no horse had been able to do all year. Ghaiyyath had always put the 'easy' into easy lead but this was a different game now.

For the first time in a long time, without the comfort of daylight surrounding him, Ghaiyyath had an air of vulnerability, an Achilles barefoot. As the leader turned for home, Buick was hard at work, but then so was Heffernan. At the quarter-mile pole, Magical put her head next to Ghaiyyath's and left it there. One of these days, O'Brien had said.

Japan dropped away. Armory and Sottsass (what next for him?!) were too far back. It was only Magical and Ghaiyyath, Ghaiyyath and Magical, the world reduced in size to two horses running. "Roll up! Roll up!" called commentator Jerry Hannon, the old huckster's cry. Come and see, come and see. We came and saw; she conquered.

For the whole long length of a furlong the two horses were in lockstep, and then Magical nosed in front. The nose became a head, the head became a neck, the neck a half-length, the half-length became three-quarters. Ghaiyyath's grip weakened. Magical went past him like a bright bay arrow.

"Once I landed on his girth, I knew I would win," Heffernan said. "I saw Ghaiyyath having a look at her at the start, he knew we were there today. He knew we meant business."

The irresistible force of Ghaiyyath had met the immovable object. Magical simply wouldn't budge, she never gave him a moment's pause, and at the end she had the change of gear her rival lacked. Ghaiyyath was still the world leader on the basis of his York performance but, although defeat by one of the best in the business hardly points to a serious demerit, his crown had nevertheless slipped over one eye.

The 'brute in blue' was a justifiable absentee from the Arc, run on ground possibly worse than that which led to his capitulation 12 months earlier, and he wasn't under consideration for the Champion Stakes at Ascot, with his retirement to stud announced shortly after that race. Magical, on the other hand, at her best when the leaves fall, did go to Ascot as favourite for the end-of-season highlight in an attempt to repeat her victory of the previous year, the double-double of Ireland and England.

It wasn't to be; whether her Leopardstown exertions had left the tank half-empty, whether it was the fact that she was unable to sit in the front rank behind a fast pace, but she came up short in third place behind the mud-loving Addeybb, who had followed her home 12 months earlier. From such a high point, there is usually only one way to go.

But we remember the view from the peak, the things we saw. Two top-class horses, one the best in the world. One race of the season. One for the ages.

▼ The brute in blue: Ghaiyyath with William Buick in the York winner's enclosure, and how the Racing Post reported their Juddmonte International victory

GLADIATOR GHAIYYATH

Godolphin star leaves his rivals toiling

Kameko team eye mile races in autumn

William Buick enjoyed a high-speed summer on the brilliant front-runner Ghaiyyath, 12 months after serious injury had put his riding career in doubt. He spoke openly in this Racing Post interview in August

FAST FORWARD

By Julian Muscat

IT IS six days after the Juddmonte International and William Buick hasn't yet run out of superlatives. With Ghaiyyath's emphatic triumph having just been assessed as the best by any racehorse in the world this year, Buick is more than happy to add to the tributes that have rained down on the five-year-old like an autumnal squall.

The difference is that while some questioned the son of Dubawi's capacity to dismantle a top-class field, Buick harboured no doubts. The Ghaiyyath we are seeing this season has been four years in the making. He needed to evolve from a headstrong, one-dimensional galloper into a wiser, more rounded competitor.

"The way Ghaiyyath quickened again at York when he was challenged was quite visible on television, and it felt like it in the saddle," Buick says. "We saw his speed and his stamina; it was the full package coming into play. He certainly had the ability to do that last season but whether he was mature enough mentally is a hard question to answer."

But Buick makes an equally telling observation of Charlie Appleby's trainee when he notes: "The horse had done that before, especially in last year's Grosser Preis von Baden [which Ghaiyyath won by 14 lengths]. But this year he has managed to string a sequence together. That's important. It shows how much he has progressed."

At 32, Buick is wise enough to recognise how flights of fancy can take wing on the back of a top-class horse. He understands that racing devotees quickly become enchanted by a champion, especially one in the mould of Ghaiyyath, whose adversarial, front-running style dares opponents to catch him if they can.

It's a dynamic much cherished by fans who love nothing better than a horse prepared to go out on his shield. But the boot was on the other foot in the Derby, when Buick, riding Amhran Na Bhfiann, gave vain chase to Serpentine before finishing a leg-weary third. What did he make of Serpentine's pillar-to-post triumph?

"It was a funny race, for sure," he says. "I was flat out all the way and the winner had us all cooked. But you don't win the Derby like that without being a very good horse. It's as simple as that."

Asked whether the jockeys near the front of the chasing pack had talked mid-race about how they might claw back Serpentine, he replied: "No. The Derby is the most important race in the calendar. You're not going round Kempton in a maiden. It's not the kind of race where you can make a big mid-race move to get yourself on the heels of the leader."

With those words Buick neatly amplifies the dilemma faced by every jockey riding against Ghaiyyath.

****

ALL in all, it has been a challenging 12 months for Buick. This time last year he had just returned from an enforced three-month layoff after he was unseated and fell heavily from a horse on the way to post. He felt well enough the following morning to take his rides that day but unwell enough by the evening to take himself to Addenbrooke's Hospital, in Cambridge. He was subsequently diagnosed with post-concussion syndrome, a complex disorder for which the best antidote is a sustained period of rest.

In most cases the condition, often characterised by headaches and bouts of dizziness, lapses after three months, which corresponds with Buick's absence from the saddle. Nevertheless, it was a worrying time. The most extreme of racecourse rumours held that he might not return at all. On top of that, Buick had to contend with the bane of every sportsperson's life: mental inertia through inactivity.

He countered it with the support of family, close friends and his long-term partner Jane Duncan, with whom he has a 20-month-old son, Thomas. "Charlie and the whole Godolphin team gave me wonderful support, as did Jane, and my mum and dad were there, as they always are," he says.

"It aided my recovery. I was never worried I might not come back. It was just a case of getting everything right, getting as fit as I possibly could before I came back and just looking forward. Yes, I missed a large chunk of the season but I'm planning to have a long career. It was important to recover in the right way."

Buick would have returned sooner if wellbeing alone was the sole litmus test. "My life was pretty much back to normal three or four weeks before I rode in public again but there are regulations that need to be followed – and rightly so," he says.

"The BHA's doctor was very

Continues page 62

▼ Comfort zone: William Buick at home in Newmarket and, opposite page, with his partner Jane Duncan and son Thomas

helpful, as were a lot of other people. Of course I missed race-riding, the daily routine, being involved. It's a massive part of my life, but you also feel like that when you get a seven-day suspension. And now it's all in the past, it's done, finished. To be honest, I don't think at all about what happened to me last year. I look forward."

★★★★

BUICK made a winning comeback on the Appleby-trained Lazuli at Newmarket on August 3, 2019. Ghaiyyath cemented the jockey's return to the big time four weeks later with that monstrous performance at Baden-Baden, and then, on September 15, Pinatubo all but secured champion juvenile honours when winning the National Stakes by nine lengths. Buick's vista had been transformed in the space of six weeks.

He then had a productive spell in Japan before Christmas, after which he bedded down in Dubai for the carnival. That, too, was one to savour, but then followed the Covid-19 pandemic that would derail his momentum, starting with the cancellation of Dubai World Cup night.

Inevitably, the start of the turf season in Europe was postponed, yet frustration was tempered by realism. "Watching the news during lockdown, when the daily deaths were read out, you can't be selfish," he says. "What was important was that when racing restarted everybody got together to create a very safe environment."

Like everybody else, Buick misses the crowds on big days but prefers to accentuate the positives. "It's not good, we all know that, but it's important the industry is functioning," he says. "Prize-money is not great at all but again, the whole world is not in a good place. The bottom line is that I was delighted to get back to racing. I'd missed it."

Ghaiyyath made the wait worthwhile.

This is an edited version of an interview that appeared in the Racing Post on August 30

Three steps to heaven

William Buick's view from the saddle on the three wins that took Ghaiyyath to the top of the world rankings

Coronation Cup, 1m4f, Newmarket, June 5
Won by two and a half lengths from Anthony Van Dyck
RPR 125

"Ghaiyyath is an amazing horse and he has so much speed he could lay up with a six-furlong horse at home. You have to go along with him and try to keep the lid on him as much as you can. Fair play to Shane Featherstonhaugh, who rides him at home, and that was a big win as it was his first Group 1 in Britain and it was a deep field."

Eclipse, 1m2f, Sandown, July 5
Won by two and a quarter lengths from Enable
RPR 129

"He's got a high cruising speed and he knows how to use it. He's a horse that you go with what he wants to do. He's not a horse who wants to be controlled, you're best sitting against him and letting him use his big stride and then go when he's ready. He's a joy to ride and he's a very good horse. I think it will be a mile and a quarter [where he's best] as he's very fast and has a high cruising speed. Sometimes when you ride him over a mile and a half you're worried that last furlong is going to be a long one, although he always keeps going."

International Stakes, 1m2½f, York, August 19
Won by three lengths from Magical
RPR 131

"I let him get into his rhythm and then he does the rest. He has this amazing high cruising speed, but I thought what was evident today was the kick he had a furlong and a half out. He completely put the race to bed, finished it off and stamped his authority. He can do things that other horses don't do. He gives you confidence. His comfort zone is different to other horses. He can sustain his speed and then finish off a race with that turn of foot at the end. I haven't ridden many horses who can do that. He's the best I've ridden, without a doubt."

◂ World class: William Buick at Doncaster for the St Leger festival in a year when he was at the peak of his powers on Ghaiyyath, pictured top winning the International at York

THE BIGGER PICTURE

Three of Newmarket's early starters are silhouetted against the rising sun on the Racecourse Side gallops on the morning after the spring equinox in March

EDWARD WHITAKER (RACINGPOST.COM/PHOTOS)

THE ROCKET

By Steve Dennis

LIGHT a firework, step back and watch it explode in brilliance. Or not. Sometimes nothing happens. Is it still alight? Is it a dud? Everyone knows not to return to a firework once lit. The only thing is to wait.

Marcus Tregoning is very good at waiting. He's very good at training too, which is all about waiting, isn't it? Tregoning had to wait more than 14 years for another Group 1, after Sir Percy's Derby, and he had to wait more than 15 months for Mohaather to explode in brilliance. The Qatar Sussex Stakes at Glorious Goodwood provided the setting, and the waiting was well worth it.

"It's a while since I've had a champion," said Tregoning, tilting back his Panama hat to better see the happy scene at his favourite racecourse. "This is pretty special. He's a proper horse."

Tregoning first put the match to Mohaather in the 2018 Horris Hill Stakes at Newbury, then saw the flame catch in the Greenham Stakes at the same track the following April, but a severe stone bruise ruled the colt out of the 2,000 Guineas and left Tregoning watching that season's big mile races come and go from a safe distance.

▸▸ *Continues page 68*

Mohaather burned brightly but all too briefly with his explosive Sussex Stakes success

▼ Final flourish: Mohaather swoops for a thrilling victory in the Sussex Stakes on what proved to be his last start, winning from Circus Maximus (third right), Siskin (second right) and Kameko

This year was different. The old fire began to travel up the fuse with an easy victory in the Group 2 Summer Mile at Ascot and the rocket went up at Goodwood a couple of weeks later, setting the sky alight. It wasn't just the victory itself either, but the way in which Mohaather achieved it, a sensational last-to-first charge down the outside that would have brought the crowd to its feet in delight, had there been a crowd.

****

THE Sussex Stakes annually marks the spot where the generations meet at a mile, where the Classic crop takes on the older horses and the hierarchy in one of the most glamorous divisions of the game begins to be made plain. It is also habitually and alliteratively labelled the 'Duel on the Downs' by the marketing department, the race regularly luring two crack milers to go head to head. This season, though, it wasn't so much a duel as open warfare, with six of the seven runners bringing Group 1 black type to the battlefield. The exception? Mohaather.

Kameko and Siskin were 2,000

▸▸ *Continues page 70*

▲ Summer star: Mohaather with trainer Marcus Tregoning at Whitsbury Manor Stables in Hampshire
▼ Tregoning keeps a watchful eye as Mohaather (right) walks down the gallops with first lot

MOHAATHER

Guineas winners at Newmarket and the Curragh; Wichita and Vatican City were runners-up in those Classics. Circus Maximus had won the Queen Anne Stakes on his previous start, while San Donato had run third in the Poule d'Essai des Poulains in a truncated 2019 campaign. Mohaather had been well beaten on both his starts at the top level, but the nature of his Ascot win, allied to his evident talent, encouraged punters to send him off second favourite behind Siskin.

That faith looked misplaced two furlongs from home, the familiar Goodwood curse of trouble in running hanging over Mohaather after Wichita had bored in upon him, forcing jockey Jim Crowley to snatch up and pull his mount wide to challenge. At the furlong marker he had five Group 1 horses in front of him, but the picture changed dramatically in the next 100 yards as Mohaather's scintillating turn of foot propelled him to the lead and a three-quarter-length defeat of the ever-game Circus Maximus.

The formbook comment said 'cosily', underlining the likelihood of his superiority being greater than the winning margin implied. Crowley seconded that motion.

"I had to let the race unfold and then pull him around the field," he said. "When he saw daylight he just absolutely flew. I thought it was a very special performance, and the way it panned out he was exceptional. I've never had any doubt he could win a Group 1 over six furlongs and would say he's in the mould of the really good ones."

The emphatic nature of Mohaather's victory, and the way he readily overcame his lack of racing room – Kameko was another caught out by circumstance, finishing a frustrated fourth – made him indisputably the pro tem leader of the mile division, which had basically shrunk to five preceding races (both Guineas, the Queen Anne, the St James's Palace and the Coronation Stakes) owing to the loss of the Lockinge from a heavily restricted campaign.

Now the only real threat to Mohaather's dominance seemed to be the John Gosden-trained three-year-old Palace Pier, who had started the season in handicap company before squeezing the last of the air out of the Pinatubo balloon at Royal Ascot. Three weeks after Goodwood, Palace Pier underlined his growing potency with victory in the Prix Jacques le Marois at Deauville, with Circus Maximus nearly six lengths back in third.

▲ Speed machine: Mohaather wins the Sussex Stakes from Circus Maximus and Siskin

▼ Masked jockey Jim Crowley and trainer Marcus Tregoning savour their success

Here, it seemed, was the duel we desired. Send the boys around town with an armful of posters and a pot of paste, Mohaather v Palace Pier, the big fight, the decider on Champions Day at Ascot. Tregoning, slipping easily back into his long-vacated role as cornerman to a champ, would never in his life descend to the sort of trash talk that characterises the preliminaries of most heavyweight bouts, being far too urbane an English gentleman, but he came as close to it as his character allowed.

"Palace Pier has proved he's a very nice horse," he said, judiciously, before metaphorically rolling his shoulders and raising his voice, jabbing his finger. "Getting these good horses to meet is what it's all about and we'll see what's what then."

★★★★

WE NEVER had the chance to see what was what. In circumstances that typify the uncertainty of racing, the way disappointment walks in the footprints of delight, a bare week after Tregoning had called it 'on' it was 'off' with a "significant bone bruise" to Mohaather's near-hind fetlock ushering him into retirement at the height of his form. The exhalation of anguish from the racing world was almost audible, and Tregoning – so briefly back in the big time – now found himself watching from the wings again.

"He was getting better and better," he said. "I can't see another miler who would have beaten him. I've seen lots of very good horses over the years, particularly when I was assistant to Dick Hern, but I never saw one quicken like this horse could. Absolutely extraordinary acceleration – he was like a rocket."

The rocket always falls back to earth and all that remains is the brightness and beauty that is still imprinted on the eye long after the event. The mile division was now in danger of becoming a damp squib, for without defeating a peak-form Mohaather, how could Palace Pier – or any other horse – claim undisputed honours? His absence would define the cold and closing weeks of the season just as his irresistible presence had defined the heat of high summer.

"He's what we do it all for," added Tregoning, 61. "One of my owners said to me 'you'll never see a horse as good as that again, Marcus', and I said 'no, there's no such thing as never'."

Tregoning, so patient, so good at waiting, might be right. A month after Mohaather's retirement, he sent out two-year-old Alkumait – a son of Showcasing owned by Hamdan Al Maktoum, just like Mohaather – to record an impressive success in the Group 2 Mill Reef Stakes at Newbury. Parallels were drawn, comparisons made, hope rekindled.

There may never be another Mohaather but one thing is certain. There will always be the potential for fireworks.

MILERS APART

By David Carr

THERE is no doubting the creative genius of the inspired folk who come up with the Christmas gifts that raise vital funds for the Injured Jockeys Fund. Every penny counts and this worthiest of causes is needed as much now as when it was founded in the 1960s – for all the many improvements in safety, riding a thoroughbred racehorse at speed remains an inherently dangerous activity.

Ask dual former Flat champion Paul Hanagan, whose career was put in doubt when he sustained serious back injuries in a fall at Newcastle in February but who battled back to fitness and scored a hugely emotional win on Majestic Dawn in the Cambridgeshire at Newmarket in the autumn.

Or poor Jacob Pritchard Webb, an aspiring jump jockey for whom there will be no return to the saddle after he suffered a horrifying list of neck and spinal injuries in a fall at Auteuil in June at the age of just 23.

So no-one can begrudge the effort put into thinking up the enticing gifts that fill the annual IJF catalogue – a publication whose latest offerings included branded LED torch beanie hats ('great for walking the dog in the dark'), Grand National winners playing cards and a 1,000-piece jigsaw featuring Politologue and Harry Skelton landing the Queen Mother Champion Chase.

But they may just have missed a trick in not designing a Kameko/Palace Pier weather house. The season's two best three-year-old milers lent themselves perfectly to playing the parts of the characters on either side of the folk art device, taking strict turns to emerge into the light while seemingly destined never to meet.

That was never better exemplified than when a wet October meant one was safely tucked up inside while the other put his reputation on the line in the Queen Elizabeth II Stakes. Rarely can a pair of high-class contemporaries with such similar attributes have operated so much in parallel universes, each making their mark and then leaving the stage for the other to shine.

▲ Different orbits: star milers Kameko (above) and Palace Pier (opposite page)

★★★★

KAMEKO, the younger by a mere 18 days, started it off with a winning debut at Sandown in the July of his two-year-old season.

The tall, scopey colt, who was bought for $90,000 by Qatar Racing and put in training with Andrew Balding, made comfortable work of seeing off a field of maidens over seven furlongs and was then beaten just a nose in the Solario Stakes there the following month.

Tantalisingly, it was on the opening day of the Solario meeting that Palace Pier made his first appearance. The strong and athletic 600,000gns purchase landed a maiden over the same trip in smart fashion and put himself in the 2,000 Guineas picture when he and Frankie Dettori followed up in novice company at the same course the following month. But that was

Kameko and Palace Pier were the top three-year-olds in a high-class division but destined never to meet

the last we saw of him. John Gosden had to scrap plans to test him in the Prix Jean-Luc Lagardere at Longchamp due to a leg injury.

Over to Kameko, who re-emerged into the spotlight by making history at the back-end of the turf season. The Vertem Futurity was rescued from waterlogged Doncaster and switched to Newcastle as the first British Group 1 race on an artificial surface, and Oisin Murphy's mount was the first winner, emphatically so as he scored by a comfortable three and a quarter lengths.

That was where the pair stood as the entire horse population were kept inside through the pandemic shutdown, after which Palace Pier was the first to step into the daylight on the first Saturday of the delayed season.

With no chance of a Classic prep run to give the novice more experience, Gosden chose to run him in a handicap at Newcastle, where he readily made it three from three under Robert Havlin.

That was not strong form – his six rivals failed to win in 21 subsequent attempts between them by mid-October – but the sparkling turn of foot he showed to go from a couple of lengths down into utter command within a few strides hinted strongly at an extremely bright future in top company.

Yet there was little time to consider that as just 20 minutes later Kameko proved the very same point in the Qipco 2,000 Guineas 250 miles away at Newmarket. With owners at that time banned from being on course in the early days of racing behind closed doors, Sheikh Fahad had to watch from home as the colt stayed on determinedly to get the better of Wichita and odds-on favourite Pinatubo in a contest his family had sponsored for a decade.

The rest of the team more than made up for the owner's absence with their jubilation as champion jockey Murphy called his first British Classic success "the stuff of dreams". Balding was going one place better than his father Ian had done with Mill Reef 49 years previously and said: "This is a massive thrill. It's a bizarre experience, but I promise you I didn't feel any less elation than if there had been 500,000 people here."

A practically empty Epsom was no less bizarre four weeks later but Kameko never threatened to emulate Mill Reef's 1971 Derby triumph. For all that he got much less than an ideal run of the race behind Serpentine, he seemed palpably not to stay the mile and a half.

In fact, it was a decidedly anti-climactic summer for Kameko, who followed a luckless fourth in the Sussex Stakes – Murphy blamed himself for getting blocked in while Mohaather whooshed past – with a so-so fourth in the Juddmonte International.

****

WHICH meant it must have been Palace Pier's turn to shine, and he did not disappoint. Those who

▸▸ *Continues page 74*

thought the style of his Newcastle success had the stamp of a Group 1 performer in the making had their view confirmed when he landed the St James's Palace Stakes at Royal Ascot a fortnight later, readily beating Pinatubo by just a neck less than Kameko had done at Newmarket.

Whereas Kameko had been beaten when going into open-age company over a mile in the Sussex, Palace Pier looked the stuff champion milers are made of when following up in the Prix Jacques le Marois at Deauville in August, rewarding Dettori's decision to travel to France for the ride even though pandemic restrictions meant he had to miss the following week's Ebor festival.

The Deauville ground was heavy and Palace Pier "didn't like it one bit", according to Gosden, but he was still able to stretch to the line three-quarters of a length in front of Alpine Star, who had won the Coronation Stakes impressively on the same day as the St James's Palace. Another five lengths behind in third was Circus Maximus, the Sussex runner-up.

Palace Pier himself was put by for the autumn and as he stepped out of the spotlight . . . well, you've probably got the idea by now.

Kameko emerged to show his true colours once more, dropped back to a mile in the Group 2 Joel Stakes at Newmarket and defying a Group 1 penalty with a performance 4lb better than his Guineas win judged on Racing Post Ratings, although 2lb behind the mark earned by Palace Pier at Deauville.

Which set things up perfectly for their meeting in the Queen Elizabeth II Stakes, where the two best three-year-old milers would finally take each other on – the quickener against the resolute galloper in a clash of styles that promised to put the champion into Champions Day.

Until, ironically, the weather intervened. The ground was deemed too soft for Kameko to take his chance – the closest he got to the action at Ascot was the advert for his stallion services in 2021 that appeared in the racecard. And Palace Pier was unquestionably below his brilliant best in third place behind The Revenant, losing a shoe in the testing conditions and never travelling with his customary elan.

▲ Star turns: Palace Pier lands the St James's Palace Stakes at Royal Ascot ▶ Kameko gives Oisin Murphy his first British Classic success in the 2,000 Guineas at Newmarket

"You can't win a race with three wheels, you need all four," Dettori said.

It was a frustrating turn of events for those keen to see the best horses in competition with each other, but entirely in keeping with the tenor of the miling division. With Mohaather departing the scene soon after his Sussex triumph, the promise of an ultimate showdown to decide the overall champion was never delivered. More's the pity.

THE
BIGGER
PICTURE

Toro Strike (Oisin Murphy) wins the Theo Fennell Handicap on the second day of Glorious Goodwood in July. Normally the beautiful South Downs course would welcome around 100,000 racegoers over the five days of its biggest festival

EDWARD WHITAKER (RACINGPOST.COM/PHOTOS)

PLEASE KEEP A LENGTH APART
PLEASE KEEP A LENGTH APART

AL BASTI
DUBAI

CHANGE OF GEAR

Battaash completed his transition from wild thing to model professional with a perfect season in the top British sprints

By Nick Pulford

IN HIS four years of being the most electrifying sprinter around, there have been two types of Battaash moment.

There is the one where, most thrillingly, he takes the breath away with his brilliant speed. He has produced plenty of those; in many ways it is the default position. But then there is the other type where, most frustratingly, something throws him out of kilter and he doesn't perform at his best. There have been a few of those too.

Happily, in the high summer of 2020, every Battaash moment was a positive one. At the age of six he seemed finally to have come of age as a true professional, rising to every challenge with a mental toughness to match his physical talent. New places were conquered, more records were broken, and he left opponents not just racing for second place but running scared.

Battaash's dominance of the 2020 sprint division started at Royal Ascot, where he put down an important marker for the season ahead. He had come up short at the meeting on three previous visits, including two second places behind Blue Point in the King's Stand Stakes, and many questioned whether he would be able to master the track and the rain-softened conditions this time.

The answer was emphatic. Battaash pinged the gates and was soon travelling powerfully in front. Already he looked in complete control and in the final furlong Jim Crowley did not have to engage top gear to finish two and a quarter lengths clear of Equilateral, giving trainer Charlie Hills a one-two in the race that had eluded him in the previous two years.

"I was slightly tense, but I've lived every emotion with him now," Hills said. "We have been beaten twice before and, three times, I don't think I could have dealt with that. I watched the race where no-one could see in the concourse. I just thought 'Thank God for that' when he got the job done."

This time there had been no Blue Point to take on Battaash in

▸▸ *Continues page 80*

the final furlong and nor, of course, had there been a crowd to put him on edge. Both factors made Crowley's job so much easier. "He was really good going down today," he said. "He has got better as time has gone on. Obviously two years ago at York he completely blew his lid before the race. I think not having the crowd here did help. When those gates opened, he was gone. He's just such a naturally fast horse. Okay, he can throw the odd one in now and again, but when he's good, he's very, very good."

The York hoodoo had been ended in even more dominant fashion the year before with his record-breaking triumph in the Nunthorpe Stakes and this victory put Battaash in exalted company as a winner of Europe's big three Group 1 sprints over five furlongs, having started his run in the Prix de l'Abbaye in 2017.

Hills was already looking towards another historic moment. "I would be really proud if he could win the King George Stakes four times at Goodwood. It would be a highlight of the season if he could do that."

★★★★

WHILE Hills waited for Goodwood with Battaash, the rest of the sprint division was gathering pace. The two six-furlong Group 1 races at Royal Ascot, the Diamond Jubilee Stakes and the Commonwealth Cup, had fallen to Hello Youmzain and Golden Horde respectively, setting up a clash of the generations in the July Cup.

The three-year-old Golden Horde was sent off 2-1 favourite at Newmarket but he found a couple of his year-older rivals a little too strong. Hello Youmzain was not one of them, finishing fifth. Victory went to Oxted, giving Lambourn trainer Roger Teal his first Group 1 success. Irish trainer Denis Hogan, also striving to score at the top level for the first time, had to settle for second with Sceptical. Unfortunately, within a month Hogan had lost his rags-to-riches stable star to a fatal leg injury on the gallops. It was a sad end to a wonderful story that had seen Sceptical go from a £2,800 unraced Godolphin castoff to a Group 1 contender in less than a year.

▾ Winning start: trainer Charlie Hills celebrates Battaash's victory in the King's Stand Stakes

A few days before Sceptical's untimely death, Battaash strengthened his grip on the five-furlong division. Goodwood, in contrast to Ascot, is a place he has always loved and once again he was on his A-game in the King George Stakes. By dint of his King's Stand win, he had to carry a Group 1 penalty for the first time in the race he had made his own for the previous three years but it made not an ounce of difference to the outcome. In fact, he went faster than ever before down the Goodwood straight, beating the 2019 Abbaye winner Glass Slippers by two and a quarter lengths and clocking a track record of 55.62sec.

As he had predicted, Hills was a proud man. "We knew if he did what he did in the King's Stand he'd be very hard to beat on a track that suits him," he said. "You've got to give credit to the horse. For a six-year-old sprinter to have his

enthusiasm every day is wonderful. You could say sprinters are at their best when they get older and he has fully matured. Mentally he's fantastic and in a really good spot."

Just how good a spot was emphasised by Teal a few days later when discussing whether to send Oxted for the Nunthorpe. "We'd be dropping back in trip if we went to York and I think he could do that because he travels very strongly," Teal said. "The problem, of course, would be turning up against Battaash. He just destroys you in the first two furlongs of those five-furlong races. I'd like to try it but you don't really want to be taking on horses like him when you do."

None of the six-furlong Group 1 winners dropped down to take on Battaash at York and his main rival on form was Art Power, who had run away with the Palace of Holyroodhouse Handicap at Royal Ascot and then stepped up in class and trip for another clear-cut success in a six-furlong Group 3 at Naas.

Tim Easterby's hope faded in this even warmer company, finishing sixth, and instead it was another northern-trained runner and testing weather conditions that presented the biggest threat to the hot favourite. Famously, Battaash had been beaten into fourth place on his first two cracks at Britain's five-furlong championship race before winning in record time at the third attempt, while his most recent defeat in the 2019 Abbaye had come on what Hills described as "awful ground".

Now, in driving rain and gusting winds, he faced a searching test of character. The ground was good but softening and it was never going to be a blistering burn-up like the year before. Instead it was a battle and Battaash was made to fight all the way by 22-1 shot Que Amoro, representing the Michael Dods yard that had claimed the Nunthorpe with Mecca's Angel in 2015 and 2016.

Crowley had Battaash in the front rank early on as usual but Que Amoro, racing nearer the stands' rail away from the main group in the centre, was flying out in front. A furlong and a half out Crowley got more serious on the favourite and, as they closed the gap on Que Amoro,

▲ Quick fire: Battaash is well clear in the King George Stakes at Goodwood (main picture above), winning the race for the fourth time and setting a track record; a clear-cut first victory at Ascot in the King's Stand Stakes (top right); a much tougher fight to overcome Que Amoro in the Nunthorpe Stakes at York (main picture left); Jim Crowley celebrates at York (inset top left) and Goodwood

they drifted across to race next to the leader. It was neck and neck at the furlong pole but the outsider would not relent, harrying Battaash all the way. The race was finally settled when Crowley squeezed out a little more to get home by a length.

The time was nearly a second and a half outside Battaash's own track record, but this had been a day for something more than pure speed. "I was so proud of the horse today," Hills said. "For me, that was probably the best run of his career because so many things were against him. He knuckled down and worked really hard. It was always going to be tough. On similar ground he's been beaten here as a three-year-old and a four-year-old. He has grown up and matured with age."

Crowley was similarly impressed. "He had to be a man today," he said. "He stuck his neck out and galloped, he tried really hard. We went a serious gallop, there was a really strong tailwind and it was blowing us over to that stands' rail. In the past he's always won his races at halfway and fair play to the second, who ran a mighty race."

▸▸ *Continues page 82*

★★★★

THIS was the first time Battaash had reeled off three wins in a row since his rapid rise up the lower ranks as a three-year-old, a run that ended with his first Nunthorpe defeat. He had done it this time with a Racing Post Rating of 123, matching his seasonal best at Royal Ascot but significantly below the 128 and 129 (twice) he had achieved in the previous three campaigns. What we had missed in terms of pure excitement had been replaced by a consistency he had never shown before at the top level, but crucially he lacked a rival who would push him to his limits.

None of the others could establish the same mastery. The Haydock Sprint Cup went to Dream Of Dreams, who beat the outsider Glen Shiel by a length and a quarter. Glen Shiel's turn came in the British Champions Sprint at Ascot when he got him home by a nose from Brando, who had been unplaced at Haydock. Unplaced this time were Oxted – on his first start since the July Cup – and Dream Of Dreams.

In the five-furlong division, Glass Slippers, well beaten by Battaash at Goodwood, found her best form in the autumn for the second year in a row. First she went to Ireland to land the Flying Five and then narrowly missed out on a repeat win in the Abbaye, falling a neck short of the French three-year-old Wooded.

The Abbaye was meant to be Battaash's final destination but when the ground at Longchamp again came up awful, to use Hills's description of the previous year, he stayed at home. "It's a real shame but it would be silly to take a risk with him," the trainer said.

After Royal Ascot there was a sense that Hills was keen for Battaash to complete an exemplary campaign in Europe for the first time. He had his wish, and there was something else too. "I'm delighted he seems to have caught the public's imagination for the right reasons," Hills said. "It's a bit like the good National Hunt horses, they're around so long that you can't help but get attached to them. We love him to bits."

First stop Royal Ascot, then on to Goodwood and York, the Battaash love train was the perfect ride.

At home with Battaash – views from the people closest to him

Charlie Hills has trained Battaash for Sheikh Hamdan Al Maktoum since 2016

"Sheikh Hamdan asked me to pick out a couple of horses [at the yearling sales] and thank God I put him on my list. I remember he was the most beautiful walker, so athletic, and just the sort of precocious type we were looking for. He likes his routine, he's an intelligent horse and doesn't miss a trick. He likes going out first thing, he wants to be the first out of the stable door.

"He has his quirks, but I'm very proud to be involved with him and my kids – James and Eddie – love him. He's like a family pet. He's not big or imposing, but he loves the attention and he's like having a little pony in the yard."

Bob Grace, who has worked as a groom for the Hills family for 33 years, looks after Battaash at home and at the races

"I've looked after him since the very first day he came. He was quite an interesting character as a baby but, then when he was gelded, he started to look a bit special as a three-year-old. The gelding changed him because when he had his balls he could be a right bastard. It's a good thing, I suppose, otherwise we wouldn't have had him for so long.

"You could do exactly the same thing with him two days running and he'll be fine one day and the next he'll get angry. If someone in the yard turns on a radio, or has a chat on their phone, his head will come straight out of his box and he'll stand there staring.

"I think people like him because he's a bit of a git, but I'd like to think all that stuff is in the past. He has only really run badly twice in his life. Surely we can forgive him that."

Work-rider Viktoria Gatu has been Battaash's regular partner in morning exercise since March 2019, although she wasn't happy to be asked in the first place

"I had a moan, as I'm inclined to do, but Charlie asked me to try it for one week. I just wanted a quiet job, riding horses at the back of the string, and here I was being asked to ride Battaash. I'd never heard of him before I started working for Charlie but there's a lot of pressure taking on a good horse, especially when they're not the easiest.

"I've been stuck with him ever since. He has grown on me. In the beginning he was just another horse but now I realise it's a bit of a privilege to ride him. He's one of the cleverest I've ever ridden. You have to let him have his way as much as you can. Yes, he can have a buck on the gallops, but he's a lovely horse to deal with. Everyone involved has done a great job."

▸ Charlie Hills with Battaash: "He's like a family pet"

ELECTRIC BLUE

Jim Crowley enjoyed a stellar year in the Sheikh Hamdan colours, highlighted by the brilliance of Battaash and Mohaather

AT THE start of August the Racing Post published a retrospective on Hamdan Al Maktoum's 40 years as an owner in Britain. Marking his first winner, a two-year-old called Mushref, at Redcar on July 30, 1980, the article reflected on the sheikh's massive impact on British racing with luminaries such as Nashwan, Dayjur and Salsabil, and around the world with victories in major races including the Breeders' Cup Classic and Melbourne Cup.

Success had largely flowed at a slower rate in recent years but 2020 marked a reopening of the floodgates. Even as the retrospective was being written, thrilling chapters were added to the Hamdan story by Battaash and Mohaather with their brilliant wins at Glorious Goodwood in the last week of July. Those triumphs followed an even more glorious Royal Ascot, where the sheikh had six winners, and big-race success continued to flow throughout the summer and into the autumn.

For Jim Crowley, who wears the famous blue and white silks as the sheikh's number one jockey, it was also a year to remember. The champion jockey of 2016 had taken the job at the end of that year with the express ambition of riding major winners on the biggest occasions. In the first three years, principally with Battaash, he took his career to greater heights; in the fourth, he scaled peak after peak.

Battaash led the way again, not least in laying his Ascot hoodoo with victory in the King's Stand Stakes at the royal meeting, but there was a new star for Crowley in the brilliant miler Mohaather, plus a large supporting cast. The first venue where they hogged the spotlight was Royal Ascot, just over a fortnight after the resumption of racing.

Crowley got the meeting off to a flyer with victory on Motakhayyel, his choice of four Hamdan runners in the Buckingham Palace Handicap, followed up on Battaash and ended the first day with a treble after Nazeef's win in the Duke of Cambridge Stakes. The next day he won the King George V Handicap on Hukum and on the Thursday he added two more victories on Molatham in the Jersey Stakes and Khaloosy in the Britannia Handicap. Six winners might well have been enough to win Crowley the leading rider award but he was pipped by Frankie Dettori, who rode a final-day treble to match his rival's winners and beat him on places.

▲ Royal blue: Crowley strikes with Motakhayyel (above right), Battaash (left) and Nazeef (above) on day one of Royal Ascot

Crowley did not dwell on what might have been. "I didn't lose any sleep over it that night and was very pleased my boss was leading owner," he said. "All my six winners were for him and all the horses we ran performed brilliantly."

★★★★

THE blue and white streak of success was far from over. Nazeef stepped up another level to win the Group 1 Falmouth Stakes at the Newmarket July meeting, with Crowley driving her home to score by two necks, and the John Gosden-trained filly later gave him another top-level win across the Heath on the other Newmarket course in the Sun Chariot Stakes in October.

At the end of July it was Mohaather who led the charge at Glorious Goodwood with his scintillating Sussex Stakes victory, swiftly followed by Battaash's fourth consecutive King George Stakes. As the calendar turned over to August, there was more Group-race success at Goodwood with Enbihaar in the Lillie Langtry Stakes and Crowley ended the meeting with four winners.

York's Ebor festival, the next of the big summer meetings, was even better. On a fabulous Friday afternoon, he swept the first four races on the card within barely an hour and a half. Alfaatik started the ball rolling in the Sky Bet Handicap and then came Group-race successes on Enbihaar in the Lonsdale Cup, Minzaal in the Gimcrack Stakes and, most magnificently of all, Battaash in the Nunthorpe Stakes.

★★★★

ALL these winners were pushing Crowley towards a personal milestone at rapid speed and on August 30 he got there. Victory on the sheikh's Modmin in a three-year-old novice event at Goodwood took him to 2,000 winners in Britain, Flat and jumps combined, making him only the sixth current rider to reach that number.

Crowley was elated to reach the landmark at his local track. "It's been a fantastic season and it's nice to do it here," he said, adding that it was also nice "to do it in these colours" and for Marcus Tregoning, Mohaather's trainer.

Ahead of Crowley in the 2,000 club are Richard Johnson, Frankie Dettori, Joe Fanning, Ryan Moore and Jamie Spencer, in that order. All but Dettori have won on the Flat and over jumps. Crowley won 253 races over jumps before switching to the Flat, with Modmin's win the 1,747th of his career in that sphere.

At the age of 42, and having been a late starter on the Flat in his late twenties, Crowley feels there is plenty more to come. "It's not impossible [the next 1,000]. It might seem a long way away now, but so did 2,000, so did 1,000," he said. "You see lads like Oisin [Murphy] and they've achieved so much, so early, I sometimes wish I'd switched to the Flat sooner. I've always tried to be as consistent as I can and every year just keep on improving. I still feel I've got plenty of improvement in me."

Improving on an incredible 2020 might be difficult but Crowley is sure to give it a go.

IN THE PICTURE

Hanagan lands special Cambridgeshire win after brave comeback

PAUL HANAGAN has won Classics and championships but there was a special feeling to his success on Majestic Dawn in the Cambridgeshire at Newmarket in September.

The 40-1 shot stormed to victory by four and three-quarter lengths, putting his 40-year-old rider back on the big stage just six weeks after his return to action from a broken back that almost ended his career.

"That gave me so much pleasure – it was very special," said Hanagan, the 2010 and 2011 British champion jockey, after Majestic Dawn's success. "I was out for six months with the injury and I didn't think I was going to make it back at all, so I'm delighted to bag a winner like that. It was a very tough time but days like this make it all worthwhile."

Hanagan was left with three fractured vertebrae after Requinto Dawn clipped heels and fell at Newcastle in February and he required keyhole surgery, followed by months of rehabilitation aided by the staff at Jack Berry House, the Injured Jockeys' Fund's centre in Malton, North Yorkshire. He did not return to race-riding until August 18.

Speaking before his comeback, Hanagan said: "Getting fit to ride again has been the biggest challenge of my life. It's the worst injury I've had. I couldn't get up from the fall and I couldn't breathe or move anything, so it was pretty scary."

Hanagan discussed the possibility of retirement with his family and some were in favour, but he decided to fight on. "I had one of the best back specialists in the country, Daniel Fagan, performing keyhole surgery and he inserted a balloon with a type of cement into my back to fix the cracked vertebrae. He took the balloon out and it makes it twice as strong."

As well as the positive medical prognosis, Hanagan was buoyed in his rehabilitation by the prospect – ultimately achieved – of his beloved Liverpool lifting the Premier League trophy after a 30-year wait. Above all, it was his inner strength that got him through.

"It's been a character-building few months but I can safely say I'm a lot stronger for it," he said. "In a way, this was the right time to have a serious accident if you were going to have one, because lockdown meant missing far less racing than would normally be the case."

After the Cambridgeshire, Hanagan said: "I've got so many people to thank like the team at Jack Berry House, family and friends, Richard Fahey and my agent Richard Hale, who has been fantastic. I've been with him my whole career and he's been behind me from day one."

Pictures: EDWARD WHITAKER (RACINGPOST.COM/PHOTOS)

THE JOCKEY CLUB
SUPPORTING BRITISH RACING
SINCE 1750
THE JOCKEY CLUB
15

Politologue and Harry Skelton seized control from the front in a Champion Chase shorn of its headline acts

By Jonathan Harding

POLITOLOGUE was a forgotten horse heading to his fifth consecutive Cheltenham Festival, pushed from many minds by the galaxy of stars who would be in action across the four days. Even in his race, the Queen Mother Champion Chase, he was overshadowed by dual winner Altior and the younger pretenders Chacun Pour Soi and Defi Du Seuil. With a mixture of luck and consummate judgement, however, Politologue made everyone sit up and finally take notice.

The race was billed as the highlight of the week with Altior bidding for a record-equalling third success against leading Irish contender Chacun Pour Soi, a convincing winner of the Dublin Chase for Willie Mullins, and Defi Du Seuil, the dominant force in the British two-mile chasing division after an unbeaten build-up to the festival.

Politologue had finished behind Defi Du Seuil in the Shloer Chase and Tingle Creek Chase before Christmas and he also had to reverse the form with Altior, who had beaten him into fourth and second in the last two Champion Chases. Beating any of them, never mind all, looked an extremely tall order for a horse who had not managed to get his nose in front since April 2018.

But then the race started to collapse like a house of cards. Altior was scratched 29 hours before the race, while Chacun Pour Soi was withdrawn on the day. That appeared to set up a lap of honour for Defi Du Seuil, who was sent off 2-5 favourite in a much-reduced field of five, but still this was a story that would not follow the script.

With Defi Du Seuil unrecognisable from the sublime performer who had looked destined for top honours, the final twist belonged to Politologue. Paul Nicholls had never lost faith in his old warrior's ability and had tuned him to perfection, while Harry Skelton jumped in the saddle for the big day at the invitation of owner John Hales. Together they left Defi Du Seuil more than 13 lengths behind in fourth with a dominant front-running display. Finally, at the fifth attempt, Politologue was a festival winner.

****

THE result was a big surprise to many in the Cheltenham crowd but not to Nicholls, whose confidence came more from expectation than hope. He had devised a pinpoint-accurate training regime for Politologue, who had required a gentler touch after bleeding on his previous start when fifth in the Tingle Creek.

Hales left it up to Nicholls to train him completely differently. Taxing canters uphill were replaced with repetitive work on the level to bring out the best in a talented chaser who had spent the past 18 months struggling to land a blow at the highest level.

"I had rung John at Christmas and said: 'I'm not going to run him again until Cheltenham. Just leave it to me,'" Nicholls said after Politologue's triumph. "He never interfered. I love training them very fit and fresh for their big day and that's what we did. Bingo!

"I was so bullish about him because he had been looking fantastic at home. You always have to believe in your own horses and today was his day. He wasn't beaten far by Altior in last year's race, but he was nowhere near as good then as he is now. He was never going to stop."

Nicholls changed his approach to the festival too. He did not have a runner on the opening day of the meeting for the first time in 25

▸▸ *Continues page 90*

LEADING ROLE

years and it was a normal day back at his Ditcheat yard, which involved meeting Paul Barber, the yard's owner, for a Diet Coke in the pub, watching the action from the festival on TV and making plans for his runners to come. He must have slept soundly too, knowing his team had Politologue in the best possible condition.

From the pub to the winner's enclosure, it did not take long for Nicholls to reclaim centre stage. Politologue was his sixth Champion Chase winner, putting him level with Nicky Henderson and Tom Dreaper on the star-studded roll of honour, and his second for Hales after Azertyuiop in 2004.

For Nicholls the full house of festival crown jewels was long since completed – although that did not stop him from bellowing home his latest winner – but for Skelton it was the biggest day of his career as Politologue carried him to Champion Chase victory at his first attempt.

With Nicholls' stable jockey Harry Cobden opting to ride Dynamite Dollars, Hales had decided to give Skelton the spare ride rather than Sam Twiston-Davies, who knew the horse well having partnered him in 17 of his 23 British starts.

"John rang me up and said 'Harry, you're riding Politologue in the Champion Chase – you'd better ring Paul and go down and sit on him'," Skelton said. "Then I started believing. I sat down and watched every replay of his races; you just do your homework. I had a sit on him and it went great. If Paul tells you he believes in a horse, you can believe."

With confidence coursing through his veins, Skelton produced a masterpiece of front-running boldness. He utilised Politologue's pin-sharp jumping to stretch their rivals but ensured there was enough left in the tank to get him up the hill. The winning margin of almost ten lengths over stablemate Dynamite Dollars reflected their dominance from start to finish.

Winning for Nicholls made it extra special for Skelton. Along with his brother Dan, a festival-winning trainer, he had been given his big break by Nicholls and in his post-race interviews the jockey highlighted that contribution. "Me and Dan will be ever grateful for what Paul has done for our careers," Skelton said. "I spent a long nine years with him grafting away, and every single day, every minute, every hardship, has been worth it. It's just magic. As a kid you dream of winning big races like this one.

"Paul told me at the start of the season to come back and ride out a little bit. This is what he can do, he trains them to perfection. I'm so thankful to everyone for giving me the opportunity. It's all worked out perfectly."

▲ Complete control: Politologue is well clear as he jumps the last after a masterpiece of front-running boldness by Harry Skelton; top from left, another clean jump, the victory salute and Skelton with trainer Paul Nicholls and owner John Hales; below, Nicholls celebrates

★★★★

SKELTON also repaid the faith shown in him by Hales, who has known the jockey since he was a child. His wife Patricia used to take Skelton to shows when they owned showjumpers with his father Nick, a dual Olympic gold medal-winning rider.

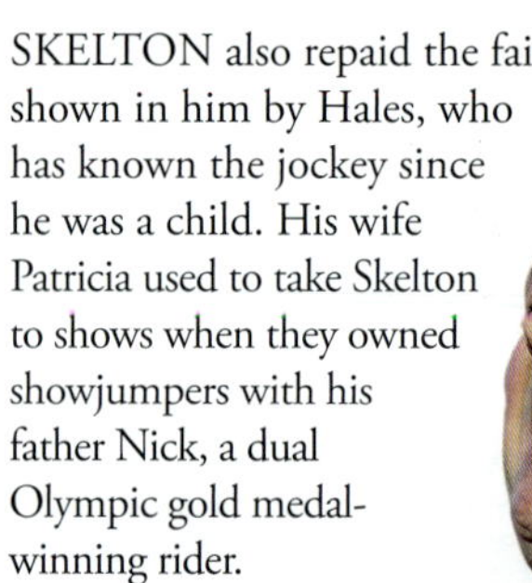

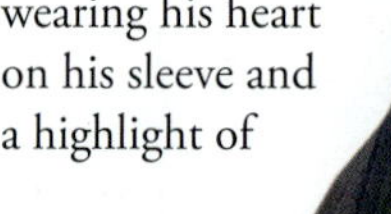

Hales is renowned for wearing his heart on his sleeve and a highlight of Politologue's win was his no-holds-barred celebration. With a flourish of his walking stick and a primal roar, he belied his advanced years with a determined victory charge alongside his beloved winner. A throng of hugs, kisses and raw emotion soon followed once Politologue crossed the line.

Hales is a jump racing stalwart and no stranger to winning big races but this was different. It represented a return to the big time for the owner, who had won the first of his three Champion Chases 22 years earlier with another grey, One Man. There were shades of his predecessor when Politologue winged the final fence, although Hales felt there was more in common with his Grand National winner Neptune Collonges, another grey.

Politologue's success was no surprise to Hales. He bought the then four-year-old in 2015 after watching him win impressively at Auteuil and being taken by his attitude, which counts for so much in top-level jump racing. Politologue's determination was there for all to see in the Champion Chase.

"That was brilliant," said Hales, trying desperately hard to get his words out as he fought back tears of joy. "I'm over the moon. We dictated the race from start to finish and Harry got it absolutely right tactically. I love all my horses and it's a privilege to own one like Politologue."

A privilege and a pleasure too for those watching. With the guidance of his masterful trainer and ice-cool jockey, Politologue finally secured his place in festival history. After all the doubts and defections, he was a worthy winner.

Six pack

Paul Nicholls became the third trainer to send out six Queen Mother Champion Chase winners, joining Tom Dreaper and Nicky Henderson

Winner	*Year*	*Jockey*	*RPR*
Call Equiname	1999	Mick Fitzgerald	167
Azertyuiop	2004	Ruby Walsh	176
Master Minded	2008	Ruby Walsh	186
Master Minded	2009	Ruby Walsh	169
Dodging Bullets	2015	Sam Twiston-Davies	169
Politologue	2020	Harry Skelton	173

Oscar was boldly sent to the front. Paisley Park was already starting to struggle in fifth but Wedge was not looking behind; he was going all in with what turned out to be the race-winning move.

Ronald Pump closed up behind him going to the last but Wedge and Lisnagar Oscar saw off that challenge soon after starting up the hill and it was clear well before the line that they would not be caught. Ronald Pump finished two lengths behind, with Bacardys a non-threatening three lengths back in third. Paisley Park trailed home more than 14 lengths in arrears.

"I was thinking, 'don't get caught, don't get caught,'" said Curtis, showing just how much this return to the big time meant to her. At the races with her was 14-week-old daughter Reeva and now the trainer's professional aspirations had moved in sync with a happy personal life. "It's come at a time when I really needed it. It was tough but we've worked hard and kept going. I'm trying to rebuild the yard. I've had four winners here before, but it's been five years, so it's just great to win another one.

"They called his last run a fluke but I knew it wasn't and I thought 50-1 was a massive price. I didn't think he'd beat Paisley Park but I was confident he'd run into a place. To see him improve that much, I'm just delighted."

★★★★

FOR Wedge, delight had become a familiar feeling in a season that had delivered his first Grade 1 win on the Evan Williams-trained Esprit Du Large in the Henry VIII Novices' Chase at Sandown. Now, at the age of 30, he had landed his first festival success for another of the Welsh stables that have supported his career development.

"I'm having a brilliant season and this is the cherry on top," he said. "I thought we'd have a very good each-way chance but I never expected that. To come here and get that is unbelievable. I'll never forget it."

Wedge, who had been given another big moment by Curtis when they won the 2018 Scottish Grand National with Joe Farrell, was warmly praised by the trainer. "Adam is what I call such a solid, solid jockey, he gave the horse a brilliant ride," she said, while he relived how that ride had unfolded: "Apple's Jade went off very hard and for the first circuit I was a bit cold, but Becky had done a fantastic job and when he came alive I was able to fill all the way down the hill. After the last I just had to hope he'd keep galloping, and he did. He's not very big, but he was fantastic."

After the jumps campaign had been brought to an abrupt end a few days later, Wedge was asked to rate his season out of ten. With 65 winners, more than double where he stood two seasons before, the answer was not surprising. "I'd have to say ten out of ten. It's been better than I could ever have imagined. Esprit Du Large gave me a lot of satisfaction, because it was from Evan and [owners] William and Angela Rucker. That meant a lot. But a Cheltenham Festival winner with Lisnagar Oscar was just unbelievable. We work every day hoping you've got a horse good enough for those races."

▲ Festival magic: Adam Wedge brings Lisnagar Oscar home in front in the Stayers' Hurdle; below, Paisley Park's rider Aidan Coleman congratulates Wedge, and Rebecca Curtis celebrates

For a long time Lisnagar Oscar did not look good enough, and there will still be many who decry the 2020 Stayers' Hurdle in a season that produced the lowest ratings for hurdlers in the 21-year history of the Anglo-Irish jumps classification, with Sharjah on 164 being the top mark. Paisley Park dropped 7lb from the previous season to 162 and Lisnagar Oscar was 160.

If nothing else, this was a victory for hard work and perseverance. More than that, it was reward for taking the bold approach rather than the easy route, both in the way he was trained and ridden. Curtis and Wedge earned their success and they deserved it.

THE BIGGER PICTURE

Gavin Sheehan is unseated in spectacular style as he goes over Itchy Feet's head in the Grade 1 Marsh Novices' Chase at the Cheltenham Festival in March. Two races later Sheehan was unlucky again in the same colours when he was beaten a neck on Saint Calvados by Min in the Grade 1 Ryanair Chase

PATRICK McCANN (RACINGPOST.COM/PHOTOS)

GUINNESS
JOULES

SECOND COMING

Samcro had been the future once but all that seemed behind him until his career was resurrected in dramatic fashion at Cheltenham

By David Jennings

AS WE awaited the judge's verdict on the Marsh Novices' Chase for what seemed like months rather than minutes, with the slowest of slow-motion replays still not conclusive and Davy Russell already scampering down the chute in front of the packed Cheltenham stands, it was tempting to wonder what the reaction might be if Samcro came out the wrong side of the photo-finish.

This, after all, was the same Samcro who was the previous season's Champion Hurdle chump. Favourite in November, not good enough to run in the race come March. This was the same Samcro who had been made to look a fool by Faugheen at Limerick over Christmas, outsprinted by a horse four years older than him. This was the same Samcro who had started at odds of 5-6, 4-9, 6-5, 6-4, 1-3, 13-8 and 4-6 since blowing his rivals away in the Ballymore Novices' Hurdle in 2018, but only managed to win one of those seven races.

This was the same Samcro who had prompted this downbeat report from Gigginstown racing manager Eddie O'Leary on New Year's Eve: "We'll have to probably end up with a handicap mark now as he's going nowhere as a good horse. A good horse, he is not. Hopefully he can prove us wrong but I think we can just forget about him at this stage." And this was the same Samcro who was supposed to be a pale shadow of the unbeatable beast who burst on to the scene by winning his first seven races.

Perhaps that is why Russell scooted down the chute so fast and wasn't waiting around for a post-race interview with ITV's Mick Fitzgerald. He presumed he would not be needed.

Samcro winning the Marsh Novices' Chase did not fit the narrative. He finds ways of losing races he should be winning, not winning races he should be losing. So when he got in tight to the second-last and handed the initiative back to Melon, that really should have been that.

Yet on this occasion he stuck out that long neck of his and answered every question Russell threw at him; ones he had never answered before. He attacked the last, landed running and found more for pressure than he had ever done to force a photo-finish with Melon.

At first glance, it still didn't look enough. Melon was definitely in front a stride after the line, and possibly a stride before it too, and the fact Russell was not waiting around suggested he feared the worst. Jockeys always know.

Then the result arrived: "Here is the outcome of the photo-finish for first place. First number nine, Samcro."

Russell looked over at Danny Cook next to him on Midnight Shadow, then turned around to Paul Townend on Faugheen to make sure. "Nine, is that me?" were how his lips read. It was Russell, and it was Samcro.

★★★★

IN SAMCRO'S novice hurdling days Jack Kennedy said he had given him "the best feel I've ever got off a horse" and there was the same level of excitement from

▲ Fight to the finish: Samcro (maroon and white) edges out Melon (yellow and black) by a nose in the Marsh Novices' Chase with Faugheen (left) close behind in third

Gordon Elliott. "We can go anywhere with him," the trainer said. "We're lucky to have him. He could be anything."

Anything was quickly dissolving into nothing as the defeats piled up, however, and even Elliott admitted to having doubts heading to Cheltenham 2020. Samcro had just a sole success in a sub-standard Down Royal beginners' chase to his name from seven outings since the end of that glorious season as a novice hurdler. "Everyone was knocking him when he was in the doldrums. You know what, I probably lost a bit of faith in him myself," Elliott confessed.

Despite that, the trainer never stopped trying things. He knew there was a superstar still in there somewhere, so Samcro was given a third wind operation as well as a different home environment.

Speaking this autumn, Elliott explained: "We just couldn't get him to scope right, so we moved him to a new stable. We built him one that allows him to walk outside if he wants. It means he can have fresh air the whole time, which after the problems of last year is a good thing. If he wants, he can go into a woodchip paddock.

"Samcro was the forgotten horse going to Cheltenham. He's one of the favourites in the yard and we all love him. It meant the absolute world to everyone in the yard when he won and the reason is because so much work went into getting him back. All the girls have put in so much work with Samcro, and Jack Madden, who looks after him every day, has left no stone unturned. They have spent day and

▸▸ *Continues page 100*

night trying to get this horse right. Thankfully it has paid off."

Samcro is now a two-time Cheltenham Festival winner. That is a sentence few would have imagined reading for most of 2018 and 2019. As a new year dawned, O'Leary certainly wasn't expecting the second coming in mid-March. The Marsh Novices' Chase was not the handicap O'Leary had predicted Samcro would be showing up in. It was a Grade 1 and, arguably, the hottest novice chase of the Cheltenham Festival.

"If he hadn't broke the second-last, he'd have won as he liked," was the post-race view of O'Leary, whose tune had changed. "This horse is very special to us. He lost his way for a while but so did Don Cossack. He's trained by a genius, so hopefully he'll come forward now.

"We always thought he was a champion. And now we've got his wind right, we can go any trip. He could go three miles, no problem."

★★★★

KENNEDY, who missed Cheltenham with a broken leg, knows Samcro better than anyone. He has been on board the giant son of Germany ten times, notching four victories, and he believes three miles might be within his compass too.

"It was obviously annoying to miss the ride on Samcro but I was delighted for the horse that he won," Kennedy said. "He deserved it. He's got an awful lot of stick over the years and it was nice for him to silence the doubters for a while. He's very laid back and does everything so easily that I doubt three miles would be a problem to him. I think he would stay anyway."

The thing is Elliott and Gigginstown already have a top-notch staying chaser in Delta Work, who in the 2019-20 season took his tally of Grade 1 wins to five and is still only seven. The recent acquisition of 2018 RSA Novices' Chase winner Presenting Percy expands Elliott's options in that division too, so it would be no surprise to see Samcro campaigned mainly around two and a half miles. "He has the Ryanair Chase written all over him," Elliott said as he looked forward to a new season with fresh hope.

It wasn't too long ago that the trip Samcro was running over didn't really matter at all, but the 'forgotten horse', as Elliott hailed him after his second Cheltenham success, is back in fashion. "I suppose you could say he is a bit like Don Cossack in that he went missing for a while and took time to develop into the horse we thought he might be," Elliott mused. "It can often take those chasers a while to reach their peak and hopefully, now that his confidence is back and he's scoping clean, we can see what he's really made of."

▲ Standing tall: Davy Russell returns in triumph on Samcro after the Marsh Novices' Chase; right from top, Samcro and Melon jump the last and go head to head for the line, while Russell turns round in surprise as the result of the photo-finish is called

And so we think back to those agonising few moments waiting for the result of the Marsh Novices' Chase to be announced. "I didn't think I was up, I thought he [Patrick Mullins, on Melon] had chinned me," said Russell afterwards. "My horse was headed and got back up, which will just show you the guts he has. He was very brave." Gutsy and brave; this was a Samcro we had never been introduced to before. All you thought you knew about him was wrong. The big question is: can he keep surprising us?

THE BIGGER PICTURE

Welsh Grand National winner Potters Corner (Jack Tudor) walks along the River Ogmore with a group from Christian Williams' string in Ogmore-by-Sea near Bridgend in January

EDWARD WHITAKER (RACINGPOST.COM/PHOTOS)

Derby, which involved closing the famous Downs for a 24-hour period and fencing off 150 hectares.

Under the 1984 Epsom & Walton Downs Act, the land is a public right of way and there was some local opposition to the closure, but the Jockey Club's submission pointed out that the act also said the Downs should not interfere with the ability to hold race meetings. The Derby's importance was recognised at the conservators' meeting and approval was given unanimously, leaving Epsom just over seven weeks to get ready for the race on July 4.

A seven-race card was drawn up, featuring the Oaks as well as the Derby. Normally Epsom would have welcomed more than 100,000 visitors to the Downs for the day, but on this occasion a huge perimeter fence was erected to keep people out. In accordance with the coronavirus regulations in place at all racecourses, only jockeys, trainers, stable staff and essential racecourse personnel were permitted inside, although there was one significant change in Derby week when it was announced owners could attend for the first time since lockdown.

The stage was set for the strangest Derby, held on the deserted Downs in near silence.

****

PREPARATIONS for potential Derby contenders were just as complicated. The traditional trials season of April and May was wiped out and bringing horses to a peak without any set dates for races tested the skills of trainers across Britain and Ireland. Eventually British racing was given June 1 as the date for its resumption, with Ireland following eight days later, and firm plans could be drawn up.

On the fifth day of the condensed Flat season, English King stamped himself a leading contender for Ed Walker with an impressive victory in the Lingfield Derby Trial, and 24 hours later Kameko took the 2,000 Guineas for Andrew Balding, setting up another Classic bid at Epsom. With several of his usual routes blocked off, O'Brien used Royal Ascot as a stepping stone for a couple of his leading hopes, with Russian Emperor winning the Hampton Court Stakes and Mogul finishing fourth in the King Edward VII Stakes, while Vatican City put himself in the picture with his second to Siskin in the Irish 2,000 Guineas.

On that Classic day at the Curragh, Serpentine was barely noticed as he finished fifth in a mile-and-a-quarter maiden. It was only the second run of his life, following his debut tenth of 11 in a Galway maiden the previous September. He had the pedigree, by Galileo out of Oaks runner-up Remember When, but his performances were lacking.

▲ Sign of things to come: Serpentine (Wayne Lordan) leaves his rivals trailing as he wins a 1m2f maiden from the front at the Curragh

▼ Seven days later Emmet McNamara does exactly the same in the Derby; the cheekpieces that were fitted at the Curragh and again at Epsom; the Racing Post front page the day after the Derby

RACING POST

Download the free Racing Post app for must-have news, tips and fast results

RETURN OF The Queen

Wondermare Enable out for Eclipse repeat – live on ITV

Preview, page 12

The king of Yorkshire

Mick Easterby in rip-roaring form

1st 25-1
2nd 50-1
3rd 66-1

Demolition Derby

- Serpentine runs them ragged in strangest Derby ever
- Record win for O'Brien – and he lands the Oaks as well

Things changed seven days before the Derby when Serpentine returned to the Curragh for another mile-and-a-quarter maiden and, wearing first-time cheekpieces, led all the way for a nine-length win. After the race O'Brien said: "He's very genuine and uncomplicated. We'll step up to stakes races next over staying distances."

There was no hint from the trainer that this might be his Derby winner, even when the stakes race quickly chosen for Serpentine's next race was the premier Classic. With hindsight, which would have been a wonderful tool for most of the Derby jockeys, the signs were there in that dominant Curragh performance but they were largely ignored. O'Brien took note, however, and briefed McNamara accordingly.

"I had a huge amount of confidence in the horse having spoken to Aidan during the week," said McNamara after cheekpieces and a front-running ride had worked again at Epsom. "He said that if things worked out well, he was one horse who could win the Derby. He said 'jump, go your own tempo, from halfway after you give him a breather from the six to the five, you keep building to that winning post, he will keep going'. God, he was right!"

The master Derby trainer called it right and McNamara executed the tactics perfectly. Whatever the other arguments, no-one could deny that.

FANCY THAT

Donnacha O'Brien made a stunning start to his training career with a Classic winner at the age of 21

By Nick Pulford

DONNACHA O'BRIEN, former Classic-winning jockey, officially became a trainer near the end of 2019. Before 2020 in all its strangeness was even halfway over, he was a Classic-winning trainer, landing the Prix de Diane with Fancy Blue at the astonishingly young age of 21. Even for a son of Aidan O'Brien, and with his elder brother Joseph having blazed a similar trail to the top both as jockey and trainer, it was a spectacular start to his second career.

There are few things his father has not done but the younger O'Brien found one of them in landing his first Classic with Fancy Blue. He became only the second Irish trainer to win the Prix de Diane after Seamus McGrath 50 years earlier and, in doing so, he kept the patriarch of the family off the roll of honour. O'Brien snr was third with his Irish 1,000 Guineas winner Peaceful in an excitingly tight finish, beaten a short neck and a head by Fancy Blue. Wedged in between them in a historic Irish 1-2-3 was Jessica Harrington's Alpine Star, who went off favourite following her impressive Coronation Stakes victory at Royal Ascot. Another head behind in fourth was Raabihah, the best of the home team.

With quarantine restrictions in place, young O'Brien had to watch the ground-breaking moment at Chantilly from Fairyhouse racecourse. "I didn't think I'd get to see the race as I had to saddle one up for the next race at Fairyhouse but I managed to find a spot to watch it quickly," he said. "The home straight felt like a lifetime, I didn't really know what was going on. Thankfully at the end of it all she got her head in front. There's so much pressure and a lot of work goes into it, but this feeling is great."

O'Brien had that feeling again just three and a half weeks later when Fancy Blue tucked a second Group 1 in the bag with victory in the Nassau Stakes at Glorious Goodwood. Again it was

Extra special: Fancy Blue (6) follows up her Prix de Diane victory with another Group 1 success in the Nassau Stakes at Goodwood, holding off One Voice by a neck

Harrington who was beaten narrowly, this time by a neck with One Voice, and again O'Brien snr had to give best to his son, with his favourite Magic Wand back in fifth.

"It's unbelievable to get a filly like this in my first year," said Donnacha, who had turned 22 the week before the Nassau. "People go lifetimes without getting anything like her. I'm under no illusions as to how lucky I am."

****

GETTING Fancy Blue to head his 35-horse team undoubtedly gave young O'Brien a head start. Owned by the Coolmore partners Michael Tabor, Derrick Smith and Sue Magnier, she had won both starts as a two-year-old when she was officially trained by his father but in reality was already the budding trainer's responsibility. Her first victory came in a Naas maiden, with Donnacha in the saddle, and the second in a Listed mile race at the Curragh when he rode the runner-up for his brother Joseph.

Her performances and pedigree – by Japanese star stallion Deep Impact out of a sister to Derby winner High Chaparral – indicated Classic potential and Donnacha set about realising it from David Wachman's former yard in Longfield, County Tipperary. First stop after racing's emergence from lockdown was the Irish 1,000 Guineas at the Curragh, where Fancy Blue was beaten two lengths into second by Peaceful. In a notable family 1-2-3-4, Aidan had the first and third, while Joseph saddled the fourth.

Before that race, Donnacha had predicted Fancy Blue would improve for the run and for a step up in trip, and he was right. Three weeks later she moved up to a mile and two and a half furlongs in the Prix de Diane and reversed the Classic form with Peaceful under a great ride from Pierre-Charles Boudot. That was a Group 1 win for O'Brien with his first French runner, and he repeated the feat in the Nassau when she was his first runner in Britain.

Continues page 112

The whirlwind start had been longer in the planning than it might have appeared. While 21 seemed young to be launching his training career, the decision had been made well before that and he ran his yard as a satellite to Ballydoyle for 18 months before starting officially. "I actually considered not riding last year [2019]," he said. "I had these horses here and I thought it might be hard to do the two things, but in the end I said I'd do another year. It worked out well and it was probably the right thing to do in the end."

That final year brought a second Irish jockeys' title and more big-race success, notably with Magna Grecia in the 2,000 Guineas and on British Champions Day when he won the Champion Stakes on Magical and beat Stradivarius aboard Kew Gardens in the Long Distance Cup, but training was already a big part of his life. Six days before Champions Day, he effectively had a Listed success with Fancy Blue's Curragh win, albeit in his father's name.

"It's so much harder to train a winner [than to ride one], it really is," he said in a Racing Post interview. "So much more work goes into training. There's so much more depth to it."

An extra layer was added with the start-stop-start of his first season amid the coronavirus pandemic. The two horses he earmarked for Dundalk's all-weather track in the winter both won, with Flower Garland becoming his first official winner in February and Mythologic following the next month, but then came the shutdown. "It is strange, very strange," he admitted. "But, to be perfectly honest, everything was always going to be strange for me. I'm not doing anything I did last year, so it's all strange to me anyway."

There was an odd end to the Fancy Blue story too. Having been beaten into third by Champers Elysees in the Matron Stakes at Leopardstown in September, she was due to have one last crack at Group 1 glory in the Prix de l'Opera on Arc weekend but was one of the withdrawals in the contaminated feed scare. Her retirement for breeding duty was announced a few days later after she suffered a tendon injury.

"She's been such an important filly for us," O'Brien said. "I'll always remember her as the horse who gave us our first big days. She's been very special to us and always will be."

★★★★

AMID the shifting sands of 2020, young O'Brien had a rock to lean on just up the road in Ballydoyle. On his relationship with his father, he said: "I fry his head every morning about things. If a horse is a bit lame, or something is coughing, anything like that. I ring him about everything pretty much. He's a genius, but he's my father first and foremost and he's always been amazing to us. He does everything he possibly can to help us. I wouldn't be anywhere near where I am now without him."

Father couldn't have advised son on how to train a Classic winner at the age of 21, though, because it was simply mould-breaking. Fancy Blue's victory at Chantilly made the most junior of the clan by far the youngest trainer to attain Classic success in the modern era in which trainers have required licences that reveal their date of birth.

He took over that mantle from Joseph, a relative slow-starter who did not claim a Classic until the age of 25 when Latrobe (ridden by Donnacha) landed the 2018 Irish Derby ahead of a quartet trained by their father, who had reached the grand old age of 27 when Classic Park got him off the mark in the 1997 Irish 1,000 Guineas.

▲ Fighting Irish: Fancy Blue (left) proves too strong for Jessica Harrington's One Voice in the Nassau Stakes ▼ Donnacha O'Brien, the youngest Classic-winning trainer of the modern era

That was the same age at which Fulke Johnson Houghton, father of current trainer Eve, landed the Irish Derby and St Leger with Ribocco in 1967, and he followed up the next year in both races with full-brother Ribero. Peter Chapple-Hyam was 29 when he won the 2,000 Guineas with Rodrigo De Triano and the Derby with Dr Devious in 1992, while Sir Henry Cecil had reached 30 when he bagged the 1973 Irish 1,000 Guineas with Cloonagh.

An alternative sense of perspective is offered by the fact that, while the O'Brien boys have opened their Classic accounts, their father clocked up his 86th and 87th successes the day before Fancy Blue's victory when he landed the Derby-Oaks double at Epsom with Serpentine and Love.

"I hope I'm some little bit similar," Donnacha said when asked whether there is much of Aidan in him. "I don't think I'm a carbon copy of Dad, or Joseph. I think we're all a bit different, but we all have the same basic values Mum and Dad have given us and we always try to do our best. I've been extremely lucky, as lucky as they come."

He was being unduly modest. Luck was only the start of this remarkable success story.

POSITIVE & NEGATIVE

Tom Marquand stepped in to land the St Leger for Joseph O'Brien on Galileo Chrome after Shane Crosse's positive test for Covid-19 cost him the ride

By Lewis Porteous

SHANE CROSSE has a special bond with Galileo Chrome. Indeed, the young Irish jockey goes as far as saying the horse is like a pet to him. Little wonder, then, that emotions were running high when he was forced to watch from home as the Classic hope he had nurtured bore glorious autumn fruit in the St Leger at Doncaster.

Crosse, who had partnered Galileo Chrome in all four of his previous runs, bellowed at the television screen, willing him to the front. Yet seconds after the Joseph O'Brien-trained colt passed the post a neck in front, Ireland's

former champion apprentice was blindsided as his roars were engulfed by anguish and all he could do was sob. It should have been him punching the Doncaster air in delight instead of Tom Marquand, his late replacement in the saddle.

One of the brightest riding talents in Irish racing, Crosse had been declared by O'Brien for the St Leger ride. The then 18-year-old could not wait for Saturday to come. He had rattled off three consecutive wins on Galileo Chrome to set up the Classic mission and felt sure he would be heading to Doncaster with a strong chance.

Then came Friday. In line with the protocols for travelling jockeys, Crosse had been tested for Covid-19 and, less than 24 hours before the world's oldest Classic, he got the result: positive. It was a blunt end to his Classic dream. For him it was the most negative outcome imaginable.

"I thought it was a mistake, it had to be," Crosse said. "I paused for a while on the phone to try to take it all in. I knew what it meant. I knew what I'd be missing. I knew I'd miss the Leger."

That one phone call had changed everything and crucially left Galileo Chrome without a rider for the St Leger. Already at Doncaster on the day before the big race was Marquand. Like Crosse, he had recently received some disappointing – if not totally unforeseen – news that his intended St Leger mount, English King, was being diverted to an alternative target in France.

That decision had been taken before Crosse received the galling news that he had to self-isolate at home and it did not take long for O'Brien to reach out to Marquand. The ride on Galileo Chrome was his, completing a most remarkable big-race merry-go-round.

Earlier in the season Marquand had been replaced by Frankie Dettori for the Derby ride on English King. At the time English King was favourite, yet Marquand kept a cool head and maintained his dignity, accepting the decision of connections with a level of maturity way beyond his 22 years.

The irony of that episode was that Marquand was then snapped up for Khalifa Sat, who went on to finish second in the Derby, three places in front of English King. While the circumstances were entirely different at Doncaster, the decision of English King's connections once again proved pivotal to the narrative of a British Classic. Preferring Longchamp to Doncaster, they had unwittingly freed Marquand to go on and land the biggest success of his career.

★★★★

PERHAPS it was not a vintage St Leger line-up but the race was nothing if not competitive. Irish Derby winner Santiago had the Classic form in the book, Great Voltigeur winner Pyledriver had the time-honoured profile and Hukum was improving fast. It was a Classic that was going to take some winning.

Although he was making his first foray into Group company, Galileo Chrome was the gamble of the race. The week before the St Leger he was a 20-1 chance, but after he appeared in the five-day entries he was as short as 6-1. On the day he went off at 4-1, with Santiago the 5-2 favourite, Hukum 7-2 and Pyledriver 9-2. His attractiveness to punters was not surprising. O'Brien, who won the St Leger as a jockey on Leading Light in 2013, has quickly established himself as a big-race trainer, while Crosse had

▸▸ *Continues page 116*

▾ Tight finish: Galileo Chrome (red and yellow) and Tom Marquand edge Berkshire Rocco (red and white) by a neck with Pyledriver (green) third and Santiago fourth

described one of Galileo Chrome's earlier wins at Leopardstown as "mind blowing".

The race proved as competitive on the track as it looked on paper. Seven of the runners were virtually in line two furlongs out but Marquand was decisive as the gaps opened in the home straight, sending Galileo Chrome to the front over a furlong from home and driving him out to deny 16-1 shot Berkshire Rocco in a tight finish. Next came Pyledriver, Santiago and Hukum.

Barely had Marquand passed the post than he was expressing sympathy for Crosse, who should have been floating on cloud nine but was instead in turmoil hundreds of miles away.

"I can't stress enough how bad I feel for Shane because we've all been in a situation where things haven't gone our way and we're both relatively young, so I can relate," said Marquand, who intuitively had predicted his chance would come after losing the English King ride at Epsom and was convinced the same thing would happen to Crosse down the line.

"He'll be sat at home in pieces no doubt and I guess the one thing in racing is that it always comes back round, so I have no doubt he'll have his day."

Marquand's conviction proved right again. The following month there was such a day for Crosse when he scored his first Group 1 win on the O'Brien-trained Pretty Gorgeous in the Fillies' Mile at Newmarket. "This is the best day of my life," he said. "This takes a lot of edge off what happened in the St Leger, which you wouldn't wish on your worst enemy." Given the strength of O'Brien's juvenile team in 2020, Crosse will have new Classic dreams over the winter.

★★★★

LOST somewhat in the commotion over the enforced jockey switch at Doncaster was the achievement of the winning trainer, yet there is no doubt this was another momentous occasion in O'Brien's fast-developing career.

Not only was this his first British Classic success as a trainer, O'Brien became the first since Harry Wragg in 1969 to achieve the rare feat of having ridden and trained a St Leger winner. His backstory does not end there either. O'Brien was the man on board Camelot, sent off at long odds-on to land the 2012 St Leger and become the first Triple Crown winner since Nijinsky, only to come up painfully short in second place behind Encke.

That piece of history can never be recovered but Galileo Chrome's victory gives O'Brien another positive memory of Doncaster's biggest race, and further Classic success will surely not be long in coming. Remarkably, Aidan O'Brien's eldest son is only at the end of his fifth year as a trainer and he made this latest mark in the record books at the age of 27, just five years older than the winning rider.

Crosse was most unfortunate to miss out, but on this occasion the stars aligned for Marquand, who along with the winning trainer has climbed to the pinnacle with giant strides.

Never mind chrome, for them the St Leger was pure gold.

▲ Change of fortune: Tom Marquand celebrates victory and lifts the trophy wearing the traditional winning jockey's cap
◀ The unlucky Shane Crosse, who would have been in the saddle but for Covid-19

▸ Major Tom: a jubilant Tom Marquand after winning the Champion Stakes on Addeybb; opposite page from left, Marquand opens his Royal Ascot account on Who Dares Wins, celebrates his first Group 1 success in the Ranvet Stakes at Rosehill on Addeybb, and scores a second victory on Champions Day with Njord in the Balmoral Handicap

By Steve Dennis

PEOPLE his age have a long list of experiences they are eager to tick off, to be there, to do that, buy the T-shirt. Tom Marquand, at 22, is surely no different. What might have been on his list at the start of 2020?

Have a great time abroad. Sure, why not? Make some new friends. Of course. But come on, what about the job, Tom? One might picture him gazing out of the window, gnawing on a pen, pondering how much he could safely wish for. A Royal Ascot winner? A Group 1 winner? A Classic winner? A run at the jockeys' title? The reputation and status of a top jockey? Tick, tick, tick, tick, tick. Marquand will be one of the very few to look back at 2020 with sheer happiness.

In almost every facet of life, Marquand has been ahead of the curve this year, out in front. Neatly, sweetly, he hasn't been out there alone, as his partner Hollie Doyle has been right by his side as they climb the ladder three rungs at a time. Even within these pages they sit next to each other, the awesome twosome we are almost contractually obliged to refer to as the 'golden couple'. And it was Marquand who struck gold first.

His spell in Australia during the spring – when his fellow riders were still coming to terms with the restrictions of lockdown in Britain – sent him stratospheric. He won the first Group 1 of his career on Addeybb in the Ranvet Stakes at Rosehill in March, a milestone for every jockey, and then went the extra mile three weeks later on the same William Haggas-trained horse in the far more prestigious Queen Elizabeth Stakes at Randwick. Possibly more satisfying than even these two

SUPERMAN

From Australia to Ascot – and Doncaster in between – this was a year of high achievement for Tom Marquand

top-level triumphs, though, was the impact he made in Sydney as a whole. Tick, tick.

The Australian circuit is a hard place for hard jockeys, yet here was this fresh-faced Pom kid showing the locals how it was done. He did so well they gave him a nickname, a demonstration of great respect from such a tough crowd, especially as it was one that showed how quickly he had become one of their own: Aussie Tom. Good on ya, mate.

"I've been really lucky," he said, sounding far more deprecating than you might expect from someone known as 'Aussie'. "There are maybe five jockeys who dominate the scene, and since I've been here I've been lucky enough to be able to get on some of the horses that crowd is trying for."

****

THAT crowd? Marquand was now securely in that crowd on merit, as displayed on his return to Britain in April when he was quoted as fourth favourite for the jockeys' championship. The champion apprentice of 2015 was right in the vanguard of the new wave of young talent that was busy pushing the elder statesmen to one side, and when racing resumed in Britain in June he gained further recognition, this time from the best in the business, when Aidan O'Brien booked him to ride outsider Royal Dornoch in the 2,000 Guineas.

The day before the Classic, Marquand had ridden English King to an impressive victory in the Lingfield Derby Trial, the colt thus becoming the Epsom favourite. On this occasion, though, he had to endure the time-honoured slap in the face – a rite of passage for so many youngsters – of being jocked off in favour of a more experienced rider, in this case Frankie Dettori. Life is all ups and downs, the true test of character being in the way one reacts to the latter. In this respect, Marquand has the right stuff.

"I respect their decision and I wish them the best of luck," he said, winning admiration for his cool handling of the situation. "I've just got to hope that I get my chance one day. I'm not going to let something like this define my year."

Dettori finished fifth on English King. Three places ahead of him was Marquand aboard the unconsidered runner-up Khalifa Sat, underlining his resilience and confidence and ability. By then he had already ridden his first Royal Ascot winner on Who Dares Wins, galvanising the veteran stayer through the closing stages of the Queen Alexandra Stakes to prevail by a neck, and had thrust himself into the championship conversation with the best monthly return (25 winners) of his career. In July he surpassed himself and that mark with 29 winners. Tick, tick, tick.

****

A LESS prolific August saw his title hopes recede, but Marquand's magical year still had plenty up its sleeve. On the morning of the day before the St Leger, he didn't have a ride. A few hours later, he was booked for Galileo Chrome after the colt's regular rider Shane Crosse tested positive for Covid-19. Twenty-four hours later, Marquand was in the winner's enclosure at Doncaster, his first Classic in the bag, very happy for something like this to define his year.

The following week he was the punters' pal after winning the Ayr Gold Cup on the well-backed favourite Nahaarr, in the same sun-yellow silks of Ahmed Al Maktoum he had worn aboard Addeybb. He wore them again on that gelding in the Champion Stakes at Ascot in October, embellishing his Group 1 haul with an authoritative success in the most valuable race of the whole season. Victory in the last race on the Ascot card, on Njord for Jessica Harrington in the Balmoral Handicap, set the seal on a wonderful day, a remarkable season. Tick, tick.

"Addeybb has elevated me to heights I thought I might never reach, never mind so quickly in my career. So many opportunities have come because of him," said the polite, personable, thoroughly likeable Marquand, while trainer Haggas had just as much praise for his jockey as he had for his horse. "I have no doubt Tom will be champion one day. He's got there very young, but he has a great future ahead of him."

Perhaps days like these, years like these, will become commonplace for Marquand. After a campaign of immense progress on all fronts, next year holds nothing but promise for him. He's been there, done that. Now to do it all again. Tick, tick, tick.

Hollie Doyle had an incredible year topped off by a first Group 1 victory on Champions Day

WONDER WOMAN

▲ Day to remember: Hollie Doyle scores her first Group 1 win on Glen Shiel (centre, gold) in the British Champions Sprint at Ascot; above right, she kicks off her Champions Day double with victory on Trueshan in the Group 2 Long Distance Cup

◀ The Racing Post front page the next day, marking the doubles of Doyle and her partner Tom Marquand

By Nick Pulford

THE glass ceiling for women riders, which once seemed so impenetrable, suddenly looks much more fragile. Several significant blows have been landed over the years, from Gay Kelleway and Gee Armytage with their ground-breaking Royal Ascot and Cheltenham wins in the 1980s to the more recent top-level breakthroughs by Hayley Turner, Lizzie Kelly, Bryony Frost and Rachael Blackmore, and now the hammer has been taken up by Hollie Doyle. It is quite possible she will make the most sustained impact of all.

Doyle was in the headlines throughout 2020 as she ticked off a young jockey's bucket list at rapid speed – first Royal Ascot winner, first Group-race success, first Group 1 winner.

She could not stop making history. The 24-year-old broke her own British record for most winners in a calendar year by a female jockey and five of them came in a single breathless August afternoon at Windsor, making her the first woman to ride a five-timer in Britain. Fourth place in the championship table was by far the best for a female rider, improving on the previous high of 13th she had achieved herself 12 months earlier.

On top of those exploits, she gained wider prominence beyond the racing audience as one half of Flat racing's golden couple with fellow rising star Tom Marquand. When they dominated British Champions Day at Ascot in October, both riding doubles that included Group 1 winners, it was a dream for feature writers as well as the two young jockeys.

Not that there was anything juicy for gossip columnists. Doyle and Marquand are dedicated to their profession and admit their celebrations tend to be a tad muted. Asked how she had celebrated her Windsor five-timer, Doyle said: "I just went for some food with Tom and had an early night. We were both pretty knackered."

It was a similar story after the adrenaline rush of Champions Day, when they had a quiet meal out on the Saturday night, followed by a spot of shopping and then roast dinner with friends on the Sunday, which was a rare day off for both of them.

"We live a pretty normal lifestyle – we're just your normal everyday people outside of racing," Doyle said on Champions Day. Inside racing, however, they are both out of the ordinary.

★★★★

FOR most of the truncated season there was simply no stopping Doyle. In 2019 she had emulated Turner and Josephine Gordon by reaching the century mark, eventually beating Gordon's seasonal record for a woman with a total of 116 winners. She got there even faster in 2020 when becoming the first woman to hit a century twice. The year before, she had moved into three figures on November 21; this time she got there on September 11 despite the loss of two and a half months of racing during lockdown. By October 14 she had gone further, beating her own seasonal record.

Three days later it was Champions Day and this was about the quality, not the quantity. No woman had ever ridden a winner on the prestigious card but Doyle was on the scoreboard immediately when the Alan King-trained Trueshan ran away with the Group 2 Long Distance Cup by seven and a half lengths, with Irish St Leger one-two Search For A Song and Fujaira Prince taking the minor placings and Stradivarius finishing a tired 12th of the 13 runners.

"I have to pinch myself really, that was absolutely amazing," Doyle said. Just over half an hour later it became even more amazing.

Glen Shiel, her mount in the British Champions Sprint, had taken her close to victory on her first ride in a British Group 1 when they finished second in the Haydock Sprint Cup in September. Despite his odds of 16-1 he clearly had a chance against several of the same opponents and Doyle was determined to take it. The strength and spirit of her ride encapsulated why trainers and punters alike have come to invest so much trust in her.

Doyle bounced the Archie Watson-trained six-year-old out of the gates and into the lead, setting out to make all the running despite the tough test posed by soft ground. From halfway she was taken on by Cieren Fallon aboard July Cup winner Oxted and, after an almighty tussle, Glen Shiel was headed entering the final furlong. Doyle refused to give way, however, and fought her way back into the lead, only to be threatened anew by the late thrusts of Brando and One Master. Brando was closing all the way to the line but Doyle just held him off by a nose. Only a length covered the first five.

"It was too close for comfort really," said Doyle, having become the third woman – after Alex Greaves and Turner – to win a Group 1 on the Flat in Britain. "I thought I hadn't won, so to have got the result was incredible. I'm a bit in shock at the moment. It's a dream come true, a massive dream come true. My aim at the start of the year was to ride a Group winner and I've always said I wanted to win a Group 1 one day. I didn't think it would come this year."

★★★★

NOTHING seemed out of bounds for Doyle in 2020. The previous year she had watched Turner bridge a 32-year gap to become only the second female jockey to score at Royal Ascot, following Kelleway's pioneering success on Sprowston Boy in 1987, and she saw her older role model do it again on the Thursday of this year's meeting. Just 24 hours later, Doyle joined Turner and Kelleway on the roll of honour when she landed the Duke of Edinburgh Handicap on the King-trained Scarlet Dragon.

"This means a huge amount to me," said Doyle after bringing the 33-1 shot from off the pace to get on top in the final half-furlong, scoring by half a length. "You walk into Ascot every year with really high hopes and try to picture in your head what it's like to ride a winner here, but it's very hard to come across winners. It was really important that I got that Royal

▸▸ *Continues page 122*

Ascot winner. It's important for any jockey and it's a monkey off my back. This is amazing for me."

Cheekily, she added: "For once in my life, I have beaten Tom to it!" Not by much as it turned out, with Marquand breaking his duck at Royal Ascot aboard the King-trained Who Dares Wins in the Queen Alexandra Stakes the following day, but her comment was a window into the private competition helping to drive them both to greater heights.

The following month Doyle took another step forward with a first Group-race success on Dame Malliot in the Group 2 Princess of Wales's Stakes at Newmarket. Ed Vaughan, Dame Malliot's trainer, was full of praise for Doyle. "She works hard and has a great record for me," he said. "She's got good hands, rides them with a good length of rein and I just love the way she rides."

In late July it was announced that Doyle had been given a retainer by owner and breeder Imad Al Sagar, whose colours were carried to Derby victory by Authorized in 2007, and she was quick to set the seal on the deal when she won the Group 3 Rose of Lancaster Stakes on Extra Elusive at Haydock a few days later.

Roger Charlton, Extra Elusive's trainer, also praised her riding. "Hollie is demonstrating her talents on a daily basis," he said. "She's brave and strong, and because she's small she has no weight issues. She's doing fantastically and it's great for her profession."

At the end of August, there was that incredible day at Windsor. Her fifth victory on Mistress Nellie gave her another entry in the record books and her achievement received widespread coverage, including on the BBC1 evening news. "I didn't know five winners in a day was a record," Doyle said. "It's a day I won't forget for a while. When you get on a roll you have so much confidence and that helps."

The roll continued the next day when she had a hat-trick at Yarmouth. One of the winners was for Kelleway, who believes Doyle will keep raising the bar. "Hollie is a go-getter. She's hungry and ambitious and I see no reason why she won't be champion one day," she said.

It is odd to think that, in a Racing Post interview during lockdown, Doyle had wondered aloud about whether the shortened season might push back some of her ambitions. "I want to ride a Group winner but that's going to be hard now," she said. "I just need to get on some quality horses to take me to the next level. That's easier said than done, isn't it?"

Yet she did it, and even after such an incredible year this brilliant young jockey is entitled to set herself the loftiest targets.

▲ Golden year: Hollie Doyle on her Royal Ascot winner Scarlet Dragon (top) and Dame Malliot in the Group 2 Princess of Wales's Stakes (bottom) ◀ Doyle after riding Certain Lad to victory in the Group 3 Strensall Stakes at York

IN THE
PICTURE

Snap! Turner and Fellowes double up in Sandringham

LET'S do it all again next year, same time, same place. The pact made by many festival regulars (in normal times at least) served Hayley Turner and Charlie Fellowes well on the Thursday of Royal Ascot. For the second year running, Turner partnered a filly trained by Fellowes to victory in the Listed Sandringham Handicap, with Onassis (*main picture*) coming home in front to repeat their success with Thanks Be (*inset*) 12 months earlier.

In 2019 Turner had bridged a 32-year gap to become only the second female jockey to score at Royal Ascot, following Gay Kelleway's ground-breaking success on Sprowston Boy in 1987, and now she had another winner in the bag.

Remarkably, the parallels in the Turner-Fellowes Sandringham successes even extended to the 33-1 starting price of both winners. There was plenty of confidence behind Onassis, however, after Fellowes spotted the chance to get her into the Sandringham near the bottom of the weights, just as he had with Thanks Be. Being drawn in stall one was the uncontrollable element for Fellowes, but Turner had her game plan all worked out, having manoeuvred to victory from stall four the year before.

"I rode a very similar race to the one I rode on Thanks Be, and that was the plan from a similar draw," said Turner, who held up her mount before bursting through on the far side in the final furlong to score by a length and a quarter. "She had the perfect profile for the race – the same as Thanks Be last year – and Charlie told me she would win it about three months ago."

Fellowes, who went on to a Royal Ascot double the next day when Chiefofchiefs took the Silver Wokingham, said after the Sandringham: "To win this race two years in a row, same weight, similarly awful draw, it's amazing. I begged the owners to have a crack at this. This was the perfect race for Onassis. She's a very good traveller and I thought the stiff mile would suit her."

The big difference from the year before was the strange atmosphere without the Royal Ascot crowds, but that was not going to stop Turner having some fun. Immediately after crossing the line, she cupped her hand to her ear as if listening for the crowd reaction.

"I thought it wasn't going to be the same [without crowds] but I'm buzzing just as much as last time," she said. "I hope everyone at home was cheering and I think I could hear my nana shouting from home as I was coming in. It's still an Ascot winner – it's just as hard to ride winners whether anyone is here or not."

Pictures: EDWARD WHITAKER (RACINGPOST.COM/PHOTOS)

BET
ROYAL

IN THE PICTURE

Mould-breaker Kelly retires from race-riding as motherhood calls

LIZZIE KELLY, who made history aboard Grade 1-winning chaser Tea For Two, announced in July she was calling a halt to her race-riding career as she was expecting a baby at the end of 2020.

"Thank you to all those who played their part, big or small. On to a new chapter," she said. "I have really had a career that I could never have imagined and I've been blessed to have been associated with the horses I have ridden. It's been a dream."

Kelly, 27, made history in 2015 when she became the first woman to win a Grade 1 race over jumps by landing the Kauto Star Novices' Chase at Kempton on Tea For Two. The pairing landed another big prize the following season in the Grade 1 Betway Bowl at Aintree, getting the better of Cue Card by a neck in a rousing finish.

She also rode two Cheltenham Festival winners, Coo Star Sivola in the Ultima Handicap Chase in 2018 and Siruh Du Lac in the Brown Advisory & Merriebelle Stable Plate the following year.

Tea For Two, now 11, is looked after in retirement in Devon by Kelly, who said: "I was a point-to-point rider who managed to turn professional because of Tea For Two. At every stage of my career he did something that made the next step easier. Winning a bumper on him as a student, an amateur against professionals, was massive for me, on a horse I'd grown up with at home. When I turned professional he won a Lanzarote for me as a 7lb claimer, then I won my first Grade 1 on him as a 3lb claimer, then the Aintree Bowl, and he took me to Gold Cups and Grand Nationals. He's the fairytale horse, my National Velvet."

Kelly said she would still be heavily involved with racing through Valentine Bloodstock, a new venture with her husband Ed Partridge (*pictured with Kelly*), and hoped to continue working with the racing media.

"When you look back at the career I've had, you remember all the good times, so it's hard to stop, you don't want to stop," she said, "but having a baby is a very nice reason to retire from a sport."

Kelly refused to rule out a return to race-riding at some point. "I'm never going to shut the door completely on that," she said. "I've never had closure. I never went out on a final winner or had a day when I announced it would be my final ride. If I do come back, though, it won't be to ride novice chasers. My career as it was is over."

Picture: EDWARD WHITAKER (RACINGPOST.COM/PHOTOS)

Jessica Marcialis made history as the first woman to ride a Group 1 winner on the Flat in France

BRAVO!

By Scott Burton

IT IS one of those rare horseracing stories that resonates with the wider world, one that brings in a far bigger audience even than tales of hat-trick bids for the Grand National or Prix de l'Arc de Triomphe.

Jessica Marcialis, 30-year-old jockey and mother to three-year-old Leo, leaves a field of riding superstars including Frankie Dettori, Christophe Soumillon and Olivier Peslier trailing in her wake to win a major race on the Arc undercard.

The first woman to ride a Group 1 winner on the Flat in France did so aboard Tiger Tanaka, who had been bought by her partner Charley Rossi out of a claimer at Lyon in June for €23,789 and who subsequently took the couple on a racing ride to the stars.

Owner Miguel Castro had insisted that Marcialis kept the ride as Tiger Tanaka rose through the ranks for Rossi's small stable near Marseille, ignoring offers to buy France's top two-year-old filly and the pleas of agents everywhere to put one of the leading jockeys on board.

Even Tiger Tanaka's companion goat, Tata, has become a part of the story, one that must have the Hollywood producers of Seabiscuit and Secretariat kicking themselves for undercooking the feelgood factor in their movies.

At the centre of it all, Marcialis freely shared the joy she felt after the Prix Marcel Boussac as she and Tiger Tanaka made their own special piece of Longchamp history, and the feelings don't seem in danger of leaving her anytime soon.

"I look at the photos of that day a lot and the sensations return very quickly," said Marcialis, almost two weeks on from her Boussac triumph. "I don't think you can ever forget something like that. It was such a great day that when I talk to people about it, it's almost as if I'm talking about someone else. But we did it, that was us! It just makes me smile."

★★★★

BORN and raised in Italy, Marcialis boasts a father and a brother who are trainers and racing was always likely to play a big role in her life. And despite the restrictions on numbers at Longchamp due to the Covid-19 crisis, almost everyone who has ever mattered in her life was there to see Tiger Tanaka streak to success, the jockey upright in her stirrups and waving her whip to the small band of supporters in the stand as the pair crossed the line three-quarters of a length in front.

"I can remember every detail of what happened before and after but the race itself was over in a flash," she said. "I knew I had a good draw and the race went very smoothly.

"I was perhaps a bit further forward than planned but I was just riding my filly for herself. It opened in front of me and we took the lead so easily. I could feel she thought the job was done and began to ease up a little but one shake of the reins and she was back at it. I was just praying for the post to come."

The post arrived and so did the joy. "The emotion was not because

I'd won the race, it was all the work that had gone before: it was seeing my father with tears in his eyes, my mother in the stands.

"Even talking about it makes me think I'll start crying again. Charley and I have been through difficult moments and our son was there as well. Charley had won Group races with Madame [Criquette] Head but he was her assistant then and now it's his name over the door. God sent us this filly, she's a gift from above."

Tiger Tanaka had been aimed at the Marcel Boussac by Rossi ever since a Group 3 win at Deauville in August but as the days ticked down, Marcialis said she was able to keep a lid on things with relative ease.

"I read an interview with Frankie where he said he didn't want to ride work on Enable until close to the Arc because she would know it was him and she would start to get revved up," Marcialis said.

"I think it was helpful that it's completely normal to ride 'Tiger' every morning. She never got to feel that rising pressure because we were aiming her at a race like any other.

"It felt normal to me as well and I knew she was well in herself, so we were both very relaxed in the build-up. If anything I was a bit worried that I was too relaxed and that I would maybe not concentrate enough for a Group 1.

"Then when I got into the parade ring I was standing next to my father and I told him I felt like throwing up. I'd had no pressure up until that point and all of a sudden it went through the roof.

"But I had a dream day up to that point because I was surrounded by positive people. I even had bacon and eggs for breakfast in the morning with a family friend.

"It could not have been any better. I really needed those people around me and I honestly didn't feel any pressure throughout the day."

★★★★

SOME of the women who have made racing breakthroughs have shied away from the notion that they were smashing barriers for anyone other than themselves.

Marcialis is well aware of the history she has made as a woman and a mother and even in the moments immediately after winning at Longchamp she was able to articulate just what a big deal it was. Now she has a little perspective on it, she can broaden her view to encompass every part of the racing family that spends most of its time in the shadows.

"Everybody felt the emotion and it was a victory that belongs to everyone. It's a win for every small trainer; for women and for young mothers; for jockeys who are not famous; for a cheaply bought filly and for an owner that nobody knows. It belongs to all.

"There is so much negativity in the world that I love sharing the story. For everyone who works hard every day, there is always the possibility that you will find your Miguel Castro, the owner who gave us all a chance."

Bravo Jessica! Bravo Charley! And bravo Tiger Tanaka! Three heroes sorely needed by a weary world.

THE BIGGER PICTURE

With Glorious Goodwood closed to the public, racefans watch the last race on day three, the Tatler Nursery Handicap, from the flint wall that runs down the side of the racecourse

EDWARD WHITAKER (RACINGPOST.COM/PHOTOS)

Brian Hughes achieved his long-held ambition to win the British jump

NORTHERN LIGHT

By David Carr

NOTHING summed up a year of tumultuous upheaval better than one of the most heroic championships in sport being awarded by phone rather than in the heat of battle. It was a year when all the old certainties became uncertain – nothing we used to rely on was reliable any more.

Of course, some things change all the time. Between 1996 and 2019, Britain had four poet laureates, five Doctor Whos and no fewer than six prime ministers. But through that whole period there were just two champion jump jockeys.

Tony McCoy reigned supreme for 20 years and when he retired the heir apparent Richard Johnson took over both AP's throne and the sense of being super-glued to it. 'Dickie' landed the title for the next four seasons and started 2019-20 as odds-on favourite to win a race that had seen only five different winners since Tom Baker occupied the Tardis.

But that championship phone call on April 6 was made to North Yorkshire, rather than to Herefordshire. Brian Hughes was the man getting the news from Great British Racing, confirmation of something that everyone really knew: with racing shut down and not going to resume before 2019-20 became 2020-21, he was the new champion.

"It was a strange way to win the

jockeys' title, becoming the first northern-based champion in 40 years

◂ Title role: Brian Hughes receives the championship trophy from Mick Fitzgerald
▴ A guard of honour at Perth in July for the new champion

championship," Hughes recalls, months after the event. "It was ironic because it was my little daughter's first birthday and on the day she was born the previous year I went on to Newcastle and got a fall in the first race. I smashed my face up, so she was in one hospital and I was in another. Clock on 12 months and how different it was."

★★★★

TO UNDERSTAND how and why the 34-year-old had come to unseat the champion, you need to go back to the beginning, which takes you to the Armagh-Tyrone border in Northern Ireland, where two decades ago Hughes took the first steps on the path that led to the no.1 spot. That is where James Lambe trained two dozen jumpers and took a shine to the 7st teenager who turned up with a burning determination to make it as a rider and a willingness to do whatever his boss asked, even if that meant schooling over racecourse fences on a four-year-old who had never previously left the yard.

"He was a great kid," Lambe recalls. "He was as good a young fella as ever came through the door. He never questioned anything, he always did exactly what I asked him to do. When I asked him to school over fences he never said 'has this jumped before?' He was like Robocop, he was relentless. At 16 he knew what he wanted. He wanted to be a jockey and he wanted to be a champion. He's done it and it's very rarely in life that people's dreams come true.

"I remember going one day to Loughbrickland point-to-point with him in the car to school horses. I said to him: 'Hughesie, what happens if you can't be a successful jockey?' He turned round and said, 'That won't be happening'. There's a difference between being cocky and being driven and Brian was driven.

"Hindsight is a wonderful thing but to me he was always destined to be champion if he got the opportunities. His work ethic and his drive were second to none. He's the closest fella that I know to AP McCoy. He doesn't drink, he doesn't smoke and all he wants to do is ride winners."

Neither hard work nor the falls that are part of the job for a jump jockey could faze the youngster. "He schooled 14 horses for me one

▸▸ *Continues page 134*

morning and he never questioned it or wanted a break and a cup of tea," Lambe recalls. "He got a purler of a fall on a mare at Down Royal one day and I said 'now you know what's in front of you'. He never flinched."

That drive was evident when Hughes moved to Britain a decade and a half ago, hailed as "exceptionally dedicated and exceptionally motivated" by one early supporter and crowned champion conditional jockey in 2007-08. The jumping technique learned under Lambe's wing plus tactical nous and judgement of pace, which owed plenty to a background on the Flat and his time as an apprentice with Kevin Prendergast, helped carry him to second, second and then third place behind Johnson in the championship in 2017, 2018 and 2019.

He was a 16-1 shot to come out on top in 2020, although the man himself was not thinking too much about the title when the action got under way. "Every year you just start out with the aim of riding 100 winners, ride a few good ones and stay in one piece," he says. "You do your best and hope the trainers you ride for are in form, but last season started like any other season."

Except that it soon got rather better than any other season and he ended September on 62 winners, a higher total than ever before at that stage. "I had a good summer and that's somewhere I've lacked in recent years," Hughes reflects, as he looks back on previous seasons when he was left with a bit too much to do. "I would get a bit behind in the summer, then in the autumn and the new year I'd always have a good run but the championship leader was gone clear."

That good form continued as autumn and winter set in and December four-timers at Carlisle and Newcastle helped him to the

◂ Friends and rivals: Brian Hughes and Richard Johnson in the weighing room at Ayr in January and, left, going out to ride; far left, Hughes after winning on Gaelik Coast at Doncaster later that month, just after Johnson was sidelined with a broken arm

front, putting him top of the table at Christmas for the first time. But January was the key month, specifically January 21 when Richard Johnson broke his arm in a fall at Exeter.

"It was to-ing and fro-ing and I remember I had a double at Ayr and drew level, then I rode three winners at Newcastle," Hughes says. "The next day I had no rides and Dickie had his fall. I was gutted for him. When a lad next to you gets a fall it really hits home how any of us can get injured at any time. I was relishing the challenge and it was looking like it was going to go all the way to the end of the season."

★★★★

AS IT was, Hughes was 20 winners clear when his resilient rival resumed 37 days later, immediately firing in a Musselburgh double on his return. "Dickie came back and had a couple of winners but I tried not to think too much about it," Hughes says. "I could only control what I was doing. There was a 20-winner gap, so all I needed to do was ride as many winners as him. The yards I ride for had plenty of spring ammunition ready to roll, plenty of nice horses looking forward to Aintree and Ayr."

Aintree and Ayr never took place and the season was halted when racing was shut down on March 17 with the challenger 19 winners clear of the champion, 141 to 122. "I was gutted not to see the end of the season but I suppose we were all a bit naive about the coronavirus," says Hughes, who got that memorable phone call 20 days later.

"I suppose I'll appreciate it more when I look back on it in 30 years' time and it hit home a bit when I got the trophy. Mick Fitzgerald came up to present it and you look at it and see the names of people I consider to have legendary status in jump racing – not for a second do I think I'm a legend, I should say!"

The fact he was the first northern-based champion since Jonjo O'Neill 40 years earlier meant plenty, including to Donald McCain, who trained 43 of those 141 winners and has never regretted teaming up with the area's top man. "It was pretty obvious in the north of England that he was so far ahead of everyone else," McCain says. "He's so dominant that it was a no-brainer: if we're the biggest yard in the north of England, we had to have him onside.

"Every time you watched him, he was always in the right place. When someone is very good at something they make it look easy and that's Brian, he makes the job look very smooth and simple. He's dedicated to a fault and he's very driven – he eats, sleeps, lives and breathes racing. He does his homework and doesn't miss anything. He knows what's going on, he knows what the opposition are doing, he knows what races are coming up. I wouldn't fancy being married to him, but then I don't know if it's great fun being married to me either."

Hughes does not believe that winning the title has changed him. "I'm no different a person, just trying to do my best and ride as many winners as I can," he says, "but it does give you more confidence and this game is all about confidence."

Lambe, who still speaks to Hughes once a week, does not expect his success to end any time soon. "I think he's the best jump jockey riding in England at the moment," he says. "He's the complete package. He's strong, he's healthy and he's still driven, he wants that winning post as much as he wanted it when he was 15."

The teenager with burning ambition is now the champion. Just as he had vowed he would be.

Faugheen was reinvented as a chaser and provided one of the best stories of the jumps season

SAME MACHINE DIFFERENT MODEL

By Lee Mottershead

THE horse tried, the trainer did not. No wonder. In the minutes that followed Faugheen's heartwarming, age-defying defeat of stable companion Easy Game at the Dublin Racing Festival, Willie Mullins did not for one second seek to mirror the effort his venerable warrior had just displayed on Leopardstown's turf.

Had he been a true diplomat, Mullins could have pretended that as he watched two members of his Closutton team tussling through the closing stages of the Flogas Novice Chase, he did so without cheering one animal over the other. Ireland's champion trainer could have told us he minded not one jot whether Faugheen beat Easy Game or Easy Game beat Faugheen, so long as one finished first and the other finished second.

He could have done that but nobody would have believed him. Like the rest of us at Leopardstown that unforgettable afternoon, Mullins was willing home only one horse – one utterly incredible horse whose rebirth provided one of the jumps season's most glorious stories.

"I was praying for Faugheen, so I was," Mullins said. "I wanted Faugheen to win in a big way. I would have been gutted if he had been beaten." The stirring reception around the winner's enclosure, plus the euphoric reaction on social media, made it clear that feeling was widely shared.

They call him Faugheen the machine but the machine that lit up Leopardstown is not about nuts and bolts but heart and soul. Machines can survive indefinitely. Racehorses cannot. On the day he won a Grade 1 novice chase at the age of 12 – which sounds ridiculous because it is – Faugheen was back at the racecourse where on his previous visit it briefly appeared heart and soul had been extinguished.

It was the Grade 1 Christmas Hurdle, not the festive two-miler of the same name he banked so easily at Kempton in 2015 but the three-mile top-flight test that takes place during Leopardstown's Christmas festival. In the three years between Kempton and Leopardstown much had happened, although an awful lot had taken place even before Kempton. By that point Faugheen had already won twice at the Cheltenham Festival, most famously when making all to capture the 2015 Champion Hurdle for owners Rich and Susannah Ricci. There was talk then about whether a horse whose debut success had come in a point-to-point would go chasing. He stayed hurdling.

He continued to be very good at it, perhaps producing the performance of his life when winning Leopardstown's 2016 Irish Champion Hurdle by 15 lengths. Fate then intervened and Faugheen was kept off the track for 665 days. He resumed with a win but thereafter there were more bad days than good days. The legs seemed to move slower than had once been the case, so Mullins moved the old boy up in trip.

◂ Pride of Ireland: Faugheen and Paul Townend soak up the applause after their marvellous Flogas Novice Chase triumph at Leopardstown ▾ Faugheen with groom John Codd

It worked exceptionally well at the 2018 Punchestown Festival but not so well a few months down the line at Leopardstown, where he lay on the grass behind the penultimate flight for a worryingly long time after crashing out with a horrible fall. Thankfully he rose. Ruby Walsh removed the saddle, walked his long-time ally in a circle and gave him a pat. We breathed a sigh of relief.

Faugheen had not said goodbye to life, nor indeed racing, but plenty of us thought he had four months later at Aintree, where Walsh eased him down and pulled him up after the pair had led over the fifth flight. "He didn't feel like he normally does," Walsh said. "He was just lifeless. He's sound but he just didn't feel right."

The superstar of old was 11 and seemingly close to retirement, certainly judged by the words of Rich Ricci, who spoke of possibly making one last trip to Punchestown, where adoring Irish fans would be able to bid their hero farewell. We assumed Ricci was talking about another outing over hurdles at the imminent Punchestown festival. That is likely also what he was thinking about. Mullins began to think about something else.

★★★★

FAUGHEEN did indeed return at Punchestown, but it was in a beginners' chase seven months later. At an age when some champions of jumping take on the fresh challenge of show classes, dressage or crochet, Faugheen was instead going to take on fences, seven and a half years after he had last jumped one in a Ballysteen point-to-point.

▸▸ *Continues page 138*

Having outlasted the now retired Walsh, Faugheen was partnered by Paul Townend in the 17-runner beginners' chase. Across the water at Cheltenham, eyes were not on Allmankind, who had just won the Triumph Hurdle trial. In the racecourse betting shop, punters began to complain loudly that the television monitors were showing the maiden hurdle at Uttoxeter, not the beginners' chase at Punchestown.

Fortunately, someone shouted that the race was on the big screen, around which the Cheltenham faithful made a big gasping noise when Faugheen almost unseated Townend at the eighth fence. They then made a big clapping noise when Faugheen came home an easy winner. From her Racing TV broadcast position, Lydia Hislop was one of those applauding. Faugheen was fantastic once more, now over open ditches as well.

On St Stephen's Day at Limerick, Faugheen became a Grade 1-winning novice chaser, causing Samcro to wave a white flag of surrender in between the final two fences. Patrick Mullins, who had ridden the then five-year-old to land his one and only bumper, was in the saddle because Townend was at Leopardstown. Townend was there again in February on day two of Leopardstown's fabulous winter weekend. So was Faugheen.

In reality, he was only a shade over a month older than he had been at Limerick, but on that day he was 11 and on this day he was officially 12. At that age, horses should not be contesting top-flight novice chases. That, however, is what Faugheen was doing. "I arrived here thinking if he came home in one piece it would be grand," Ricci admitted afterwards, adding: "I was a bit sceptical but the yard was confident and the horse was on song."

The owner's racing manager was in a state of continuous tears. Faugheen did that. Truth be told, he neither jumped nor travelled as well as he had at Limerick. Through most of the contest he appeared to be moving slightly less easily in second than market rival Battleoverdoyen was in the lead. A clumsy leap at the penultimate fence should have knocked Faugheen back. Instead it propelled him forward and up the inner of Battleoverdoyen, who faded as the field turned for home and eventually fell at the last fence.

Easy Game was now the challenger to a stable companion twice his age. With Faugheen against the far rail and Easy Game close to the stands' rail, they committed to a duel that sent the decibel levels soaring. No more than half a length separated them at the line. Faugheen passed it in front.

People cheered. People sprinted to the winner's enclosure. People sprinted and cheered at the same time. It was absolutely marvellous.

★★★★

JOE CHAMBERS, the sobbing racing manager, never really dried up over the ensuing few minutes. His boss appeared not to cry, although behind his dark glasses there must surely have been some moistening, not least due to the reception his white-faced warrior received.

"It was magic, super, fantastic," Ricci said. "Golly, Faugheen was brilliant. It's spectacular and wonderful for all the people here."

Mullins borrowed one of his client's adjectives, while also admitting to some pre-race anxiety. "Coming here I was worried he'd have a bad fall or get injured or something like that, but he came up trumps," he said, before describing the scenes we had witnessed as "fantastic" and adding: "He has got everything. He has stamina, he has speed and he can jump. He has got it all. He has got a will as well. He's a bit like Un De Sceaux – every morning the two of them go up the gallop and they want to train, they want to get at the job."

The desire to work, to race and to perform was no less obvious in March at Cheltenham, where Faugheen went around the paddock with the enthusiasm and excitement of a young buck and competed with no less verve. Despite giving his all in the Marsh Novices' Chase, Faugheen suffered his first defeat over fences, but although the elder statesman was unable to add to his 11-strong Grade 1 haul, he ran a cracker, finishing a close third behind Samcro and Melon before receiving the sort of ovation normally reserved for winners.

Asked about Faugheen's reinvention as a chaser, Mullins said: "I should have done it last season but I got sidetracked. I then didn't want to retire him without going over fences because that's what we bought him for. Now just look what he can do at 12."

What he did at 12 still seems scarcely believable. It may yet turn out that anything Faugheen achieved over hurdles was a bonus.

WINNERS UNITED

By Nick Pulford

GOING through a season undefeated is an impressive achievement for a top-level jumper, especially if it includes victory at the Cheltenham Festival. Champion Hurdle winner Epatante did it in her three races of 2019-20, along with Al Boum Photo in his short Gold Cup campaign, and Honeysuckle and Envoi Allen were two more who earned a high tariff by rounding off impressive seasons with a Grade 1 festival victory.

In fact, Honeysuckle and Envoi Allen reached the early end of the campaign still unbeaten in their careers after two seasons of racing and with their connections excitedly looking forward to even greater success. It is a measure of their class that both were in the top five of the 2021 Champion Hurdle betting following their festival victories, even though it was already open to question whether that race would turn out to be the target for either of them.

An impeccable racing record was not the only thing these Irish-trained hurdlers have in common. Both were born in 2014, just two months apart, and the same time gap separated their eyecatching wins on their sole point-to-point starts, which put them much in demand at the sales. Envoi Allen went for a whopping £400,000 at Tattersalls' Cheltenham February Sale in 2018 and two months later (again) Honeysuckle fetched a not inconsiderable €110,000 at the Goffs Punchestown Sale. Thereafter their paths diverged, with Honeysuckle immediately going over hurdles while Envoi Allen had a season in bumpers that culminated in Cheltenham Festival victory, but both continued to head upwards.

****

HONEYSUCKLE was long touted as a Champion Hurdle contender in the 2019-20 season, with the calls growing ever louder after her Grade 1 wins in open company in the Hatton's Grace Hurdle in December and the Irish Champion

▸▸ *Continues page 142*

Envoi Allen and Honeysuckle completed undefeated campaigns with Grade 1 successes at the Cheltenham Festival

◂ Double top: Davy Russell wins the Ballymore Novices' Hurdle on Envoi Allen (opposite page) and Rachael Blackmore savours Mares' Hurdle success with Honeysuckle

Hurdle in February, but in the end trainer Henry de Bromhead and owner Kenny Alexander took the easier option of the Mares' Hurdle at Cheltenham.

Not that it was much easier, if at all, in a season when the mares took high rank among the elite hurdlers. Benie Des Dieux, who also had the talent to go for the Champion, was diverted to the Mares' Hurdle against Honeysuckle, leaving another outstanding mare, Epatante, to claim the Champion crown on the same afternoon.

Explaining the decision to send Honeysuckle for the Mares' Hurdle, De Bromhead said: "Mainly it's that her most impressive performances have been over two and a half miles. That's the trip she's got her highest rating at." Despite her obvious class after seven consecutive wins, three of them at Grade 1 level, Honeysuckle was only second favourite at 9-4, with Benie Des Dieux rated one of the bankers of the week at 4-6.

Benie Des Dieux had let down odds-on backers in the previous year's race when she fell at the last and she was a costly loser again in another dramatic race. The crucial moment came on the home turn when Rachael Blackmore crept up the inside of Stormy Ireland to seize the lead on Honeysuckle while Paul Townend had already committed to taking Benie Des Dieux the longer way round the outer of her stablemate. There was an almighty battle all the way to the line but Honeysuckle bravely held on to her advantage and made it eight wins from eight with half a length to spare over Benie Des Dieux.

While the brickbats rained on Townend and Stormy Ireland's rider Robbie Power for messing up the race on the Willie Mullins-trained runners, there was delight in the Honeysuckle camp. "Thankfully we came up with the right race between us," De Bromhead said. "What a ride by Rachael. My God, the way she got up the inside coming around the last turn. It was two amazing ladies together. Suddenly the gap appeared and she was gone. It's fantastic."

****

TWENTY-FOUR hours after Benie Des Dieux's defeat, Envoi Allen was an even bigger Irish banker at 4-7 in the Ballymore Novices' Hurdle. He did not disappoint. Like Honeysuckle, he took his perfect record to eight but with the difference that nothing could get close to him in the closing stages. His winning margin of four and a quarter lengths over stablemate Easywork was only a loose measure of his superiority.

Not that trainer Gordon Elliott could relax for much of the race, such was the pressure heaped on him not only by his own expectations but those of an entire racing nation. There was also the question of whether he had made the right decision in sending Davy Russell's mount for the Ballymore over two miles and five furlongs on soft ground, rather than the shorter Supreme Novices' Hurdle the day before.

"I was nervous the whole way through the race," admitted Elliott, who watched with Colin Bowe, the man who had trained Envoi Allen to win his sole point-to-point and then sold him for that massive sum. "I was asking Colin the whole way 'Will he stay? Will he stay?' and he said he would definitely stay no bother. If I had picked the wrong race, I was going to blame him."

Elliott had a few moments of concern as Envoi Allen swung off the home turn around six lengths behind The Big Getaway and Easywork, but the favourite quickly showed his class to storm into the lead before the final flight. "I thought Davy had given them too much lead coming down the hill but he knew the horse well," the trainer said. "He was our big runner for the week, so this was the big pressure. He was our best chance and everybody was here to see him."

▲ Irish cream: from top, Envoi Allen puts in a mighty leap in the Ballymore Novices' Hurdle; Davy Russell celebrates; groom Seainin Mahon greets Envoi Allen; Honeysuckle takes the final flight in the Mares' Hurdle; Rachael Blackmore returns victorious

****

WHERE everybody would see Envoi Allen in the new season was a topic for debate immediately after the Ballymore. Richard Thompson, son of owners David and Patricia Thompson of Cheveley Park Stud, said: "You'd like to think he'll kick on to chasing next season. I don't think we'll be aiming him at the Champion Hurdle, I can't see that."

Asked about Envoi Allen's potential and how he might compare with some of his best horses, Elliott said: "I'm not going to answer that question. He's a very nice horse and as long as he keeps winning I'm happy." As for future targets, his answer was succinct. "He was bought to be a three-mile chaser, that's all I'm saying."

Chasing was mooted for Honeysuckle too, but in the summer Alexander's racing manager Peter Molony said the plan was to keep her over hurdles. "I'd imagine we'll treat the season in two halves," he said. "She could start off in the Hatton's Grace at Fairyhouse before going on to the Irish Champion Hurdle, just like last season. There's a chance she could go a different route to last season after that depending on how everything unfolds."

Whichever paths they take, Honeysuckle and Envoi Allen should be heading back to the Cheltenham Festival with many hopes pinned on them again.

PICTURE PERFECT

By Nick Pulford

ON THE day of her christening Maxine O'Sullivan was pictured with her father Eugene and the enormous trophy for the Foxhunter Chase, which was in his possession thanks to Lovely Citizen's triumph at Cheltenham the year before. The County Cork trainer never gave up hope of another victory in the race known as the 'hunters' Gold Cup' and, growing up to become an accomplished amateur rider, Maxine dreamed of winning the race for him. Finally, 29 years after Lovely Citizen, it came to pass.

On a glorious March day, their dreams were fulfilled with a horse who had been bought specifically for the Foxhunter. Trained to the minute by Eugene and ridden to perfection by Maxine, It Came To Pass blew away his 20 rivals with a power-packed performance. He may have been a 66-1 shot but there was no hint of a fluke about his impressive ten-length success over the favourite Billaway, whose trainer Willie Mullins had won a second Gold Cup with Al Boum Photo over the same course and distance 40 minutes earlier.

That this meant as much to the O'Sullivan family as winning 'the big one' did for Mullins was made plain by Maxine's breathless post-race comments. Down the years she had marvelled at the stories and the photos of how Lovely Citizen, who was not only trained by her father but ridden by her uncle Willie and owned and bred by her grandfather Eoin, had conquered Cheltenham. Now she had played a central role in another chapter of the family history.

"This is our Gold Cup and it just means so much," she said. "For my family and the lovely owners of It Came To Pass, it's such a big family thing. It's a really special race for us and it's just brilliant. This is off the scale. I dreamed of winning this but I didn't think I would. This is just amazing. I will remember this day forever."

★★★★

IT CAME TO PASS'S big odds reflected not only the David v Goliath storyline as the O'Sullivans took on the Mullins-trained Billaway but also the difficulty they had in getting him there. He had been bought in January 2019 with the Foxhunter in mind but had not been qualified for the race that spring and instead stayed at home to win two point-to-points followed by a pair of important hunter chases at Cork and Killarney.

Keen-eyed punters would have noted he beat Billaway at Cork, by a similar distance as he would at Cheltenham 11 months later, and

Eugene O'Sullivan and his daughter Maxine fulfilled a long-held dream with a memorable Foxhunter Chase triumph for It Came To Pass

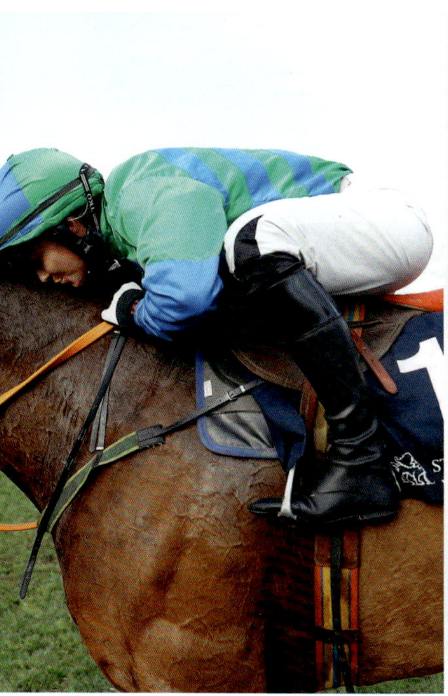

came out on top against dual Foxhunter Chase winner On The Fringe at Killarney.

That was so far, so good, but his form seemed more up and down in the new season. Having unseated Maxine at the first fence in a point-to-point at Dromahane in November, he was turned out quickly to win a hunter chase at Cork seven days later but then blotted his copybook again with a lacklustre seventh in a hunter chase at Down Royal and a pulled-up disappointment in a point-to-point at Kilfeacle on his last run before Cheltenham.

The O'Sullivans' faith in him was unshakeable, however.

"When he won he always did it very well and we always felt he was a very good horse," Maxine said. "He wasn't 100 per cent fit when he won at Cork in the autumn and it was a great run to do that when we thought he might need the run, and after that he had excuses.

"The track at Down Royal was very tight that day and even on the outside there wasn't much daylight, and after Kilfeacle he was very sick and we had to leave him out in the field for two weeks."

This was a testing period for Eugene, who faced a race against time to have It Came To Pass back in peak condition for Cheltenham less than seven weeks after the Kilfeacle run. In the last fortnight before the festival, their stable star suddenly started to brighten again. "He really came back to himself and we were confident when we left home that he was as good as we could have him," Maxine said.

"We were confident then that if he produced his form from last year he would have a very good chance."

There was another obstacle to overcome even before It Came To Pass tackled the 22 fences and 3m2½f of the Foxhunter. Maxine, who rides him all the time at home and had partnered him with varying degrees of comfort in his ten races for the stable, was well aware he needed careful handling.

"He's a tricky horse," she said. "He's very sensitive and he won't leave the yard in front. He's very nervous and everything scares him, he won't do anything on his own. At Cheltenham he wouldn't go down the chute to the gallops. It's not badness, it's pure fear. He gets very worried and kind of freezes and doesn't know what to do. Once he's going he's fine.

"He did it on the day of the race going out of the chute; he wouldn't move. We tried to get a lead off another horse, but four or five came past us and he wouldn't go, so we did a quick 360 and then we took off cantering down to the start and he was fine after that."

▸▸ *Continues page 146*

★★★★

HAZEL HILL, the previous year's winner, was missing from the start line having been withdrawn on veterinary grounds but there was still a formidable line-up headed by Billaway, the 2019 runner-up Shantou Flyer and Minella Rocco, who at his peak had finished second to Sizing John in the 2017 Gold Cup. Only five of the 21 runners started longer in the betting than It Came To Pass but he was soon to make a mockery of the odds.

For the first circuit he raced close to Billaway in midfield, with Maxine keeping to the outside to give him clear daylight. Making the climb up the far side of the course on the final circuit, the pair gradually crept closer and they were handily placed in fourth at the top of the hill. "When we went down the back the last time that was when he really started to motor and enjoy himself," she recalled. "Always from about three or four out he turns into a cheetah and you can see him eyeing up the fences and he gets faster and faster. He just sees the stride himself and attacks the fences."

While Maxine was growing in confidence, in the stands her father was nervous at the sight of Billaway and Minella Rocco tracking It Came To Pass. "I was like a Jack-in-the-box the whole way, feeling nervous for Maxine and nervous for the horse," he said. "But I knew if he came around the final bend anywhere near the front he would stay and quicken up."

On that final bend It Came To Pass was poised to challenge and by the second-last fence he had jumped into the lead. There was no stopping him now. "I know my horse inside out and, having done my homework on the other horses, I just knew he would stay going and maybe even quicken a bit going up that hill," Maxine said. "So I really enjoyed the last two fences. It's unusual to feel like that in a race but I was fairly confident."

The ten-length margin was ample reflection of the winner's superiority and the spark for a memorable celebration. As with Lovely Citizen, the family roots ran deep. Eugene oversees the training, ably assisted by Maxine, while his brother Willie runs the farming side of the family business. It Came To Pass was led up by Willie's sons Michael and Alan, and Maxine's brothers Eoin and David had played their part at home whenever college commitments allowed.

"The most special part for me was seeing the people I care about and knowing how much it meant to them as well," Maxine said. "My two cousins were leading up the horse and it was a special moment when they were running over to me. I just wanted to see all the people who mean so much – my family and friends and the owners. I was dying to see my dad and he was so happy."

It was some achievement. The only other names apart from Eugene O'Sullivan who appear on the Foxhunter roll of honour alongside two different winners in the past 30 years are Enda Bolger and Richard Barber, powerhouses of the Irish and British point-to-point scene, and Paul Nicholls, long associated with the Barber set-up.

Dad, in turn, paid tribute to the daughter who had delivered this cherished victory. "Maxine has done an awful lot of work on him at home and she gave him a savage ride. All the big guns were queuing up behind but Maxine knew what she had, she rode him accordingly and I'm very proud of her," he said.

A mark of that pride soon followed. Just as he had in 1992, Eugene held Maxine in his arms for a photo with the famous old trophy. The bond and happiness they shared was plain to see. This was another special treasure for the family album.

▲ Forward pass: Maxine O'Sullivan takes the final fence in the lead on It Came To Pass; previous page from left, flying home in front; father and daughter with the trophy 28 years apart; Maxine is congratulated by Patrick Mullins; celebratory scenes on the course and in the winner's enclosure; the trophy lift

That winning feeling

Maxine O'Sullivan on the after party

I was buzzing so much afterwards that I didn't sleep for about 48 hours. I had a flight to Dublin booked for 10.30pm but my dad and Alan [her cousin] were taking the horse back home and I went in the lorry with them. Because it was our horse and my dad, I wanted to be with them and not be on a plane on my own. We left Cheltenham at 6pm and the ferry was at midnight from Fishguard. We were all on such good form and we had great fun on the way back. It was the best journey ever.

The six runners break from the stalls for the Sky Sports Racing HD Virgin 535 Handicap at Windsor in June. Third from right is the winner of the race, the John Gosden-trained Grand Bazaar
EDWARD WHITAKER (RACINGPOST.COM/PHOTOS)

THE BIGGER PICTURE

43

THE BIGGER PICTURE

Steam rises from Western Victory after the Grade 2 Coolmore NH Sires EBF Mares Novice Chase at Thurles in January. The Declan Queally-trained seven-year-old fell two out in the race but came back from a lengthy break to open her chasing account at Roscommon in the summer

PATRICK McCANN (RACINGPOST.COM/PHOTOS)

FAIRYTALE PRINCESS

Princess Zoe's journey from low-level handicapper to Group 1 winner in the Prix du Cadran took her connections on an incredible adventure

By Nick Pulford

TONY MULLINS said it was unbelievable and no-one was going to disagree with him. Willie Mullins' younger brother had just seen Princess Zoe complete her incredible rags-to-riches story by winning the Group 1 Prix du Cadran in the most stunning fashion and yet he was still rubbing his eyes. "I'm pinching myself to make sure I'm awake," the trainer said. So was everyone else.

Just for Princess Zoe to be at Longchamp on Arc weekend was remarkable enough. Less than four months earlier, after she was beaten off a mark of 64 in a minor handicap at Navan on her first start for Mullins, nobody could have envisaged a trip to Paris. Four straight wins and a 45lb rise took her there, which was amazing in itself, but what she did in the Cadran was on another level.

At the top of the home straight, Princess Zoe and her apprentice jockey Joey Sheridan had around eight lengths to make up on runaway leader Alkuin. For an 18-year-old rider making his Longchamp debut it was a formidable task to win from there. Sheridan did not give up hope, however, and slowly but surely he began to make ground. It was attritional and stamina-sapping on the heavy ground, more like the finish of a jumps race with the nine runners all strung out, but Sheridan timed his run to

▼ Prize catch: Joey Sheridan drives Princess Zoe to Prix du Cadran victory in a dogged pursuit of long-time leader Alkuin up the home straight

perfection. With just 30 metres left to cover, Princess Zoe hit the front and the celebrations could start.

"I knew they were going too hard for the ground and the trip," said Sheridan, whose emotions poured out once the winning line was crossed. "It means everything to me. It's a dream come true and I want to take in every second. I'm going to cherish this for the rest of my life."

Mullins will cherish it too. In 1984, just down the road at Auteuil, he had ridden the great Dawn Run, trained by his father Paddy, to win the French Champion Hurdle. That was the pinnacle of his riding career and now Princess Zoe had taken his training operation to extraordinary heights.

"It's all unbelievable," he said. "I nearly had a heart attack in the last 100 metres. I thought we weren't quite going to get there. The relief when she put her nose in front was a feeling I've never had before, even with Dawn Run." A feeling better than Dawn Run? Now that's saying something.

★★★★

THE Princess Zoe story was as wonderful as it was unlikely, and it might not have happened at all if Mullins had set eyes on her before she joined his stable.

Discussing how the five-year-old came to his yard after two unremarkable seasons in her native Germany, Mullins revealed she had been bought sight unseen by him. "Bernard Cullinane [bloodstock agent] found her for me in Germany," he said. "When I looked up where she was, the flights were so difficult I didn't go to see her. It was lucky I didn't as she's quite crooked and I wouldn't have bought her if I was there. The first day I worked her I knew she was okay, though."

Before that initial piece of work, there was a phone call to Simon Minch, the manager of Gestut Hony-Hof, in Hessen, north of Frankfurt, who had sold the mare through Cullinane. "At that time, it was an absolutely legitimate offer for a horse of that standard, they didn't pay a huge amount, but I didn't need her," Minch later told

▸▸ *Continues page 160*

the Racing Post. "She went off in October [2019] and I got a phone call from Ireland basically saying, 'WTF is this?' I said, 'Look guys, you had a vet on her here in Germany, bought as seen sort of thing'."

Not that Minch thought Princess Zoe was that bad. "She was a bit pigeon-toed. She's not wickedly crooked or anything, but she just turns in a bit in front," he said, adding: "She was just what she was."

Nobody yet knew exactly what she was, but before she ran for Mullins there was a twist of fortune in her story related to the pandemic. "She was ready to run in March, but the lockdown was the making of her. Those extra three months really helped her," the trainer said.

Things did not start smoothly for her when racing resumed in June as she was in season before her scheduled first run and was then beaten into second place at Navan off that low mark of 64 when she finally got going, but after that there was no stopping her.

She won the Ladies Derby at the Curragh off a revised mark of 70 under Jody Townend in mid-July and within a fortnight she had doubled up in two of the Galway festival's hottest handicaps.

Her Ladies Derby victory at the Curragh was over a mile and a half and, having gone up 13lb, she then stepped up to 2m1f to land the amateur riders' Connacht Hotel Premier Handicap under Finny Maguire at Galway nine days later. "If she hadn't got the 13lb for the Ladies Derby, she wouldn't have got in," Mullins said, adding: "To win a feature race here is like a Cheltenham winner to me."

After another four days and a further 7lb rise in the ratings, the remarkable mare gave Mullins another feature success when she dropped back to a mile and a half to claim the Galway Shopping Centre Premier Handicap, which marked the start of Sheridan's partnership with her. This was less than six weeks since her first run in Ireland and the trainer now knew he had an exciting prospect on his hands.

"We were thinking of the Cesarewitch for her, but we'll now have to consider the Group 1 Prix du Cadran on Arc weekend," he said. "She has a nice pedigree and it's now very much on the agenda. I don't think she'll run before then."

Princess Zoe was up to a mark of 101, a rise of 37lb in 39 days, but she was far from finished and she was doing so well that Mullins did run her again before the Cadran. On September 8 she returned to Galway and took the step up to Listed company in her stride to land the Ardilaun Hotel Oyster Stakes by a length and three-quarters.

▲ Living the dream: Princess Zoe in the Longchamp winner's enclosure with trainer Tony Mullins (centre), owners Paddy Kehoe and Philomena Crampton, and groom Jackie Carter

★★★★

THAT confirmed Longchamp as the next stop but there was also another big meeting under consideration by Princess Zoe's part-owner Paddy Kehoe, as Mullins revealed. "Paddy has had some very good horses for relatively handy money but he's never had a Cheltenham winner, although Grabel was placed for him in the Triumph Hurdle [in 1987]. He's expressed an interest that regardless of her value and black type, if she jumps well he'd like to aim for Cheltenham."

Speaking about his long and fruitful relationship with Kehoe, who owns Princess Zoe with his sister Philomena Crampton, Mullins added: "I've known Paddy nearly 40 years and nearly every horse we've had has won. The luck we've had is unbelievable."

The unbelievability factor was about to go off the scale. Speaking before the Cadran, Mullins was optimistic of a good run from Princess Zoe, who was 5-2 second favourite for the two-and-a-half-mile contest. "We're stepping up to a Group 1 now and she'll be running over a mile further than she's run over on her last two starts," he

▸▸ *Continues page 162*

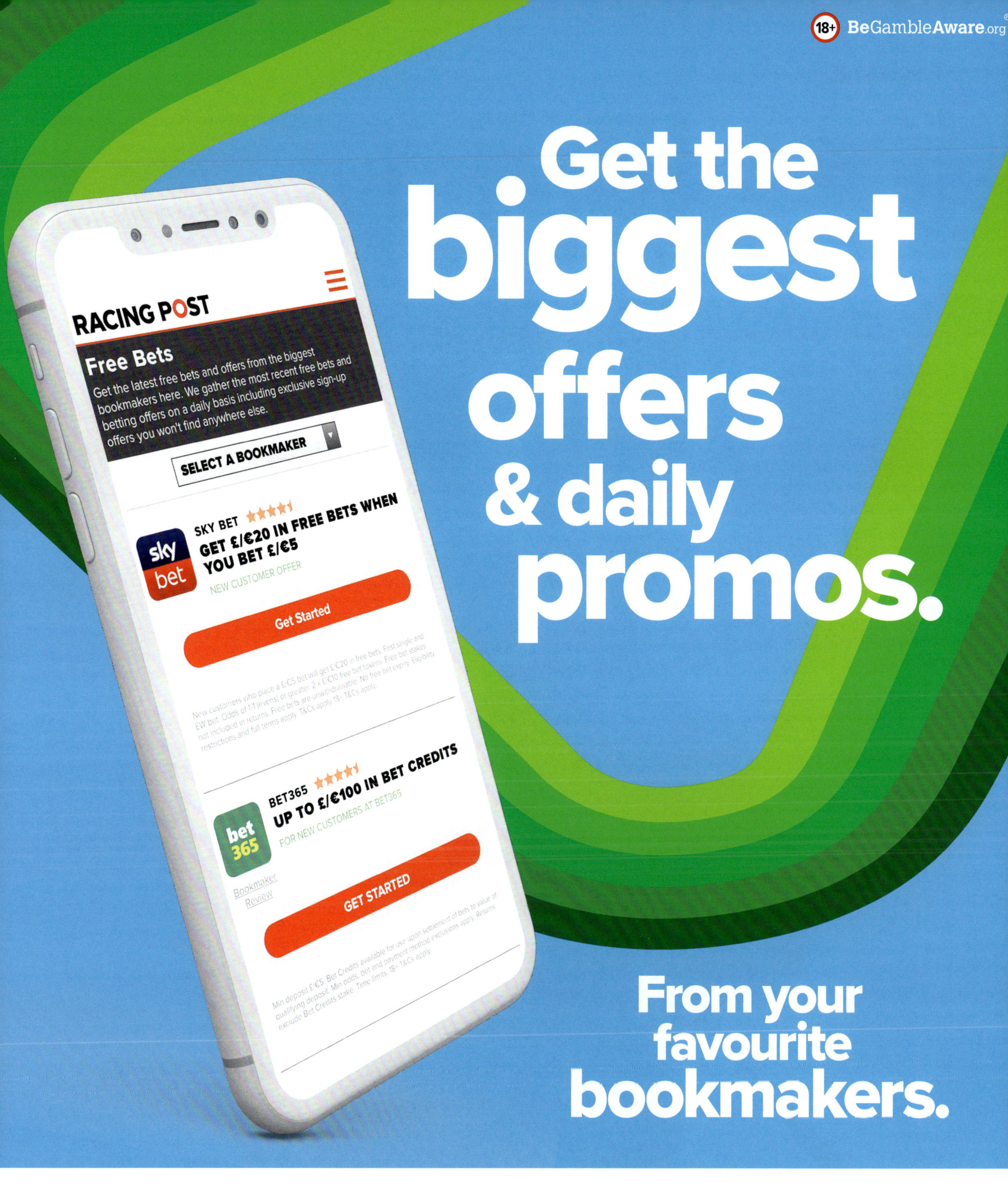

18+ BeGambleAware.org
Get the biggest offers & daily promos.
RACING POST
Free Bets
Get the latest free bets and offers from the biggest bookmakers here. We gather the most recent free bets and betting offers on a daily basis including exclusive sign-up offers you won't find anywhere else.
SELECT A BOOKMAKER
SKY BET
GET £/€20 IN FREE BETS WHEN YOU BET £/€5
NEW CUSTOMER OFFER
Get Started
BET365
UP TO £/€100 IN BET CREDITS
FOR NEW CUSTOMERS AT BET365
Bookmaker Review
GET STARTED
From your favourite bookmakers.

said, "but the burst of speed she showed me at the end of the amateur race at Galway in the summer told me she'll stay. She has a realistic chance of winning a Group 1. It's unbelievable really."

Over in Germany, Minch was hoping for a good result for his own reasons and he paid tribute to Mullins. "We'd have never gone down the route she has gone, so we would never have got her to that level, and hats off to them," he said. "It's great for us as we have the mother, the half-sister, and if she even got placed in the Cadran, it would be amazing."

Mullins kept Sheridan on board for the Group 1 mission, despite the fact the teenager was not allowed to use his 5lb claim, and his faith was repaid in glorious style. The jockey had to dig as deep as his mount in the exhausting and nerve-shredding run to the line, but he got her home by half a length from Alkuin. Call The Wind, the 5-4 favourite, was another 15 lengths behind in third and there was more than 100 lengths from first to last.

"It's an astonishing story, I know, but I really have been so confident all week," said Mullins, who has been training since 1987. "It's so rare to have no problems when you're training a horse for a race. Normally when you push them things go wrong. Not one thing went wrong with this horse."

The dreaming goes on. There is Kehoe's Cheltenham ambition and, even if that is ruled out for a Group 1 winner with valuable broodmare potential, there is the Gold Cup at Royal Ascot next summer. Nothing seems out of bounds after her incredible journey to that wonderful Longchamp triumph. In the space of a few weeks, Princess Zoe had made anything seem possible.

▸ Teenage kicks: Joey Sheridan lets out a roar of delight at the end of the Prix du Cadran; below, at Galway

'I will cherish it for as long as I live'

Joey Sheridan, the 18-year-old rider of Princess Zoe, spoke to the Racing Post's David Jennings a few days after the Prix du Cadran

I'm still in dreamland, I can't believe what's happened to me. I've been walking around in a daze for the last few days wondering has this actually happened to me? I never expected to win a Group 1 so soon. It's hard to get your head around it all.

I could barely breathe when I was pulling her up. It wasn't tiredness either; it was just pure disbelief. I couldn't believe what had just happened. I've never had a feeling like that before and I doubt I ever will again. I will cherish it for as long as I live.

I cannot thank Tony [Mullins], Paddy [Kehoe] and Philomena [Crampton] enough for allowing me to keep the ride on Princess Zoe. I wouldn't have thrown my toys out of the pram if they had got someone more experienced for the big day. I know the way it works, so I was privileged they still wanted me.

Tony kept it very simple beforehand and left it up to me. I wanted to have her bang there and ready to pounce at the end of the false straight. I didn't want to kick any sooner than on the home turn, so it worked out well. It was a strange race in that half the field were beaten about 1,200 metres out and I knew I only had one horse to beat.

There was one stage when he [Alkuin] was about 20 lengths in front of me. But my instinct told me there was no possible way a horse could go that quick, on that ground, over that far, and not come back. I knew he had to come back at some stage.

I will admit that for about 20 metres inside the final 100 metres I thought I might have misjudged it and wasn't going to get there. Luckily, I did.

I got quite emotional on the way back to the winner's enclosure as Jayo Kinane, Mick's brother, congratulated me. He, along with a few others, basically taught me how to ride. I went to Ballydoyle when I was just 13 and Jayo was a massive help to me, and here he was congratulating me on winning a Group 1. That's the stuff dreams are made of.

Ger Lyons scored his first Classic win with Siskin and quickly added another with Even So

CLASSIC DOUBLE

ALL winter Ger Lyons dreamed of having his first Classic winner. Spring came and went with no racing, but when summer arrived he was ready. He seized his opportunity with Siskin in the Irish 2,000 Guineas in June and then for good measure did it again with Even So in the Irish Oaks the following month. Together with stable jockey Colin Keane, who had become champion under his guidance, he had cracked the Classic code.

Siskin had looked a clear Classic candidate in an unbeaten four-race juvenile campaign and duly went off 2-1 favourite for the Guineas, but the waiting for the season to start had left question marks. Just over ten months had elapsed since the last of his wins, in the Group 1 Phoenix Stakes, and there had been no time for a prep run with his Classic date at the Curragh coming on a Friday night just four days after the resumption of racing in Ireland.

That meant there was no answer to whether Khalid Abdullah's exciting colt would repeat the unruly antics of the previous autumn when he had refused to load for the Middle Park Stakes, which was supposed to be his final juvenile run, or whether he would handle the step up from six furlongs to the Classic mile.

Lyons did plenty of stalls work with Siskin and opted to fit a hood for loading in the Guineas, and there was confidence the colt would stay the Curragh mile, but nobody could know for sure how he would perform on the night. As Teddy Grimthorpe, the owner's racing manager, put it: "It's slightly strange timing this year and we're not as knowledgeable as we'd like to be about where we all are."

More doubts had arisen when the final field was declared. Aidan O'Brien, who was going for a 12th Irish 2,000, had six of the 11 runners and Keane's tactical difficulty in countering the Ballydoyle battalion was compounded by Siskin's draw in stall two. Only two Irish trainers had taken the Guineas off O'Brien since he moved to Ballydoyle more than two decades ago. This was not going to be easy.

****

THE way Siskin and Keane came up with all the answers was breathtaking. As many had feared, Siskin ran into trouble from his inside berth. With two furlongs to run, Keane was surrounded by Ballydoyle rivals. Fort Myers, Royal Lytham and Vatican City were in front of him and Armory was on his outer, and then Seamie Heffernan on Lope Y Fernandez came around them all to tighten matters further.

This was the time to act. Keane swooped out from behind Heffernan, forcing Armory aside, and set off in pursuit. Lope Y Fernandez was in front going into the final furlong but Siskin was motoring just behind him and now Keane put him into overdrive, powering clear to win by a length and three-quarters from the fast-finishing Vatican City.

Lyons, who started training before O'Brien even went to Ballydoyle, had completed the long journey to join him as a Classic winner, and had beat him in doing so. "This means everything," he said as he choked back tears. "It's been 30 years of hard graft and to win a Guineas was my number one objective, and hopefully it's the first of many."

Later he added: "Martin Horan, my head lad, and Shane [Lyons' brother and assistant] have been with me from the very start, so we appreciate this. We know what it's like not to have this quality. It's just huge. It was strange with nobody there, but I loved it all the same."

Keane has been a key part of establishing the County Meath yard as a major force in recent years and Lyons paid tribute to his skill in delivering Siskin to Classic success despite being outnumbered by Ballydoyle. "Full credit to Colin, because he was out there on his own against a football team," he said. "Tactics were our worry. We were drawn two and in real terms it can be a nice draw, but I knew with the football team that was taking us on that it might not be the best draw in the world. Colin had to be on his game and he had to have a horse who was going to take him out of trouble. The horse did that and Colin had the balls to do it."

****

HAVING beaten the Coolmore army in one Classic, Lyons was in league with them a few weeks later to land the Irish Oaks with Even So. The day after Siskin's success, she had finished fifth in the Irish 1,000 Guineas behind the O'Brien-trained Peaceful but she made great strides when upped in trip, winning a Listed race at Naas over a mile and a quarter to set up her second Classic mission.

O'Brien had the numbers as usual with four of the eight Oaks runners, while the favourite was the Jessica Harrington-trained Cayenne Pepper, but Lyons and Keane had the winning answer again. Cayenne Pepper was in front passing the furlong pole but, as in the Guineas, Keane was in hot pursuit and soon swept to the front, scoring by two lengths.

Lyons had not expected victory from the 10-1 shot and there was none of the pressure that built up around Siskin. "It was lovely to watch, very different to Siskin," he said. "I couldn't watch Siskin at all, but I watched this one and I thoroughly enjoyed it."

Asked if there was any pressure training for Coolmore, he replied: "None whatsoever. They're unbelievably straightforward to train horses for. They let us do our job and they picked us for a reason."

It was the same reason he had been sent Siskin, one of the prized Abdullah homebreds, and this higher calibre of raw material had allowed him to show his prowess at the top level. "We want to be having runners in these races," Lyons said after Even So's victory. "It's been a long time coming and we're going to enjoy it."

After such a determined climb, Lyons deserved to savour the view from the highest peak.

◀◀ Happy days: opposite page, Colin Keane on Siskin and Ger Lyons celebrate victory in the Irish 2,000 Guineas
◀ Keane strikes again on Even So in the Irish Oaks

HIGH FLYER

Shane Foley took another big step up in a 2020 season that mixed class and consistency

QUANTITY versus quality. That is the eternal conundrum facing every jockey who makes it to the upper ranks of their profession, but in 2020 Shane Foley found himself in the happy position of chasing a first title while reaping the big-race rewards of riding Jessica Harrington's ever more powerful Flat string.

By the autumn, it was clear which ambition was uppermost in his mind. "It's every rider's dream to be champion jockey," he said in a Racing Post interview. "The big races are important too, don't get me wrong, but a championship shows you are doing the job consistently well."

Foley, 32, has been fulfilling that part of the job description for his whole career, having been in the top ten in every season of the past decade, and when he was starting out he had the unusual distinction of finishing runner-up three times in the apprentice championship. If that gave the impression of a dependable nearly man, he showed he was more than that with Classic triumphs on the Adrian Keatley-trained Jet Setting in the 2016 Irish 1,000 Guineas and Ken Condon's Romanised in the 2018 Irish 2,000, but they were his only Group 1 winners before the link-up with Harrington at the start of 2019. That career move provided the ammunition that enabled him to prove his class as well as his consistency.

Speaking this year about their relationship, Foley said: "Jessie is a great woman because she listens to you, which is a big help. You build confidence in each other then. You're all on the same team and everyone wants the same thing – winners."

They clicked in their first year together and Foley stormed to a personal-best 75 winners during the 2019 turf season, while doubling his Group 1 tally with

Cheveley Park Stakes and Prix Marcel Boussac victories on Millisle and Albigna. Year two brought even better numbers despite the truncated season, giving him the chance to get involved in the championship race for the first time.

★★★★

FOLEY was helped in his title challenge when chief rivals Seamie Heffernan and Colin Keane took the forfeit of 14 days' quarantine in Ireland for the chance to ride in big races in Britain and France, but there was a price to pay himself in this most challenging of years. In choosing to stay at home rather than ride at Royal Ascot, he had to watch Frankie Dettori enjoying the scintillating Coronation Stakes success that would have been his on Harrington's Alpine Star.

Emulating her half-sister Alpha Centauri's runaway Coronation triumph of 2018, Alpine Star streaked clear under Dettori to win by four and a quarter lengths on her first start of the season. Foley had played an important role, helping to prepare her at home and phoning Dettori on the morning of the race to discuss the ride, but the glory belonged to the supersub on his first outing for Harrington. Alpine Star was part of a final-day treble for Dettori that secured the leading jockey award at the royal meeting and the Niarchos family's filly was his first Coronation winner, giving him the complete set of Royal Ascot Group 1s.

For all the joy among the Harrington team, everyone had thoughts for Foley. The trainer, also forced to stay at home in Ireland, said: "I'm sitting here, I can't go racing, and watching it on the telly is very hard. It's sad for Shane that he isn't allowed to go over and ride, but we're in very strange times."

Richie Galway, Harrington's son-in-law, was the most senior member of the team to make the trip to Ascot. "Frankie Dettori, what a sub to have," said the assistant trainer, "but the amount of work that Shane has done on the filly at home has made today possible." It was a mark of Foley's down-to-earth character that instead of being at Royal Ascot he went to Naas that afternoon and rode Harrington's juvenile filly Sussex Garden to a debut victory, driving her up close home to score by a neck. The next day he rode a double for the stable at Leopardstown, including the Group 3 Blue Wind Stakes on One Voice.

★★★★

SOON there were bigger consolations for Foley, and plenty of them. He landed another Group 1 with Lucky Vega in the Phoenix Stakes and the stable's strength in the two-year-old department was also evident on Irish Champions Weekend when Cadillac won the Group 2 Champions Juvenile Stakes at Leopardstown, followed on the second day by the year-older Cayenne Pepper's victory in the Group 2 Blandford Stakes at the Curragh.

The day after that was September 14, which marked the third anniversary of the evening when Mick Halford, Foley's boss of more than a decade, let him know that he would no longer retain a stable jockey. That just made the carpenter's son from Graiguenamanagh in County Kilkenny even more determined to succeed.

"At a time like that obviously you think the worst," Foley reflected this year of his response to adversity in 2017. "But what are you gonna do? I just got the bit between my teeth and decided I was going to work hard and prove myself. It gave me a drive really – maybe that's what I needed."

It is a drive that has taken him into the top rank of Ireland's jockeys.

▼ Dash of Pepper: main picture, Cayenne Pepper and Shane Foley land the Group 2 Blandford Stakes by four lengths at the Curragh on Irish Champions Weekend
▲ Top from left, Foley in winning action for Jessica Harrington on Protagonist at Fairyhouse; Sussex Garden at Naas; Millisle in the Group 3 Ballyogan Stakes, also at Naas; One Voice in the Group 3 Blue Wind Stakes at Leopardstown; and for Kieran Cotter on Inflection Point at Bellewstown
◀ Left from top, high-class two-year-olds Lucky Vega and Cadillac

TEARS OF JOY

Kevin Stott could not contain his emotions after a breakthrough Group 1 win at Royal Ascot on Hello Youmzain in the Diamond Jubilee

IN JUST over 73 seconds on the Saturday of Royal Ascot, Kevin Stott powered to victory on Hello Youmzain in the Diamond Jubilee Stakes. Not only was it his first winner at the royal meeting, it was also his first Group 1 triumph. A little more than half an hour later, the 25-year-old had his second Royal Ascot winner when he took almost exactly the same amount of time to land the Wokingham Handicap on Hey Jonesy. These were career-boosting, life-changing moments and the effect on Stott was overwhelming.

As he pulled up on Hello Youmzain and turned back towards the empty stands, the Danish-born jockey collapsed in floods of tears. This was a ride that had carried a heap of pressure and all the pent-up adrenaline and emotion surged out of him. Even after the walk back from the course under the stands, he was still wiping away the tears as he came into the hallowed winner's enclosure.

After his quick follow-up on Hey Jonesy, trained like Hello Youmzain by his mentor Kevin Ryan, Stott was a little more composed as he put into words the importance of what he had just done. "It's very emotional," he said. "It means so much, and to my family at home in Denmark as well. They aren't here, I can't fly out to see them, they can't fly over here – it means a lot that they're watching at home. It has been absolutely amazing. An hour ago I didn't think this would ever happen and now I'm standing here with two Royal Ascot winners, my first Group 1 as well, things you could never dream of."

The margins that made all the difference were small. Hello Youmzain prevailed in a three-way photo, scoring by a head from Dream Of Dreams with Sceptical a neck behind in third, and one of the key elements in his victory was Stott's quick jump from stall two, which gave his rivals ground to make up from the start. It was even closer in the Wokingham as Hey Jonesy got up to beat Summerghand by the minimum distance. With Stott's mount on the far side and Summerghand coming from the larger nearside pack, it was impossible to call until the photo revealed Hey Jonesy had finished a nose in front.

Both wins were as well deserved as they were hard earned for a rider who has marked himself out as one of the emerging talents of the weighing room.

★★★★

IN HIS teens Stott dreamed not of Royal Ascot but of Old Trafford and White Hart Lane. His father Ken was an English journeyman jockey around the world, which is how Kevin came to be born in Scandinavia to a Danish mother, but Kevin's first sporting passion was football.

A Manchester United fan, he showed enough talent to go for a two-week trial with Tottenham Hotspur but he was rejected because he was too small. It was then that he decided to turn to racing.

"I said to Dad when I was 16 that I wanted to ride horses, and within a week he had flown me over and dropped me off at Kevin Ryan's yard, and I have been there ever since really," Stott said. "My family at home are all horsey people. My dad used to ride a lot in Scandinavia and went to India, Africa, places like that. One brother trains, the other rides in Scandinavia."

Stott made an early mark in Britain when he picked up a spare ride for Godolphin and won the Future Stars Apprentice Handicap at Newmarket on Winter Thunder in October 2014. That led to a season in Newmarket with Luca Cumani, but things got tougher as his claim reduced and he decided to go back north. In 2016 he had a career-best 39 winners and jumped another level to 61 and 57 in the next two years. By then Hello Youmzain had come into his life.

Stott steered him to victory in two of his three starts as a juvenile and early the next season gained his biggest success in Britain to that point when Hello Youmzain landed the Group 2 Sandy Lane Stakes at Haydock. That set up a tilt at the Commonwealth Cup but there was disappointment at Royal Ascot when he was third behind Advertise.

James Doyle took over on the Jaber Abdullah-owned colt for two further Group 1 missions in the autumn, winning the first in the Haydock Sprint Cup while Stott finished seventh on outsider Major Jumbo, also trained by Ryan. Fortune twisted again, however, when Hello Youmzain was purchased for a future career as a dual-hemisphere stallion by Haras d'Etreham in France and Cambridge Stud in New Zealand. He was left with Ryan for a 2020 campaign in the top sprints and the trainer had no hesitation in putting Stott back on board for Hello Youmzain's seasonal debut in the Diamond Jubilee.

★★★★

THE ride came with pressure for Stott, not just in wanting to prove Ryan right but with a stallion career at stake for the joint owners. He rose to the occasion magnificently at Royal Ascot, fending off Ryan Moore on Dream Of Dreams and Frankie Dettori on the favourite Sceptical in that frantic finish. It was confirmation of Stott's talent, as well as Hello Youmzain's, and justification of Ryan's faith in him.

"Getting jocked off for a higher-profile jockey happens and I feel blessed to be back on him after his change of ownership," said Stott, who reached a new career-best total in 2020. "Kevin gave me a lot of confidence going out to ride him. He said: 'Ride him like the best horse in the race.' I can't describe how thankful I am."

There was joy all round at what Stott had achieved. Ryan's son and assistant Adam said: "The owners have been great. It was very important for us to get a win for them, and for his stud career, and they left it to us [who should ride].

"We've got ultimate faith in Kevin. In my opinion, he is one of the most up-and-coming young jockeys and has just proved it on the biggest stage. He completed his apprenticeship with us and I'm delighted he has ridden his first Group 1 winner for the yard."

That first big horse, that first Group 1, is so important for a jockey's career. Stott's tears left nobody in any doubt about that.

▼ Marginal gains: Hello Youmzain and Kevin Stott edge a photo-finish in the Diamond Jubilee Stakes, leading to emotional scenes for the winning jockey

IN THE PICTURE

Orr repays Weld's faith with Classic victory on Search For A Song

CLASSIC success was nothing new for Search For A Song and her trainer Dermot Weld, but it was for jockey Oisin Orr when he teamed up with them to land the Irish St Leger in September.

Orr, Ireland's champion apprentice in 2017 and joint winner in 2019, is the latest young jockey to benefit from Weld's tutelage and trust and he took another big career step with his Classic breakthrough on Search For A Song. The mare had won the race 12 months earlier under Chris Hayes but had been handed over to Orr for 2020 and the main target was a repeat success at the Curragh.

Things did not entirely go smoothly on the way. The four-year-old was a well-beaten sixth when joint-favourite on her reappearance and then had the rare indignity of being pulled up on the Flat after clipping heels and stumbling in the Munster Oaks at Cork. She bounced back to finish an honourable third behind Magical in the Tattersalls Gold Cup and Orr was later applauded by Weld for the way he had looked after the filly at Cork.

When Magical beat Ghaiyyath in the Irish Champion Stakes the day before the Irish St Leger, Weld became quietly confident his filly would win. If that put pressure on Orr, the 23-year-old rider did not show any trace. He switched off his mount at the rear of the field and rode a patient race, eventually wearing down Ebor winner Fujaira Prince to score by two lengths.

"Dermot has shown a lot of faith in me," Orr said. "It's great to get opportunities like this and then be able to repay him. This was something I could have never dreamed of when I was young."

Weld, whose stable jockeys have included Mick Kinane and Pat Smullen, was impressed. "I thought Oisin switched her off beautifully," he said. "That's Oisin, he gets horses to relax for him. He has wonderful hands, rides a very relaxed race and fills horses with confidence. You might be worried watching him as very often he hasn't moved on horses. I love horses getting into a rhythm, gradual progress and ride them to come, and that's what he does very well."

It was also a special day for Weld (*pictured, inset left*) who had kicked off a Group 1 double with Tarnawa's Prix Vermeille success at Longchamp an hour earlier and for whom Search For A Song was a ninth Irish St Leger winner. That put him level with Vincent O'Brien as the most successful trainer in the 105-year history of the race, having also won with Vintage Crop (twice), Vinnie Roe (four times) and Voleuse De Coeurs.

Pictures: PATRICK McCANN (RACINGPOST.COM/PHOTOS)

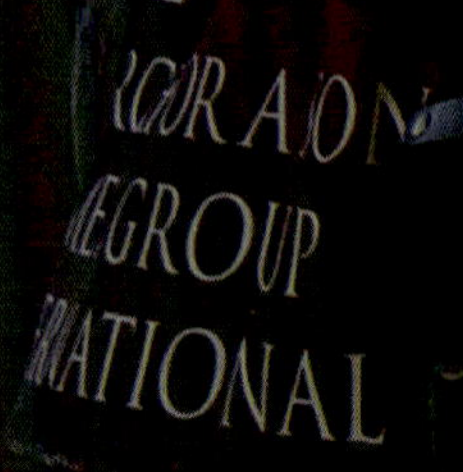

COMER GROUP INTERNATIONAL
1st
7

The coronavirus pandemic altered the shape of the world, and with it the sport and business of horseracing. This special report and a series of on-the-spot snapshots tell the story of racing's response to the crisis

THE YEAR WHEN EVERYTHING CHANGED

By Lee Mottershead

IT WAS the best of times. It was the worst of times. As the last horses galloped up the famous Cheltenham hill on the festival's final afternoon in March – Friday the 13th of all days – we knew we were on the cusp. The world was changing. The world had changed.

We knew it then but we had also known it as the roar went up for the start of the Supreme Novices' Hurdle. Racing's most fabulous four days were duly completed, and for those four days we immersed ourselves in the sheer joy of it all, while questioning whether we should really be there, whether it should really be happening.

Rightly or wrongly, it did happen. Thereafter, and for a period of time far longer than we could have imagined, nothing else did.

Racing had been talking about the coronavirus for at least a month before the festival. On February 11 in Liverpool, subsequently one of Britain's Covid-19 hotspots, the subject had been raised at the Grand National weights launch. Later the same day it was discussed in Doncaster racecourse's Hilton Garden Inn,

following the second act of the Racecourse Association's medical, veterinary, racing and turf management conference. Managing turf was not on the minds of the two medics who had asked to see RCA chief executive David Armstrong.

BHA chief medical adviser Dr Jerry Hill and his RCA counterpart Dr Iain McNeil were already worried about the virus. They put forward their concerns to Armstrong, describing what he remembered as "a nuclear scenario". If anything, what actually panned out was even more nuclear than they had feared.

Fast forward to Cheltenham on the Monday of festival week. Among those journalists already working from the track's press room there was a sense of unease. Senior members of the racecourse team insisted there was no expectation that the season-dominating fixture would not take place. That view strengthened when news came in from London, where a Whitehall meeting with sports governing bodies concluded there was "no rationale" for cancelling sporting events. The Cheltenham Festival was a runner.

The government was not simply

▸▸ *Continues page 174*

allowing racing to make up its own mind, it was actively encouraging the BHA and Cheltenham to press on. Likewise, the Irish government did not seek to stop racing professionals and fans from making their annual pilgrimage to the Cotswolds. It is true some sports were calling a halt to proceedings, and more did so as the festival progressed, but shopping malls were still welcoming shoppers, curtains were still going up in theatres and lives were still being lived relatively as normal.

And yet the festival did not feel normal. It felt different because it was different. Hand sanitisers were situated all around a racecourse whose attendances slipped. Some members of the Irish racing media took the decision to make an early exit and returned home. A number of those who did were greeted with hostility for having visited Britain.

The speed of the narrative was increasing elsewhere. Two days before the festival began, northern Italy went into lockdown. On the festival's opening day, the World Health Organisation declared the coronavirus to be a pandemic. It became increasingly obvious racing, like countless other industries, was on a precipice.

★★★★

EVEN so, we would soon know much more than we knew then. Social distancing was not a thing, which is why the members of the sport's Covid-19 group saw nothing wrong with squeezing together in a tiny BHA hut at the back of the Cheltenham weighing room, Hill just about able to breathe in one of its corners. That sort of intimate get-together would soon be banned for the rest of the year.

What then transpired can be told through three consecutive Racing Post front pages. On Monday, March 16, the newspaper's main headline stated: "All racing in Britain to go behind closed doors". In Tuesday's edition readers were greeted with three shocking words: "Grand National cancelled". On Wednesday there were three different words, capitalised and even more shocking: "RACING SHUTS DOWN". For more than two

▸▸ *Continues page 176*

Cheltenham, March 13: Gold Cup day at a packed Cheltenham Festival, while elsewhere activity was already stopping

THE unrelenting emotion was guilt. That horrible, nauseating feeling in the pit of your stomach; knowing you were doing something you probably shouldn't be doing. And, to make it worse, we enjoyed every single second of it. All 68,859 of us.

The most cherished chunk of land in the Cotswolds bathed in glorious sunshine all afternoon. The eyes of two nations, and possibly even more around Europe, were glued to our jump racing haven for Gold Cup day, and it never looked better. It takes a tan so well when the sun shines.

Cheltenham is usually fond of all the attention for its most important Friday of the year, but this was a different sort of scrutiny in the line of coronavirus. There was rage in addition to rapture when the fourth and final day of the festival got the green light.

There will not be a football kicked in the Premier League for at least three weeks, nobody will be teeing off at the US Masters next month, the cars have been clamped ahead of the Australian Grand Prix tomorrow and yet here we were watching Al Boum Photo emulate Best Mate, Arkle and others by retaining the Gold Cup.

There was something surreal about the whole thing. Even Cheltenham chief Ian Renton admitted as much. "It does feel a little surreal and I suppose we are in a bit of a bubble," remarked Renton. "It feels a little bit like that. It has been fantastic to get on with the racing and to see a Magners Cheltenham Gold Cup with such excitement and such a great finish was unbelievable."

Unbelievable indeed.

DAVID JENNINGS

RACING POST

Wednesday, March 18, 2020 — Download the free Racing Post app for must-have news, tips and fast results — £3.50

The Betting Masterclasses — James Willoughby on turning speed figures into profit. Part three of our new series, pages 6-7

RACING SHUTS DOWN

•British racing suspended until May •Chancellor announces £330 billion support package

▼ The new normal: masks and social distancing at Newcastle on June 1

Newcastle, June 1: British racing returns after almost 11 weeks in lockdown

THE opening race at the opening fixture of the strangest Flat campaign ever staged was restricted to horses rated 65 and below and worth just £2,782 to the winner but it might as well have been the Derby as far as racing was concerned.

"The wait is over!" called commentator Darren Owen as the stalls crashed open for the Betway Welcome Back British Racing Handicap at Newcastle. And 102 seconds later the fast-starting Zodiakos was crowned the first winner of a British horserace for 76 days as professional sport returned to the country.

But this was a very different scene to that which greeted racegoers who were at tracks in March. For a start there were no racegoers, with racing taking place behind firmly closed doors and admission restricted to 'key personnel' who had done an online course in Covid-19, answered a medical questionnaire and passed a temperature check on arrival.

The sense of anxiety had been palpable in the build-up to Britain's first meeting since Taunton and Wetherby had raced on March 17, an event which had ITV, BBC and Sky camera crews camped in the golf-course car park next door and Arena Racing Company's Martin Cruddace doing four TV interviews before breakfast.

Quite a gruelling start for a man who admitted to having had just a couple of hours' sleep – his group's 16 courses may race 550 times a year but this was a day like no other. "If we don't do it right, it could be taken away," he said. "That's quite a responsibility."

DAVID CARR

months, the Racing Post's print edition did likewise.

The BHA announced a suspension of activities until at least the start of May. Ireland ploughed on for a little longer, with ITV Racing even broadcasting five races from Thurles on March 23. It was a short-lived survival. In Britain, there was disappointment but generally an understanding that action had been necessary, particularly when Boris Johnson took the country into lockdown. Amid fears the NHS could be overrun with Covid cases, it seemed frivolous for a sport to risk placing further strains on the emergency services. Not everyone, however, was happy.

In April, BHA chief executive Nick Rust was preyed upon by coronavirus and two of his fiercest critics. He spent the majority of a week sleeping and losing weight, neither out of choice. The virus attacked him directly. Not so leading trainers Mark Johnston and Ralph Beckett, who both emailed BHA chair Annamarie Phelps, calling on the BHA board to end Rust's employment immediately. The board backed Rust.

The two trainers had been unhappy with the decision to halt the sport and what they perceived as a lack of urgency to bring it back. Yet across the political divide in Westminster there was praise for the moves made by the BHA and the industry's principal stakeholders. In Britain and Ireland racing's leaders spoke continually with their respective governments, offering detailed proposals for how racing could resume safely.

The same happened in France but Emmanuel Macron's administration was quicker to listen, approving a resumption on May 11. Among those to race on the comeback card was Sottsass, subsequently victorious in the Prix de l'Arc de Triomphe.

By that point the racing casualties of Covid included the Punchestown festival and major meetings at Ayr, Sandown and Chester. By far the most notable loss was the Grand National and the three-day Aintree festival. Instead, at exactly the time when Tiger Roll had been expected to chase a place alongside Red Rum in sporting

▸▸ *Continues page 178*

Newmarket, June 6: The 2,000 Guineas, like the following day's 1,000, is run on its latest date ever

THERE was almost nobody there to see it happen, yet by wearing the colours of his boss, Sheikh Fahad, and riding a horse trained by Andrew Balding, the man who did so much to launch his career, Oisin Murphy enjoyed a practically perfect first Classic success when guiding Kameko to Qipco 2,000 Guineas glory.

In late November, Murphy, by then already crowned Britain's champion jockey, landed the Japan Cup in front of 80,826 frenzied fans. There were no fans at all on the Rowley Mile, just a smattering of essential professionals, but as Kameko galloped past the winning post in front, the 24-year-old let out a roar to rival the noise made in the huge Tokyo grandstands on that autumn afternoon.

If that was a memorable triumph for Murphy, this one was unforgettable, for it was achieved in the most weirdly unique circumstances on a racecourse that resembled a ghost town and in a race staged five weeks late, on what should have been Derby day.

A neck separated first and second, with a length back to last season's outstanding champion juvenile Pinatubo, who held every chance but was beaten fair and square as 5-6 market leader. The winning time of 1min 34.72sec was a record for the 2,000 Guineas.

"This is the stuff of dreams," said Murphy. "There isn't the same atmosphere – in fact there's no atmosphere – but it means just as much to me. When I look back on this race in a few years' time, I won't remember there was no crowd. I'll just remember Kameko gave me my first win in the Qipco 2,000 Guineas."

LEE MOTTERSHEAD

▾ Ghost town: Kameko crosses the line first in the 2,000 Guineas at an empty Newmarket

Naas, June 8: Having started the Flat season in March before quickly halting all racing, Ireland resumes after a 76-day shutdown

THE scene was strangely quiet. However, that old anticipation still lingered in the air. The call for riders to mount had never been so welcomed.

Stronger protocols made the day quite different to the opening day of the Flat season here on March 23. Still, the old adage that the more things change, the more they stay the same certainly rang true.

Our last race here in March ended with a Seamie Heffernan and Aidan O'Brien maiden winner and the first contest back featured the same outcome. Saxon Warrior's half-sister More Beautiful was simply brilliant. This is what we had been craving so dearly in lockdown's often colourless existence.

Just over half an hour later there was another Jessica Harrington-trained juvenile jet in the shape of Lucky Vega to raise the pulse a notch in another high-quality maiden. Suddenly things started to feel a little more normal at the sun-kissed Kildare venue.

The reminders to socially distance, which were taken to an extreme by King's Stand contender Sceptical, were constant throughout the fixture and the track's chairman Dermot Cantillon believed the meeting had been a success. "There were plenty of people making sure the protocols were properly followed. Sometimes you can fall into a false sense of security but that wasn't happening. I think everyone in racing can be very proud of the way they conducted today."

Irish racing rolls on to Leopardstown off the back of a positive beginning to this strange new world. Two metres apart, but one step closer to experiencing in full the sport we love.

MARK BOYLAN

history, viewers on ITV watched Potters Corner win the Virtual Grand National. The television audience of 4.8 million was more than twice as big as any actual horserace would achieve once racing returned.

★★★★

THAT return happened on the first day of June. Racing would be "first out of the gates", declared culture secretary Oliver Dowden – and the gates did indeed open at Newcastle. They continued opening with increased regularity as the week went on, with Kameko claiming the 2,000 Guineas on what should have been Derby day. In Ireland the long wait for racing to restart ended on June 8.

RACING POST

BACK WITH A BANG

British racing returns – and so does the Racing Post!

IN TODAY'S BRILLIANT BUMPER EDITION

ALASTAIR DOWN WHAT TODAY MEANS FOR THE SPORT

LESTER PIGGOTT INTERVIEW WITH THE RIDING LEGEND

RICHARD HANNON A WINNER-PACKED STABLE TOUR

PRICEWISE 2,000 GUINEAS ANTE-POST SPECIAL

None of it was racing as we had known it. This was racing behind closed doors and the doors would stay closed. Attempts to get paying spectators back on racecourses starved of their principal income stream were continually frustrated. A few lucky souls were reminded how it felt to go racing with trips to Doncaster and Warwick in September but both trial events were one-off flashbacks to the past, while also being reminders of the present, given there was social distancing, restricted movement and masks.

Initially in Britain – and for most of the year in Ireland – even owners were forbidden from going racing. That meant the most eerie of all the year's crown jewels was Royal Ascot, where the media presence was also at its most restricted. From the top of the roof you could hear the jockeys shouting as finishes were fought out in front of almost deserted grandstands. For the first time in her reign even the Queen was absent, although there was still a daily playing of the national anthem and a royal message in the racecard. It was not long before copies of those extremely rare books began popping up on eBay.

Continues page 180

Royal Ascot, June 16: The opening day of Flat racing's showpiece occasion

ROYAL ASCOT looks like you might expect it to look in this coronavirus year. Strange, unnerving, empty. On the most pristine turf, some of the world's finest horses and jockeys are competing in an atmosphere that has no atmosphere. It is akin to watching Gielgud or Olivier produce an award-winning performance in a near deserted Palladium. For the spectator there is a sense of immense privilege and awkward embarrassment at the same time.

It is Royal Ascot without the royals but there is still a personal message from the Queen in one of the limited number of racecards that have been printed. There is also the national anthem, played at 1pm as the horses for the opener walk around the paddock. The person in charge of the volume controls keeps it distinctly muted, rather in keeping with an occasion that, as one of the fortunate few, you're never quite sure should be enjoyed or simply experienced.

"Don't worry, we'll still celebrate with the same enthusiasm we normally do," says Richard Hannon after winning the revived Buckingham Palace, while there are celebrations from Eve Johnson Houghton when she sees Accidental Agent has come out of the stalls in the Queen Anne Stakes.

"Go on old boy!" she then bellows as he begins to launch a challenge. The cry echoes, as does the noise made by two people applauding when Circus Maximus enters the winner's circle.

"Well, I gave him a shout, and I don't care who heard me," she says. "We're racing – and hats off to everyone who made it happen. It's not racing as we know it but we're racing, they are fabulous horses and we should enjoy them for what they are."

Nobody in racing is more fabulous than Frankie Dettori, who enjoys a runaway Ribblesdale triumph on Frankly Darling and then soars into the sky, executing a flying dismount that is greeted by nothing.

"I wasn't going to do one but the TV people asked me," he says. "It's not the same without me jumping off the horse, is it? It wasn't my best effort, a six out of ten, to be honest."

LEE MOTTERSHEAD

Flying solo: Frankie Dettori performs his famous dismount without an audience after Frankly Darling's Ribblesdale Stakes victory

Epsom, July 4: Four weeks later than scheduled, the Derby is run for the 241st time

IT HAS come later than we would have liked but at long last this historic day has dawned. Hairdressing salons have finally reopened. In a further bit of welcome news it's Derby day.

The fact Epsom is open on this 241st Derby day is testament to the excellent relations between the racecourse and local politicians, who in May sanctioned the erection of metal fencing all around the site. There is normally a heaving mass of people, drawn to the Hill by a sporting treasure, fairground rides, the Smell-A-Likes perfume stall, a hair extensions lady from Hartlepool and overpriced burgers. This year the Hill is empty, save for a few cars parked on the infield.

Knowing that pictures of large gatherings outside the racecourse would have delivered negative publicity for the sport, Epsom pleaded with people to stay away. In very large numbers they have done exactly that. One passing driver estimates a total perimeter attendance of maybe 100 people. They are doing no harm. The occasion has been done no harm.

Yet we do not want another like this one. The Derby cannot be sold as the people's race if the people are not here. Even the Queen is missing, as are the fortune tellers. Had they been present on this most peculiar Derby day, we could have asked how Epsom will look when the 242nd running is staged on June 5, 2021. Busier would be better.

LEE MOTTERSHEAD

At Ascot, as everywhere else, prize-money was badly hit, much to the annoyance of some owners and trainers. Thankfully, the Levy Board repeatedly rode to racing's rescue, injecting millions of pounds from its reserves. There was less cash and hardly any people but there was still racing. Epsom even managed to stage the Derby, albeit a month late, and from midsummer onwards the vast majority of the major contests in Britain, Ireland and France were held when and where they had been scheduled. They were also witnessed by bumper audiences on ITV, which added to its planned portfolio by covering many extra days, mostly on Sundays.

That was one positive in racing's Covid-struck year. There were others. A rule limiting jockeys to riding at a single meeting per day was, in the main, warmly received by members of the weighing room. For punters, the extension of 48-hour declarations to jump races was a significant step forward.

Mostly, though, it was grim, including headlines and stories that repeatedly blamed racing for spreading a deadly disease through holding the Cheltenham Festival, the authors seemingly ignorant of the fact the sport had simply been following government directives. We can be confident directives will still be in place when the 2021 Cheltenham Festival is staged. How many people are allowed to be at Cheltenham is anybody's guess.

To say the sport is vulnerable is not a guess. Without revenue from racegoers, hospitality customers and non-raceday activity, racecourses are going to find themselves in ever more perilous positions. It is likely not all trainers will survive the crisis in business and, although the autumn yearling sales fared far better than most expected, there will be owners who decide racehorses are now too much of a luxury.

As these words are written it is impossible to predict what happens next. Those of us at Cheltenham in March felt horribly uncertain about the future. That feeling continues to this day.

York, August 21: Day three of the Ebor festival

THE Knavesmire can never be completely behind closed doors. This wonderful racecourse has been forced to keep its doors shut, yet as it occupies an expanse of public land the public can still come to those bits of the Knavesmire that are outside of the doors, fences and running rails. Some have watched in family groups close to the stands' side midway up the home straight, while others have taken a peek down the back. None, however, have had a better view than John and Linda Douglas.

Without in any way encouraging you to follow their lead, for it is important that visitors do not descend en masse, John and Linda have been here for all three days of the fixture so far. The Douglases have brought four camping chairs, their son Jonathan, and a friend called Richard. They have parked themselves on the infield, near to the furlong pole, just beyond the closed Clocktower Enclosure. It would be a surprise if any fans have been closer to the action in this most singular of Flat seasons.

"We've been coming to this meeting for 20 years," said John. "I know it's not the same this time but beggars can't be choosers. It's just been lovely to be part of it. To see the horses is fantastic but what we've also found is with nobody around you can hear everything, every bit of the hustle and bustle. You can hear the sound of the whips and the jockeys shouting at the horses. It's amazing."

LEE MOTTERSHEAD

Doncaster, September 9: Racegoers are allowed in Britain for the first time in six months but the trial is cancelled abruptly after just one day

SHOULD they be here? Were they doing the right thing? One local racegoer even revealed their family did not agree with them heading to the course. But come they did. Factory managers, builders and childcare workers. All satisfying the same urge to do something they haven't been able to do since March.

Racing might have been brought back to life on June 1 but it has been missing its heartbeat. No hullabaloo. No fanfare. Just the eerie sound of silence, a sterile sport played out in a sterile environment.

For a brief moment that changed with an estimated 2,500 people taking their place in the designated zones in front of the stands and in hospitality marquees at the centre of the track. People dressed up in their finery, studying the form and enjoying drinks in the sunshine.

But the occasion was about to become all too brief for the sport as a whole, as Doncaster council instructed the track to go back behind closed doors following a spike in coronavirus cases in the area. Course officials, frantically trying to glean an early steer before prime minister Boris Johnson's news briefing at 4pm, did not see the curveball coming.

To say they were gutted would be an understatement. Through a massive planning operation they had met all the requirements, but ultimately suffered due to circumstances beyond their control.

ANDREW DIETZ

The Curragh, September 13: The second day of Irish Champions Weekend

IT HAS probably been a while; March for some of you, longer for others. Watching live racing in front of your very own eyes is such a luxury these days that it would have been a sin not to savour the action from as close as one could get on a weekend as big as this one.

The Irish St Leger was watched leaning on the rail, just inside the final furlong, and it was here that you realise just how strangely serene these big races are.

The final Classic of the season was won in complete silence; certainly not the way 23-year-old Oisin Orr imagined winning his first Group 1. The atmosphere would not have been any different had the race been staged in the back garden of his Rathmullan home on the Fanad Peninsula in County Donegal.

A crowd would have camouflaged the quiet, but empty enclosures ensured racing was stripped back to its bones, condensed to horse and rider. Thousands would have loved to have been in my position for the Irish St Leger – 10,075 of them using last year as a guide – and the truth is that this day was a pale shadow of the buzzing, vibrant and unforgettable occasion of 12 months ago.

A shame, really, as the Curragh has never looked so beautiful.

DAVID JENNINGS

Contrail's Derby showstopper in front of empty house

IN THE PICTURE

NO racing nation felt the absence of crowds more keenly than Japan, whose fans are among the most vibrant and passionate in the world. The action continued on the track amid the coronavirus pandemic but the magnificent racecourses were empty shells without the noise and colour that makes Japan's big races so special.

The fans missed something exceptional at Tokyo on May 31 when Contrail cemented his superstar status with a breathtaking three-length victory in the Japanese Derby. More than 117,000 had been at the Derby 12 months earlier but this time the race was behind closed doors and Contrail's superlative success was completed in near silence.

Racecourses had been closed to spectators for three months by then, robbing fans of the chance to hail Contrail's progress from champion juvenile to Classic hero. After winning all three races at two, including the Grade 1 Hopeful Stakes, the Yoshito Yahagi-

trained colt opened his Classic season with a smart victory in the Japanese 2,000 Guineas at Nakayama in April, although some felt the half-length margin over Salios left some questions. The runner-up had also been a leading juvenile and his connections argued the Guineas had not gone right for him, mainly because he ended up racing on the worst ground.

Contrail had the opportunity to settle the debate conclusively in the Derby and punters had faith in him, sending him off at 2-5 with Salios the 17-5 second favourite. From a good draw in stall five, Contrail's jockey Yuichi Fukunaga found a prominent position on the rail in the 18-runner field, while Salios was held up in midfield after breaking from stall 12.

In the home straight Fukunaga remained motionless as the son of Deep Impact cruised up to the leaders before surging into the lead just over a furlong out. Salios made a late charge down the outside but he was easily held by Contrail, who stretched out to the line without breaking sweat.

The comprehensive victory took Contrail's winning run to five and Fukunaga said: "Although he still has room for improvement – he tends to lose his focus when he's leading – he's still able to win like he did today. So he's got great potential and there's a lot to look forward to."

This was a second Derby win for Fukunaga, who had celebrated wildly in front of a full house after his victory on Wagnerian in 2018. This time was very different: he pulled up in front of the empty stands, removed his helmet and bowed his head. It was a silent tribute to the missing fans.

Picture: GETTY IMAGES

BACK IN ACTION

The Racing Post went behind the scenes on the day ITV Racing returned to our screens in June after more than two months away

By Lee Mottershead

ON JUNE'S first Friday in 2019 ITV Racing director Paul McNamara was diagnosed with bowel cancer. On June's first Friday in 2020 he is sitting in one of the bedrooms of his family's north London home in Crouch End, readying himself to steer the troops through a live television experience that could be testing even for such a master of the craft.

In front of him are two pairs of spectacles, a keyboard, any number of switches and a huge monitor on which individual screens are showing pictures from Newmarket, Lingfield and four members of the ITV Racing talent team, most of them working from home. McNamara is wearing carpet slippers. Ed Chamberlin and Francesca Cumani may be as well but we never get sufficiently close to their feet to find out.

In normal circumstances they would all be at Newmarket. There is, however, nothing normal about these circumstances. In the early stages of this racing-behind-closed-doors era, the sport's mainstream broadcaster is not going through the doors, although Richard Hoiles and a few production team members are carrying out their duties from Ascot, where the commentator has encountered a pre-programme problem.

"My chair sinks," Hoiles tells McNamara. "That's why I gradually go down." Quick as a flash, Jason Weaver interjects, declaring: "Richard's chair goes down because he's next to the food truck." This prompts Hoiles to offer words of reassurance. "If things get desperate I've got a Scotch egg over there," he informs everyone. On a day like this, things could certainly get desperate.

This is an ITV Racing programme that depends on everyone's wireless connection working. Yet even when the wireless functions there are numerous traps lying in wait. For a start, there is a three-second delay between Chamberlin and McNamara. The delay between Crouch End and Oli Bell is seven seconds, meaning that in between Bell saying something and

McNamara hearing it the suave broadcaster's now lengthy locks could grow another inch.

A voice on the programme's talkback facility offers a positive message to Cumani. "Make-up looks good, outfit looks good," says the voice, just as McNamara's wife, Sarah, pops in to wish him luck. Her husband was nominated for two Baftas earlier in the week but luck is still likely to be needed between now and 4pm.

"Let's keep it light and bright," he says. "If something does happen, we'll roll with the punches. We'll roll with the broadband. It is what it is."

★★★★

AT JUST before 1.30pm it is time to start broadcasting. The early wireless signs are good but as Cumani does her first piece to camera a strange background noise becomes apparent.

"Cesca's got bangles on her hand, hasn't she?" asks McNamara. "She'll need to take them off." After Cumani stops talking her director passes on the instruction to remove all bangles. Other jewellery items are allowed to remain.

As the programme gathers pace it becomes obvious McNamara – known throughout the industry as Macca and acclaimed for his work in racing, football, rugby and much more besides – cannot for a second lose concentration. It also becomes obvious how adept he is at feeding ideas and lines to his squad.

Prior to Newmarket's first race a horse is being led to the start, the jockey a few yards behind. "That's what we like to see – they're on message and taking social distancing very seriously," he says to Chamberlin, who then says something similar to the viewers.

A little while later he suggests to Weaver that a few words about Cumani's dress might not go amiss. "What about those shoulder pads?" asks Weaver. "They wouldn't look out of place on a wide receiver." Cumani gets her own back immediately. McNamara laughs and then exhales during a much-needed commercial break.

"They're all willing to look at the

▸▸ *Continues page 186*

lighter side and they have a great ability to laugh at themselves," he says. "They can ping back and forth from each other really quickly. You can't do it all the time because it would become draining, but there are times in the show when we can have fun and also show how much fun racing is."

One feature of the programme is the regular contributions made from owners, who producer Tim Williams has organised to appear via Zoom before and after races. For Newmarket's Paradise Stakes, Williams has snapped up Middleham Park Racing's Mike Prince, who can be seen in a corner of McNamara's screen. Much of his face is covered by a large lockdown beard.

As the horses walk around the paddock a volley of words come out of Macca's mouth: "Graphic in . . . lose the graphic . . . change the box . . . graphic in . . . lose the graphic . . . change the box . . . cue Cesca." When he asks for something it gets done. He also gets his wish when Prince's horse, Marie's Diamond, springs a 14-1 shock. The bits of Prince that are not covered by whiskers look extremely happy.

As the programme begins to enter its closing stages, script supervisor Vicky Andrews passes on an important update to her colleagues. "Just as a heads up, all races are running five to six minutes late," she says. "We might have to lose the end break. I'll inform the snooker team as well." The snooker team is duly informed. Ghaiyyath then runs away with the Coronation Cup but he does not run fast enough to make up the six-minute deficit. Andrews secures an extra minute.

"We're jumping to item 110 next – a two-box with Ed and Oli please," says McNamara, before realising he needs to pass on a request to the man in box number four on his screen. "Hoilesy, you're in vision but not looking at the camera," he says when seeing that Hoiles has his head at 45 degrees to the audience, possibly so he can keep an eye on the Scotch egg.

As the programme enters its final furlong McNamara rolls his shoulders before firing off quietly and calmly the last items of direction. The programme is finished, day one of ITV Racing's return completed both remotely and impressively.

"Unbelievable!" he tells the team, pride and delight in his voice. "Sterling work. Fantastic. One down everyone. At least you haven't got to travel far to get home. Well done. Great work. Pat yourselves on the back."

Pictures: ITV RACING

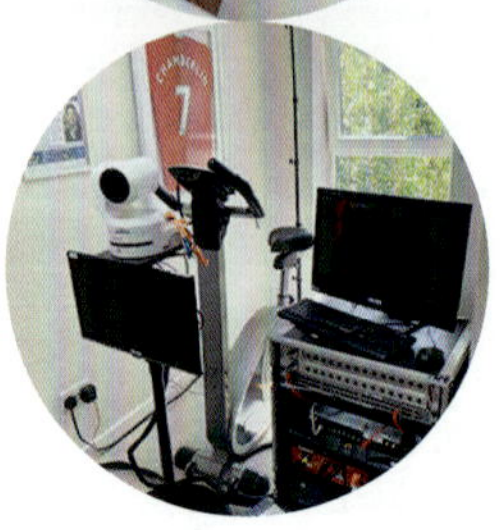

▲ Working from home: ITV Racing director Paul McNamara; below, presenter Ed Chamberlin and his 'studio' set-up

★★★★

MACCA is a modest man but his back undoubtedly deserves a pat as well. He moves from his director's seat and into a more comfortable leather chair. Then he tells his story.

"Ironically, today is bang on a year to the day since I had my diagnosis," he says. "I only went in for a routine check because I got one of those things through the post telling me I was entitled to a check-up as I had just turned 55. I thought it would just be a quick scan but within 20 minutes I was told I had bowel cancer. I was diagnosed at 12 o'clock and then had to get the train up to Haydock."

Not long after a consultant's appointment on the Friday of Royal Ascot he went into hospital to undergo surgery. He was supposed to be there for five days but instead stayed for three weeks. Six months of chemotherapy followed and, although the cancer has now thankfully gone, there will be a further operation on Friday, meaning today's programme from Newmarket and Haydock will be his last for a while.

"I was meant to do the Grand National and then have my second procedure but lockdown happened," he explains. "I was called ten days ago to say they could fit me in on June 12, which I obviously had to take because we don't know if there will be a second wave of the virus that could block me out again. I'm going to miss doing the programme next Friday. Today was a unique experience on every level and I really enjoyed it."

He expresses a hope that the viewers also enjoyed it. Although he did not know it at the time, the number of those viewers was around double what ITV4 would normally get on a midweek afternoon, with just over 500,000 people watching the Coronation Cup.

Like the ITV Racing director, many of them will have been wearing carpet slippers too.

'I sold my false teeth on the internet and got £120 for them. I'm a legend, you see'

By Lee Mottershead

APOLOGIES in advance for these occasional interruptions. It's not me you want, it's him. This is perfectly understandable, for Mick Easterby is an interviewee who needs little help from his interviewer. On a sublime summer morning in Sheriff Hutton, North Yorkshire, the interviewee is in particularly fine form.

Michael William Easterby is not your normal 89-year-old. Truth be told, he is not your normal anything. In 2021 he will celebrate his 60th anniversary as a racehorse trainer, one who has consistently punched above his weight, often at the expense of battered bookmakers.

He is a Classic winner, having sent out Mrs McArdy to land the 1977 1,000 Guineas, one year after Lochnager swept the King's Stand Stakes, July Cup and Nunthorpe. He is Britain's oldest current trainer and the caricature of the seasoned Yorkshire farmer, careful with his cash, direct with his language. Alongside his older brother, Peter, he owns an impressive portion of God's Own County. If God has any more of it for sale, Easterby remains ready to buy, assuming the price is right.

When he talks, people listen and television directors tremble. As we await his arrival, son and assistant David goes about his business alongside Fin the cocker spaniel – "he's a double portion of stupid" – and Patsy the Patterdale terrier, a hound collected one night in the car park of Wolverhampton racecourse alongside a box of meat, both supplied by a Welsh butcher called Alwin.

Patsy first lived with David but now shares New House Farm with Easterby snr and Alice, Mick's wife of 62 years. Alice has Alzheimer's but also a near permanent smile, particularly when watching Last of the Summer Wine, in which her husband might well have starred. That man's mind continues to be razor-sharp, while the body is still sprightly, although when he appears the onlooker's eye is unavoidably drawn to his sole remaining tooth, for which its owner has much pride and affection.

As well as the tooth, he wears trainers, a flat cap, baggy trousers and a large hole attached to the remnants of a jumper. This is how you expect Mick Easterby to look. What then follows is how you expect him to sound and behave, although he kicks off by talking plain and simple about the coronavirus.

"This is a hard thing to say because so many people have lost their lives, and I feel desperately sorry for those left behind, but in some ways this virus has done the

▸▸ *Continues page 190*

Mick Easterby, Britain's oldest trainer, will reach 60 years in the job in 2021. He was in typically forthright and entertaining mood for this Racing Post interview in July

Family circle: Mick Easterby with his wife Alice and granddaughter Joanna Mason

country good," Easterby says. "For a start, people have been shopping local. Supermarkets had pushed out all the small shops but those shops have been needed again. You can also get a doctor's appointment now as well.

"This has sharpened us all up. We had got too complacent. We were living in a false world but I think the virus has pulled us back into reality. What do you think about that then?" Well, it's undoubtedly food for thought.

★★★★

ALSO now thinking is Easterby, who gives instructions to the riders of five horses in between posing for pictures at the request of photographer Edward Whitaker.

The tooth is flashed and the tongue stuck out. You might think this was a variety act from the golden age of music hall, yet here is a trouper who needs no boards to tread. That becomes magnificently evident as we head away from the house. It is all laid out before us, a kingdom set green and glorious in front of the Howardian Hills. This is Easterby's place to perform, to breathe, to exist. It is his theatre, his Yorkshire, his world.

"I haven't left the farm since this all started but I'm very fortunate because I can ride around the place," he says. "I feel so sorry for people living in towns who haven't been able to get out." He then pauses to consider that frightening urban thought. "Oh, terrible!" he says with force before returning to his own experience.

"I haven't been one bit frightened. If I die, I've had a good run, but, you know, I've been so confident I won't get it. Mind, if I do get it they'll say: 'He was a clever bugger!' You'll put that in, won't you?" I say I shall and I did.

"The one thing I have missed is going to the pub," he admits, a wistful look in his eyes. "I used to go every night of my life from ten o'clock to 11 o'clock. I'm a social man. I drink any kind of beer but nothing else, except maybe a Pimm's. I've never had a glass of wine. I've never smoked either. I once bought a packet of cigarettes when I was 16. I smoked one and thought if I was going to get on in life I couldn't be buying cigarettes at this price. I sold them to a pal and never smoked again."

As he counts the heads on a strand of spring barley, there are further happy reflections on things he has not had or done. "I was brought up to do without," he declares. "I've really gone through hard times. To me, this isn't a hard time. Not at all. I grew up without a shilling in my pocket. Both my grandfathers went bankrupt. My brother says our father couldn't go bankrupt because he had nothing to lose. You can put that down. Dad told me I was very lucky because he was going to leave me the wild world to roam in. Unbelievable!"

His father would surely have been proud to see his son amass so much from so little. In typical Easterby style, he has kept most of it, although plenty has been raised for others, with over £120,000 given to the Yorkshire Air Ambulance thanks to the point-to-points staged on his land. On both the personal and charity front, Easterby is excellent with money. He is sadly not so blessed on the dental front.

"This is the only tooth I've got and I'm keeping it," he says, showing it off for another picture. "I can still eat fish and chips, rice pudding and eggs. I always boil my eggs in the kettle while I'm making tea, you know. With the same water from the same kettle I used to be able to get washed and shaved, plus I'd gently clean my plate as well. Do you know, I did have four sets of false teeth but I sold one on the internet and got £120. I'm a legend, you see. You'll have to write that." I wrote that.

"Even to this day I love just making do," Easterby adds, suddenly coming over rather evangelical. "It's the most wonderful thing. Life shouldn't be about how much you can spend. Why make money and then spend it? I can live on fresh air. If I started treating myself to things it would kill me."

★★★★

FORTUNATELY, Easterby lives in the freshest of fresh air. He breathes some of it in and surveys his splendid kingdom. "Take a photograph of all this land," he instructs Whitaker. "Oh, it's fantastic, out of this world. I couldn't dream of living anywhere else. When I wake up in the morning, I look up at the hill and see the churchyard. I own the land all around it as well. That churchyard is where I'm going. Mind, I think I'm going to live forever. I'm absolutely certain. If I do have to say 'bye-bye' I'll be going to that churchyard, nowhere else, unless I change my mind and end up on my point-to-point course. That way I could overlook all my land.

"Oh yes, I really enjoy everything about life and living here. I've got everything I need. Do you want to see my sheep?" We've seen the barley, some of the horses and will soon admire his peas, so it's about time the sheep had their turn. We head closer to the hills and stop at a beck, across which the aforementioned sheep are passing the time by eating grass. Asked how many there are, Easterby takes a panoramic view of the flock and comes up with 500 as an answer.

Behind him are three horses about to get sweaty on a gallop constructed of cloth. The horses speed along, watched by a trainer driving a Mitsubishi Shogun, on one ledge of which a nervous journalist precariously embraces social distancing and prays the man at the wheel avoids bumps.

Happy with what he has seen, Easterby takes us in the direction of the top yard and the peas, which are currently developing in suitably dry soil. "When you farm, you ask the land what it wants to grow," says Farmer Mick, who then offers more wise words accrued from a lifetime of learning.

"You mustn't be frightened of making mistakes," he states simply, producing an equally clear statement when asked what his own biggest mistake has been.

Continues page 192

"Selling things," he says, absolute certainty in his voice. "If you keep things you get growth. Once you sell them you don't benefit from the growth.

"When I first came to Sheriff Hutton in 1960 I gave £1,600 for a little thatched cottage, but then I swapped it for a new house in the village. That cottage I sold was up for sale not long ago for £700,000. My heart almost stopped when I saw that. 'Michael, how stupid can you get?' I asked myself. They had built an extension, mind."

It was, thankfully, a rare reverse. "I've done some wonderful deals," he says. "I've also never done a wrong deed in my life. Not intentionally, anyway. Put that down.

"I remember there was once a chap driving up the road just as my horses were about to cross it. I waved him down and asked him to wait. He pulled up and we started to chat, so I invited him in for a cup of tea. I had never met him before but he was a carpet dealer and I do like dealers. While he was having his tea I sold him a horse. As he left he kept saying he couldn't believe what had just happened. A nice chap he was."

Plenty more nice and similarly stunned chaps have been sold horses by the countryside carbon copy of Ronnie Barker's Arkwright, albeit one with a much bigger corner shop. There is always room for more, but with around 60 thoroughbreds in the squad – one of whom sprang a 28-1 shock at Thirsk on Monday – Easterby is not short of owners.

"I grow all my own hay and corn, which is why I can train 'osses so cheap," he explains. "Trainers charge far too much. It's ridiculous. I'll give anyone a big reduction. I just want to keep my clients happy. I love racing, you see."

As we make our way back from the peas we see two horses on Easterby's all-weather gallop, one of them ridden by fellow trainer and near neighbour Ruth Carr, also successful on the Thirsk card. "You must be learning plenty from the Boss," she says in advance of Easterby making a formal introduction. "This is Ruth Carr," he announces. "She uses my gallops and pays me." A large smile forms on his face.

****

SOMETHING else that has made him smile over the years are winning bets. He claims not to dabble these days, but those in the know insist if you see him nervously chewing his hanky, the money must be down. It most definitely was at Haydock on Saturday, June 7, 1975, when the then three-year-old Lochnager contested the Bass Apprentices' Handicap.

"I fancied three horses that day," says Easterby. All three won, all three were sent off favourite. "This is absolutely true," he continues. "I took £1,000 in my pocket. I knew it was just a case of how far Lochnager would win by, maybe ten or 20 lengths. Eight of us went in together for a punt, including Nicholas Wrigley's father, Mr Wrigley.

"I put Alice on the grandstand and told her when she gave the signal of taking off her hat we would all back the horse at the same time. While he was waiting, Mr Wrigley went over to the Ladbrokes pitch and asked for a price about Lochnager. The bookie told him 5-1. He kept looking up at Alice, like we all did, but she wasn't taking her hat off.

"A minute later Mr Wrigley asked again and the price was down to 4-1. Alice still had her hat on. He asked twice more and by then the price was 6-4. 'The silly cow still hasn't taken her hat off,' he said to the man at Ladbrokes. What we didn't know was Alice had pinned the hat on her head and couldn't get it off.

"I finished up only having £100 on. I'm sure someone found out about our plan and pinched the price. I think it was Peter O'Sullevan. I couldn't blame him."

Back at the farmhouse, Easterby tries to sell us the leg of a Telescope filly but is distracted by his son – a prolific point-to-point-winning trainer – who explains what happened following his father's announcement in 2013 that he would be passing on the licence to his heir.

"After he won the Ayr Silver Cup he said I should take over but then he changed his mind," says David. "He enjoys racing and he's even more enthusiastic than he was 20 years ago. People don't want to come here to interview David Easterby. They want to interview Michael Easterby."

Interviewing Michael Easterby has been a joy, another item ticked off the racing writer's bucket list. As an added bonus, Mrs Easterby has popped out to say hello, escorted by granddaughter Joanna Mason. Alice sits alongside her husband and beams with delight. In their 1958 wedding photos they were such a beautiful couple. They still are.

Another photo taken, she returns inside to Compo, Clegg and Foggy, while her spouse and son reveal that nobody knows her age, perhaps now not even Alice.

"You just have to adjust," says Easterby of their shared new normal. "She does forget things. A chap who we both know came in one day – you can put this down – and he said: 'Hello, Alice, how are you?' She looked up at him with a confused expression. 'Who are you? I don't know you.' So I said to her: 'Alice, do you know me?' Quick as a flash, she looked back at me and said: 'Who the hell could forget you!'"

Who indeed? Mick Easterby is a legend, trainer, farmer, salesman, collector of land and fountain of wisdom. With his wife no longer safe at a stove, he can even knock up a tasty stew.

"I quite enjoy it," he says. "You don't need a brain to cook. It's common sense. Life is common sense. We're getting that back now. What's been going on in the world has made us realise how lucky we've been. Even I started to grumble. I had to say to myself: 'What's wrong with you, Michael? Get a hold of yourself.' In that way this has all done me a lot of good."

An hour or two in his company would do anyone a lot of good. At some point he will end up in that churchyard or on his point-to-point field. Not yet, though, and hopefully not for a good while. Long may Michael reign.

Mick Easterby: "Take a photograph of all this land. It's fantastic, out of this world. I couldn't dream of living anywhere else"

MANSIONBET
MANSIONBET
MANSIONBET

THE BIGGER PICTURE

A rainbow frames the battle between Django Django (nearside) and Notachance as they jump the final fence in the Harwell Trophy at Newbury in January. Django Django, trained by Jonjo O'Neill and ridden by his son Jonjo junior, goes clear on the run-in to win by four and three-quarter lengths

FAMILY BONDS

Cieren Fallon and Roger Teal combined for a Group 1 breakthrough with Oxted in the July Cup

A FIRST Group 1 triumph is a treasured prize whether you are a young jockey on the up or a long-standing trainer battling against the big yards on a limited budget. Oxted's July Cup win linked these two threads of the racing tapestry with a memorable success for Cieren Fallon and Roger Teal and, while the winning duo come from different backgrounds, what also united them was the strong family bonds that helped them to reach the highest level.

At the age of 21, Fallon was quick to put his name on the Group 1 honours board with Oxted and his rapid progress from champion apprentice to top-level jockey, and later in the summer to the position of number two to Oisin Murphy with Qatar Racing, came as no surprise. As the son of six-time British champion jockey Kieren Fallon, he has a royal lineage and the talent to match.

Fallon snr is both house companion and mentor for his son and he played an important role in Oxted's success. The July Cup was one of the few big races to elude him during his glittering career but years of experience at the top level made his advice worth heeding when he walked the Newmarket track with his son before racing.

"I always remember what Dad has said in the back of my mind," said Fallon jnr, whose mother Julie was also a professional jockey in the 1990s. "He told me to keep it simple, stay straight and make sure I had him well balanced going into the Dip. He's very proud and has helped me a lot this year and last year. He was going to move to America to start training but stuck around to look after me. I can't thank him enough."

The young jockey deserved plenty of credit himself for a positive ride that was laced with the strength that seems to be a family hallmark. More than two furlongs out Fallon had Oxted battling for the lead with Hello Youmzain, the Diamond Jubilee winner, and he was soon in a three-way battle as Commonwealth Cup scorer Golden Horde joined the fray. Hello Youmzain was the first to wilt and Golden Horde could not match Oxted's power either as Fallon drove his mount up the hill. It was left to Sceptical to throw down a late challenge under Frankie Dettori but the Irish raider never looked likely to catch Oxted, who scored by a decisive length and a quarter.

Reflecting a few days later on his Group 1 success, Fallon said: "I never thought I'd be riding in a Group 1 so early in my career, let alone actually win one. It was such a big moment for me and I was in complete shock. I woke up the following morning and had to look at my phone to double-check it hadn't been a dream."

▸ In the pink: Oxted comes home a length and a quarter clear of Sceptical in the July Cup; right, Roger Teal and Cieren Fallon in the winner's enclosure

Fallon's Group 1 breakthrough came just three years after the first time he sat on a racehorse and less than two years since his first ride in August 2018, but he has set his sights high. "I want to emulate my father's accomplishments and do even better. It's a very big statement and it won't be easy but I'm not scared to admit it's something I want to do. I want to set big goals," he said.

On the importance of his relationship with his father, he said: "It means the world to have his support. We often play golf together and it takes me out of the racing world. We talk about my rides but also just life in general. It's a great relationship and he wants me to succeed as much as I do, if not even more. He left racing when he retired but now he's getting back into it. I want to do well to make my family proud."

****

FAMILY also lies at the heart of Teal's side of the story. His son Harry is assistant trainer and wife Sue does everything from mucking out at their Lambourn yard to dealing with invoices. "Do we have office staff? Yes, you're talking to her," she told the Racing Post's Peter Thomas this summer.

Teal, who started training in 2007, doubled his string to 50 horses over the winter following his move to Windsor House Stables but he was still punching above his weight in the July Cup. The stark reality of a small training operation was clear when Teal told Thomas: "Us mucking out or driving the box means we can save money and maintain standards. We've worked our way up the ladder and we want to stay here."

Oxted took them to the highest rung after years of hard toil and, while it was their misfortune to win the July Cup at a time when prize-money cuts meant victory was worth £140,000 less than the year before, Teal's delight knew no bounds.

"This is the race we've targeted all year," he said in the Newmarket winner's enclosure, his mobile phone pinging with congratulations. "Harry said to me last week: 'This wins the July Cup.' I told him to keep his feet on the ground but when we tacked him up today, he said: 'Dad, this will win.' I didn't want to get myself too carried away but this horse is amazing. When he hit the front I thought: 'Oh my God, he's going away here.' Then I thought: 'Keep him going, Cieren, just keep him going.'"

Out on the track, at a near deserted Newmarket, Fallon was keeping going. "I was half a furlong out and I knew I'd won," the young jockey said. "Then I could hear Harry and Roger screaming, and I let out a little one myself. I'm delighted for Roger winning his first Group 1. He gave me so much confidence going into the race. He took me aside and told me Oxted was going to win. I believed it too."

Teal also had great belief in Fallon, trusting the youngster with a rare Group 1 opportunity for the yard. "Cieren has natural talent," he said. "He's not been riding that long and had to do a lot of catching up but there's people who have ridden all their lives who don't have a racing brain like his. His dad has definitely educated him well and they have a similar riding style. Hopefully he'll be winning top races for many years to come."

Surely he will, but this one with Oxted will always be a special memory for Fallon, and for Teal too.

Johnny Murtagh landed his first Group 1 win as a trainer with Champers Elysees in the Matron on Irish Champions Weekend

CHAMPERS CELEBRATION

IN HIS stellar career as a jockey Johnny Murtagh rode more than 100 Group 1 winners, lighting up a host of big occasions with his brilliance and self-assurance. He was just as confident of his ability to deliver at the highest level as a trainer, but deep into the eighth year of his second career he was still waiting. He never wavered from his conviction that all he needed was the right horse, and then along came Champers Elysees.

Like her trainer, Champers Elysees proved she had the talent and temperament to perform in the unforgiving spotlight of the main stage when she turned up at Leopardstown on the first day of Irish Champions Weekend. It had been a long road to get this far and she was taking a big jump in class for the Matron Stakes, but Murtagh had her ready for her Group 1 moment. In beating two Classic winners in Peaceful and Fancy Blue, she showed it was where she belonged.

Murtagh left no doubt it was where he felt he belonged too, just as much as he did when he operated at the highest level as a jockey for two decades. "I'm a very good trainer – and I just need better horses," he said with trademark conviction when asked to explain his stable's surge to its best-ever season in 2020. "And when I get them, these are the results. It's very hard to source horses in Ireland but, when you do, I don't mind telling people we're able to do the business."

★★★★

MURTAGH had done well to source Champers Elysees, picking her up at the yearling sales for €28,000. He always believed she would make up into a stakes filly but for a long time dreams of a Group 1 victory would have been fanciful. She failed to win in her first three starts as a juvenile, although the last of those runs brought a creditable sixth place in the highly valuable Tattersalls Ireland Super Auction Sale Stakes when she was second-best of the home contingent against the pot-hunting British raiders.

That was on the second day of Irish Champions Weekend 2019 but it seemed highly unlikely she would be returning a year later for one of the big events. She finally opened her account on her next start, winning a six-furlong auction race on heavy ground at the Curragh, but ended her first season with defeat as a short-priced favourite in the Birdcatcher Nursery at Naas off a handicap mark of 84.

Her race record at that stage was promising enough but, with only one entry in the win column, there were no takers when she was sent to the sales. As a three-year-old, however, her value rose ever higher as Murtagh polished her from a rough diamond into a gem.

In the first week of the resumption of racing in Ireland, Murtagh made good use of her handicap mark and apprentice Danny Sheehy's 5lb claim to start her season on a winning note at the Curragh. Now was the time to test her in higher company and she passed with flying colours in the Listed Corrib Fillies Stakes at the Galway festival, powering clear to win by seven lengths.

After both races she was sold to go abroad only for the deals to fall through, the second time after failing the vet when she was trotted up, but ultimately the syndicate that had owned her from the outset, Fitzwilliam Racing, had the greatest reward of all.

A month later Champers Elysees stepped up again to take the Group 3 Fairy Bridge Stakes at Gowran Park, this time by half a length. "She deserves her shot at a Group 1," Murtagh said, but in the Matron she faced a formidable task against three fillies who had already won at that level. They were headed by Fancy Blue, who had landed the French Oaks and Nassau Stakes, and Irish 1,000 Guineas winner Peaceful, but Champers Elysees' rapid progress was recognised with third place in the betting market and she went up another gear on the track.

Colin Keane settled her near the back of the 11-runner field, with Fancy Blue close by, while Peaceful was closer to the pace set by stablemate Love Locket. In the straight Keane soon had his filly motoring down the outside and she passed rival after rival before finally catching Peaceful inside the final furlong to win going away. Fancy Blue, who had been unable to match the winner's pace from the back, was third.

Up in the near empty stands, Murtagh cheered so loudly with his wife Orla that Wayne Lordan, riding sixth-placed So Wonderful, said he could hear him out on the track and knew who had won.

"It was one of the great days, so satisfying for everyone involved," Murtagh told Racing TV's Luck On Sunday the next morning. Relating how he had dropped in to visit some of the syndicate members with the trophy after the race, he added: "People were saying, 'Johnny, it's one of the best days of my life'. It just shows there is a chance to be there on the big day."

Having enjoyed their big raceday, albeit while watching from home, the Fitzwilliam members finally took their big payday when Champers Elysees was sold privately to leading Japanese owner Teruya Yoshida shortly after the Matron.

Her first start in new colours brought a running-on fourth in the Group 1 Sun Chariot Stakes at Newmarket in October and the plan is to keep her in training with Murtagh in 2021. Having built her up into a top-level performer, he has good prospects of more big days ahead with her.

▲ Sweet success: Johnny Murtagh greets Champers Elysees after her Matron triumph
◀ Colin Keane brings the filly home in front by a length and a quarter

★★★★

MURTAGH'S first Group 1 win as a jockey was in 1993 on Manntari in the National Stakes, which is now part of Irish Champions Weekend. The initiative had not been started when he retired from the saddle and, after attending the first couple of editions as a guest, he reflected the week before the 2020 event how he soon grew bored of being there "just for the free lunches". He vowed to Orla he would strive to change that and, with Champers Elysees, he reaped the fruits of his labours.

"I'm sick of everybody saying 'Oh, you had such a great career as a jockey.' That's in the past," he said after the Matron. "It's the now I'm worried about and it's great to win this with her. To win a Group 1 on Champions Weekend, it means everything. That's what we get up in the morning for – we want to be here on this stage."

It was a stage Murtagh made his own as a rider and he was finally back there as a trainer. That taste of Champers was so sweet.

IN THE PICTURE

Authentic advert for micro-ownership with Kentucky Derby win

AMONG the many unusual aspects of the 2020 Kentucky Derby was the make-up of the ownership group behind Authentic, the Bob Baffert-trained winner. The majority owner is billionaire B Wayne Hughes, owner of Spendthrift Farm in Kentucky, but there are also 5,314 'micro-owners' who each paid $206 for a tiny share through MyRacehorse.com, which is aimed at "the democratisation of racehorse ownership".

None of them could be at Churchill Downs for the delayed and behind-closed-doors 'Run for the Roses' on September 5 but they celebrated across America and around the world as Authentic (*pictured leading*) won by a length and a quarter.

Among them was Irishman Jack Cantillon, himself a proponent of such ownership through his syndicates.racing group, who wrote on Twitter: "I paid $206 to buy a tiny share in this horse, loved following him all year and I've just won the #KyDerby sitting on my couch in Ireland. What a sport."

Another micro-owner, Valli Johnson from Regina in Canada, said: "All the way down the stretch, I had tears streaming down my face." She also told CTV News that she had wanted to have a mint julep, the cocktail famously associated with the Kentucky Derby, but had no idea how to make it and settled for a mint Baileys instead.

MyRacehorse.com was founded in 2018 by Michael Behrens, a former marketing and advertising executive, and Hughes is a partner. Having started out with more modest horses, Behrens soon realised people wanted a shot at the biggest races. The company bought 12.5 per cent of Authentic in June and then sold the micro-shares, each worth 0.001% of the breeding and racing rights.

By then Authentic was already a strong Kentucky Derby contender and at Churchill Downs, where he lined up as third favourite under John Velazquez, he foiled the Triple Crown bid of Tiz The Law, the 7-10 favourite. Normally the Kentucky Derby is the first leg of the US Triple Crown with the Belmont Stakes coming last, but in this unusual year the Belmont had been run in June and won by the Barclay Tagg-trained Tiz The Law.

The Kentucky Derby came second in the series, delayed by four months, and finally there was the Preakness Stakes at Pimlico, four weeks after the Kentucky Derby.

Authentic was 6-4 favourite for the Preakness but this time he was beaten a neck by the filly Swiss Skydiver, trained by Kenny McPeek. For his thousands of owners, however, the disappointment of that near miss was as nothing compared to the joy of the Kentucky Derby.

Picture: GREGORY SHAMUS (GETTY IMAGES)

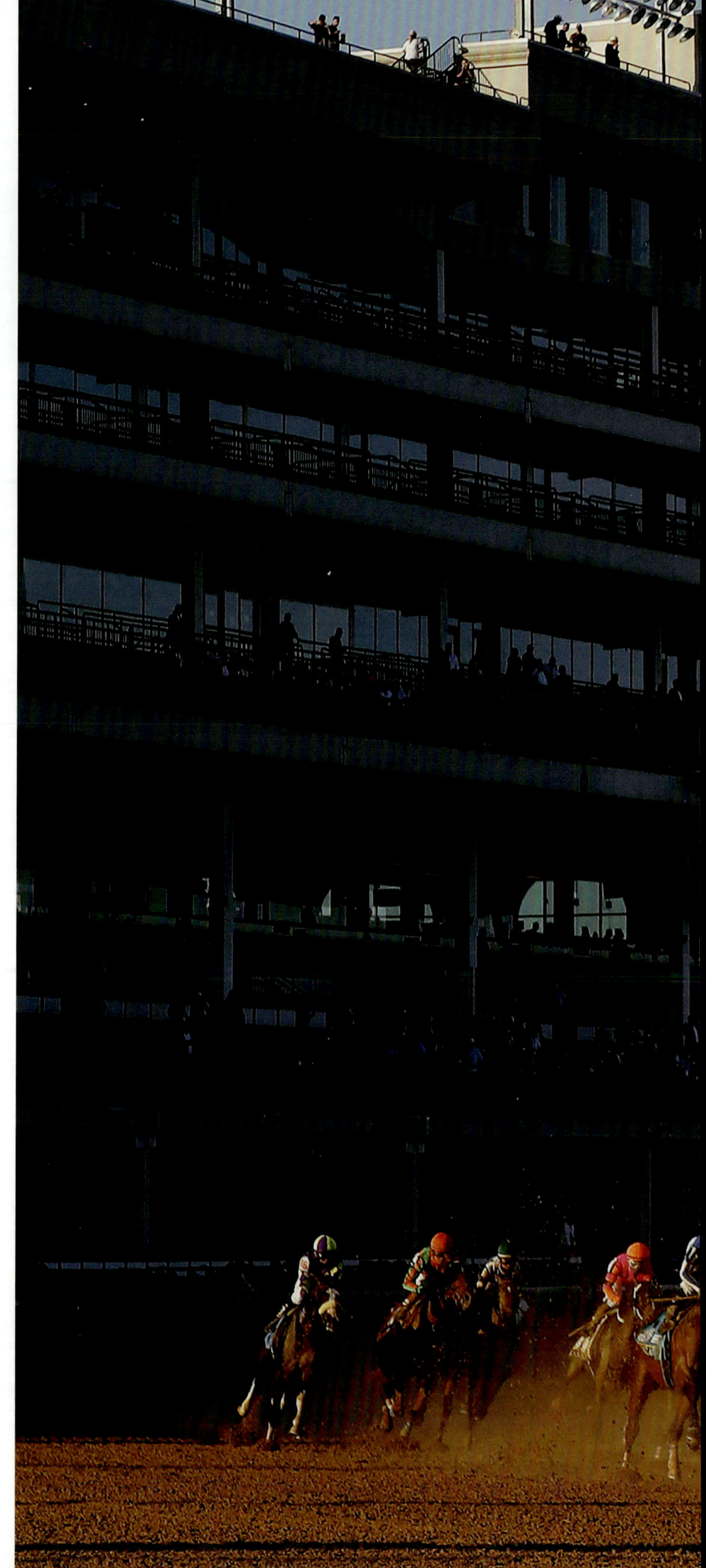

From racing icon to national treasure

Pat Smullen, nine-time Irish champion Flat jockey, died on September 15, aged 43. His indomitable spirit on and off the track, epitomised by his fundraising efforts for Cancer Trials Ireland, is remembered in these extracts from the Racing Post

By Richard Forristal

PAT SMULLEN'S time among us came to an end when he breathed his last breath surrounded by close family in St Vincent's Hospital in Dublin. His body is now at peace, having been subject to such a cruel onslaught since his diagnosis with pancreatic cancer on March 26, 2018. Pat's mind, though, had long since been at ease.

He never rode in public following that fateful day two and a half years ago, yet our respect and the public's affection for him grew exponentially with every passing day. We empathised with him because he was ill, of course, but the overwhelming outpouring of support for him was founded on the manner in which he embraced his plight. He stared his destiny in the eye and smiled.

At a very early remove, Pat resolved not to wallow in self-pity and that he wouldn't conceal his ordeal. In doing so, he became a national treasure, a beacon of light who refused to be defined by his illness. Somehow, despite his shocking predicament, he empowered people to feel better about themselves. A totem of the racing world, he was now an ambassador for hope and positivity.

The cascade of tributes paid to him, including from our head of state President Michael D Higgins and the Taoiseach Micheal Martin, is testament to the extent to which he touched such a diverse range of people.

Pat wanted some good to come of his hardship, so he set about breaking down barriers and raising awareness and funds to support the unending scientific quest to advance the unequal war on cancer. He had been subjected to the most traumatic fate, but reconciled himself with his situation so that he could help others. It was a graceful and dignified response that epitomised him.

At his lowest ebb, there was no bitterness, resentment or recrimination. Instead, he put his energy into making the most of what he had. That, more than any of his exploits in the saddle, will be his most enduring legacy.

For 25 years, as he pursued single-mindedly and relentlessly his ambition to lift himself from humble origins as the son of a farm labourer in Rhode, County Offaly to make the most of his potential as a jockey, he cut a detached, cool and somewhat aloof figure. Such discretion was a by-product of his overwhelming desire to succeed, infused as well by a nagging lack of self-belief that prevented him from ever fully accepting he was worthy of his lofty status. It meant he was always on edge, which, he would later suggest, was his edge.

Pat's pursuit of winners manifested itself in a staunch dedication, and there is a passage from a Kieren Fallon interview some years ago that gets right to the kernel of their contrasting approaches. In illustrating his own mercurial and often hell-raising ways, Fallon pointed to Pat's straight-laced temperament as a foil. "The person who gives his whole life to the job to the best of his ability," Fallon said of his colleague. "No distractions. Great professionalism. I don't know how they do it. I've had my quirks. Pat has had his tractors." That humility and integrity were his core values.

Counter-intuitive as it may seem, it was only after he had been forced to abandon a career that yielded such glorious

▸▸ *Continues page 204*

accomplishments that he came into his own. Character reveals itself in adversity, and how that rings true in the case of Pat Smullen.

On learning of his affliction, and knowing how aggressive pancreatic cancer can be, he shed the defence mechanism that had served him so well for so long. As the world closed in around him, Pat opened his heart. He never looked more comfortable in his own skin and carried himself with a lightness of being that was at odds with the assault on his physical wellbeing.

Such philanthropy of spirit saw him morph from a champion jockey to a champion in the truest sense of the word. He had earned a position of privilege, so what could he do with it?

Consider this, from Cancer Trials Ireland's chief executive Eibhlín Mulroe and its clinical lead, Professor Ray McDermott, on behalf of the association's staff: "Earlier this year, Comic Relief reached out to the entire country and raised almost €6m with the help of a host of celebs across several hours of primetime TV. Pat Smullen and the horse racing community raised almost half that – €2.6m – for pancreatic cancer clinical trials alone.

"People diagnosed with pancreatic cancer in Ireland will feel the benefit of it for years, if not decades, to come. The low incidence of pancreatic cancer (around 560 people diagnosed in Ireland each year), the fact that it is not usually diagnosed early, and the relative difficulty of treating the disease effectively with the usual tools

Continues page 206

Acute tactician who stayed cool under pressure

IN A career that spanned 25 years, Pat Smullen left an indelible imprint on the fabric of the Irish racing scene. He was champion jockey on nine occasions, winning his first title in 2000 having previously won the apprentice championship in 1995 and 1996.

Smullen's association with Dermot Weld will be remembered as one of the most powerful combinations in Irish racing history. Weld had a crucial impact on his career, along with Mick Kinane, to whom he acted as understudy in his early days at Weld's Rosewell House stables.

In adopting the same thoughtful and uncomplicated approach to race-riding that Weld had previously instilled in Kinane, Smullen played the percentage game, keeping the error count low and maintaining a high level of consistency based on excellent judgement of pace, an acute tactical brain and the ability to retain composure under pressure.

Weld and Smullen teamed up for a host of major domestic and international wins over a 20-year period, culminating with the rider's career highlights on the Aga Khan-owned Harzand in the Derby and Irish Derby in 2016.

They also won the Irish Derby with Grey Swallow in 2004, as well as capturing the Irish 1,000 Guineas twice, with Nightime in 2006 and Bethrah in 2010, and the Irish St Leger with Vinnie Roe in four consecutive years between 2001 and 2004.

Although the mutual loyalty between the two men was unshakeable, Smullen followed a path beaten by Kinane and Johnny Murtagh to achieve the rare distinction of winning acclaim as a major international jockey while operating from an Irish base.

This was well illustrated in 2015 when his big-race wins included the Irish Oaks and Prix de l'Opera on Covert Love for Hugo Palmer, Royal Ascot success for Weld on Free Eagle in the Prince of Wales's Stakes and on Snow Sky for Sir Michael Stoute in the Hardwicke Stakes, the Champion Stakes on the Weld-trained Fascinating Rock, as well as the Tattersalls Millions Trophy on Gifted Master for Palmer.

His last Pattern-level win was on the Weld-trained Tocco D'Amore at Leopardstown in November 2017. The name of that event, the Finale Stakes, strikes a poignant chord now.

Smullen made his final riding appearance at Dundalk on March 16, 2018, giving Togoville a typically strong ride to land a six-furlong conditions event for County Monaghan trainer Anthony McCann. Two days later he was reported to be suffering from gallstones when missing the opening turf fixture of the season at Naas. The following week came the shocking news of a cancer diagnosis.

Strength of character and underlying fitness helped him to negotiate an initial spell of treatment and he was determined to return to the saddle. However, by May 2019 he had to bow to medical advice and announce his retirement.

In the months that followed, he threw himself into the organisation of the Pat Smullen Champions Race for Cancer Trials Ireland, staged at the Curragh on the second day of Irish Champions Weekend. The occasion was an unimaginable success, raising in excess of €2.5 million, and he took considerable pride in announcing in July that €100,000 had been allocated to St Vincent's Hospital for a next generation sequencing machine to enhance diagnosis and management of pancreatic cancer.

Sadly, soon afterwards he had to be readmitted to St Vincent's when his condition deteriorated. His legacy there, and so far beyond, is one that will endure in his absence.

ALAN SWEETMAN

'You always did your best. Always'

Pat Smullen's funeral was on September 18. His wife Frances made this eulogy

My heart is broken. I've lost my best friend, my soulmate. Hannah, Paddy and Sarah have not just lost their lovely dad, but their mentor, friend, ally and rock. You should know that Dad was so proud of each of you and the people that you have become. He's carried you and I know you will continue to carry him with you every day.

I would like to acknowledge the support of the wider racing community, particularly for Pat's fundraising gig for cancer research at the Curragh. He died on September 15, exactly one year after that amazing day. I think that symbolises how much that meant to him.

Strong, brave, tough, fighter. All those words were used to describe Pat, and here are a few more: insecure, scared, vulnerable, sad. For he was only human and knew a body could only take so much. His spirit never gave up, but in the end it wasn't quite enough.

Pat's death will come as a big blow to many cancer sufferers in Ireland. I have a message to you from him: keep going, don't lose heart; please don't let this knock you back.

To all the cancer team at St Vincent's Hospital, we will be forever grateful. Every night when I looked at Pat I knew he was going to be treated with kindness and respect. The disappointment on their faces when they saw him fade was obvious. Pat could feel it too. I'm doing my best, he would say.

We know you did your best in everything you did, Pat. You always did your best. Always.

"My best friend, my soulmate": Frances Crowley with Pat Smullen

(chemotherapy, radiotherapy) make for a challenging, sparse research environment.

"But as a direct result of the funds Pat helped raise, Cancer Trials Ireland received nine research proposals this year. Three studies are now being advanced or explored, one of which will open in Ireland in a matter of weeks. That is the work Pat has enabled us to do.

"But that is not all that Pat did for Cancer Trials Ireland. Last November, he helped us to raise more than €120,000 for ovarian and prostate cancer trials. Earlier this year, he gave us the go-ahead to fund a next generation sequencing machine (€100,000) for St Vincent's Hospital, Dublin. This machine will allow doctors to genetically sequence pancreatic cancer tumours, and other tumours, potentially opening up treatment options for thousands of people with all types of cancer.

"On a more personal level, Pat continually made himself available for interviews, photo calls and phone calls – anything that might help people in a situation similar to his own."

In extremis, at his lowest ebb, Pat gave more than he took. It is that selfless generosity of time, energy and emotion that has inspired so many of us who knew him, and so many who didn't.

In the midst of such harrowing grief for his wife Frances and their children Hannah, Paddy and Sarah, as well as their extended family – many of whom we also know so well – that feels like no consolation. A husband, a father, a brother and a son is gone too soon. That bad things happen to good people will forever be something we struggle to accept, but these matters are indiscriminate.

Last May, as we sat in the kitchen of their beautiful Brickfield Stud home on the banks of the Grand Canal in Rhode, where he had found great solace since his diagnosis, Frances was minded to temper the talk of Pat's bravery. Conscious that so many, not least their late friend John Shortt, had been similarly brave, they were both keenly aware that courage and fortitude aren't always enough.

If they were, Pat would surely still be with us. He will live forever in our hearts.

'A brilliant horseman and an unbelievably decent man'

Full name Patrick Joseph Smullen

Born May 22, 1977

Wife Frances (nee Crowley), former trainer; sister of Annemarie, wife of Aidan O'Brien

Apprenticed to Tom Lacy, Tullamore, County Offaly

First mount Power Source, ninth at Listowel, September 21, 1992

First winner Vicosa, Dundalk, June 11, 1993

First Group winner Token Gesture (1996 CL Weld Park Stakes)

First Group 1 winner Tarascon (1997 Moyglare Stud Stakes)

First winner in Britain Takwin, Doncaster, September 9, 2000

Derby winner Harzand (2016)

Irish Derby winners Grey Swallow (2004), Harzand (2016)

2,000 Guineas winner Refuse To Bend (2003)

Other Classic winners Vinnie Roe (2001, 2002, 2003 & 2004 Irish St Leger, 2001 Prix Royal-Oak), Nightime (2006 Irish 1,000 Guineas), Bethrah (2010 Irish 1,000 Guineas), Covert Love (2015 Irish Oaks)

Ascot Gold Cup winner Rite Of Passage (2010)

Champion Stakes winner Fascinating Rock (2015)

Other Group 1 winners Refuse To Bend (2002 National Stakes), Grey Swallow (2005 Tattersalls Gold Cup), Benbaun (2007 Prix de l'Abbaye), Casual Conquest (2009 Tattersalls Gold Cup), Chinese White (2010 Pretty Polly Stakes), Emulous (2011 Matron Stakes), Free Eagle (2015 Prince of Wales's Stakes), Covert Love (2015 Prix de l'Opera), Fascinating Rock (2016 Tattersalls Gold Cup)

Breeders' Cup winner Muhannak (2008 Marathon, non-Graded)

Most prolific Pattern winner Famous Name (13 Group wins 2008-12, including 2012 Royal Whip)

Dermot Weld, Rosewell House trainer and Smullen's main employer We had a wonderful relationship for 19 years. He was an outstanding stable jockey, the professional's professional. His loyalty, integrity and honesty were key factors of the man he was.

Aidan O'Brien, Ballydoyle trainer and Smullen's brother-in-law He was an incredible man, an irreplaceable person. Pat had everything. He was a brilliant horseman, a great jockey, but an unbelievably sincere and decent man.

Mick Kinane, 13-time Irish champion jockey We'll see a lot of good riders come and go, but a handful of great ones. He was a great one.

Eva-Maria Bucher-Haefner, Moyglare Stud owner For me, he was not just our number one rider, he became a friend. He was loyal, reliable, ambitious, humorous, courageous and inspiring. A thoroughly good person, husband, father, friend, and a great jockey.

Last winner Togoville, Dundalk, March 16, 2018

Main trainer Dermot Weld 1999-2018

Champion apprentice 1995, 1996

Champion jockey 9 times (2000, 2001, 2005, 2007, 2008, 2010, 2014, 2015, 2016)

Group/Grade 1 wins 25

Royal Ascot wins 8

Most wins in a year in Ireland 129 (2016)

Total wins in Ireland 1,845

Total wins in Britain 47

Compiled by John Randall

◂ Starring roles: anti-clockwise from main picture, Grey Swallow, Harzand, Refuse To Bend, Famous Name and Fascinating Rock

IN THE

PICTURE

'Utter disbelief' for one-eyed jockey following historic Goodwood win

GUY MITCHELL made a remarkable mark in history at Goodwood in August when he became the first jockey with one eye to win a race in Britain.

The 46-year-old racecourse doctor, who was having only his fourth ride, passed the post a length in front on the Simon Dow-trained 50-1 shot The Game Is On in a 1m1f amateur jockeys' handicap. He had been allowed a riding licence just 12 months earlier, having been turned down more than once without being given a proper explanation.

Mitchell, who has been blind in one eye since the age of three, was still stunned when speaking after his big moment. "Disbelief, utter disbelief," he said. "I've waited a long time. I never thought it would happen. Last year when I had my first ride, I couldn't walk after it – it was ridiculous. I've worked much harder to get fit. I've made giant strides."

The Goodwood race almost went badly wrong, however. "I nearly fell off at the start," he admitted. "They said 'blinds off' and I had one hand on the reins and the other on the blind and he [The Game Is On] just went with them. I was slightly out the side door for a bit, which actually benefited me as it got me in a good position.

"I thought they were getting away from me coming down the hill, but I edged him out on to what I thought was a bit better ground, nursed him along a bit, started riding him and to my surprise he picked up.

"Before I knew it I was in a situation where everything around me went silent, which I thought must mean I was in the lead, but I really didn't know. I was so knackered at that stage, pushing as hard as I could. I could hear Serena [Brotherton] coming but my horse stayed on. I was relieved, utterly relieved."

The doctor, son of former trainer and champion amateur rider Philip Mitchell, has followed the lead of Guy Disney, who in 2017 made headlines as the first amputee jockey to win a race in Britain, and referenced his fellow amateur when touching on changing attitudes in British racing.

"I just think it's become more open to people," he said. "It's well known that [jump jockey] David Crosse is a type-1 diabetic, and 30 years ago there's no chance he would have been riding. You've got Guy Disney, riding with half his leg off. We can still ride and we can still ride safely, and as long as that's the case, why not?"

Pictures: EDWARD WHITAKER (RACINGPOST.COM/PHOTOS)

Dow
4

FRANKEL BIG BUCK'S SPRINTER SACRE HURRICANE FLY GOLDEN HORN

Ten years of the

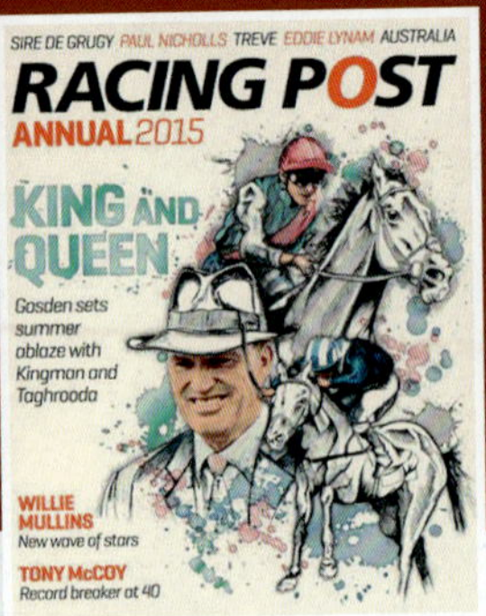

COVER STARS Flat giant Frankel and outstanding young chaser Long Run. Frankel is hailed as 'The Wonder Horse' in the headline on Brough Scott's inside story of a glorious three-year-old campaign in 2011 featuring four Group 1 triumphs from an eye-popping 2,000 Guineas to the Queen Elizabeth II Stakes. Long Run, aged only six, wins the Cheltenham Gold Cup and King George VI Chase, breaking trainer Nicky Henderson's duck in both races.

OTHER HEADLINERS
Ruby Walsh with star hurdlers Hurricane Fly and Big Buck's, Hayley Turner's Group 1 breakthrough with sprinters Dream Ahead and Margot Did, Donald McCain's chapter in family history with Grand National winner Ballabriggs and Mickael Barzalona's daring Derby-winning ride on Pour Moi

KEY EXCERPT 'That Frankel stride. Burn it in the memory. For it's a fair bet you will never see its like again' *Brough Scott*

COVER STAR Frankel again. As a four-year-old he scales even greater heights for Sir Henry Cecil, completing his perfect 14-race career, and his magnificent season and the aura around him is detailed across ten pages under the headline 'Frankel puts the rest in the shade'. On the cover he is simply 'Out of this world'

OTHER HEADLINERS
Neptune Collonges edges out Sunnyhillboy by a nose in the closest Grand National ever, Camelot wins the 2,000 Guineas and Derby but is denied the Triple Crown by Encke in the St Leger, Australia's darling Black Caviar conquers Royal Ascot in heartstopping fashion and the Annual spends seven days on the title trail with Richard Hughes as he becomes champion Flat jockey for the first time

KEY EXCERPT 'For me, after so many years searching for the ultimate thoroughbred, this really seemed to be the one' *Brough Scott on Frankel*

COVER STAR Sprinter Sacre. Nicky Henderson's great chaser joins the pantheon with a perfect season featuring festival wins at Cheltenham, Aintree and Punchestown and a stunning RPR of 190 on two occasions. The headline inside hails him simply as 'Superstar'

OTHER HEADLINERS
Hurricane Fly also completes a perfect season as he achieves the rare feat of regaining the Champion Hurdle crown; Bobs Worth gives Henderson another Cheltenham Gold Cup success; The Queen reaches the pinnacle at Royal Ascot with Estimate's Gold Cup triumph, becoming the first reigning monarch to win the race; Treve storms to a brilliant Arc victory; Auroras Encore produces a 66-1 shock in the Grand National

KEY EXCERPT 'By the end Henderson knew he wasn't just training the best horse of his 35-year career. This was a phenomenon' *Graham Dench on Sprinter Sacre*

COVER STARS John Gosden with his king and queen, Kingman and Taghrooda, Britain's top three-year-old colt and filly of the season. Kingman is beaten in the 2,000 Guineas but then dominates the mile division with four brilliant Group 1 wins in a row, while Taghrooda lands the Oaks and King George in a glorious summer

OTHER HEADLINERS
Kingman's jockey James Doyle announces himself on the big stage in his first full year as Khalid Abdullah's retained rider; Treve wins her second Arc in a brilliant training performance by Criquette Head; four-time Stayers' Hurdle winner Big Buck's bows out after his record-breaking career; Quevega becomes a six-time winner at the Cheltenham Festival; Richard Hannon wins the Flat trainers' title in his first season after taking over from his father

KEY EXCERPT 'Kingman was the miler with such a deadly turn of foot that his trainer readily and repeatedly asserted he had enough speed to win the July Cup' *Nicholas Godfrey*

COVER STARS Golden Horn with Frankie Dettori and Coneygree with Nico de Boinville. Golden Horn wins the Derby and Arc in a glorious campaign that marks Dettori's return to the big stage after a troubled few years, while the novice chaser Coneygree completes a fairytale rise with Cheltenham Gold Cup victory for Mark Bradstock's small yard

OTHER HEADLINERS
AP McCoy wins his 20th jump jockeys' title and has a final Cheltenham Festival win on Uxizandre in an emotional swansong after announcing his retirement; Many Clouds carries the biggest weight since Red Rum to Grand National victory; Faugheen wins the Champion Hurdle in brilliant style; American Pharoah becomes the first US Triple Crown winner in 37 years

KEY EXCERPT 'Many 'experts' maintained that as a three-race novice he should not even be running in the Gold Cup. It only made what happened better' *Brough Scott on Coneygree*

2012 2013 2014 2015 2016 2017 2018 2019 2020 2021

2012 2013 2014 2015 2016 2017 2018 2019 2020 2021

Racing Post Annual

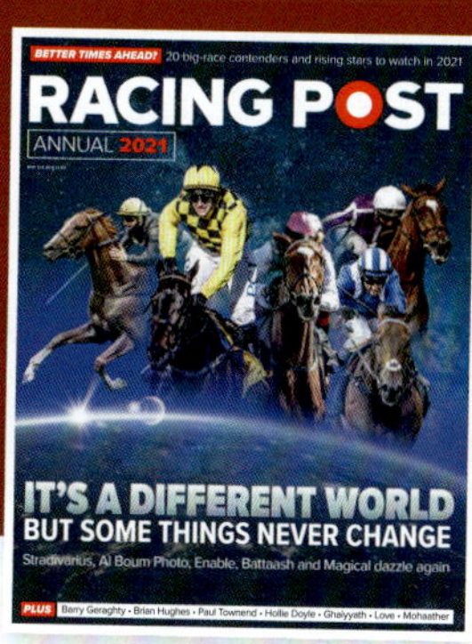

COVER STARS A whole host of them: Sprinter Sacre regains the Champion Chase crown; Richard Johnson finally becomes champion jump jockey; Willie Mullins enjoys success from Cheltenham to the Classics; Thistlecrack runs away with the Stayers' Hurdle; Paul Nicholls wins an epic battle with Mullins for the British jump trainers' title; Found leads an amazing Arc 1-2-3 for Aidan O'Brien

OTHER HEADLINERS
Harzand gives Dermot Weld and Pat Smullen their first Derby success; Don Cossack and Annie Power take the Gold Cup and Champion Hurdle honours; Mouse Morris lands the Grand National with Rule The World; six-time British champion jockey Kieren Fallon ends his glittering and at times controversial career

KEY EXCERPT 'There is an unofficial list of great Cheltenham Festival celebrations – Dawn Run, Desert Orchid, Imperial Call, Istabraq – and Sprinter Sacre went into it, somewhere near the top' *Steve Dennis*

COVER STARS Four hotshots: on the Flat, Enable rises to every challenge for John Gosden as a three-year-old, winning the Arc, King George and two Classics, while stablemate Cracksman produces an astonishing performance in the Champion Stakes; over jumps, Sizing John lands the Cheltenham Gold Cup for Jessica Harrington and Robbie Power, while Buveur D'Air wins the Champion Hurdle in an outstanding season for Nicky Henderson

OTHER HEADLINERS
Battaash makes a rapid ascent to the top and Harry Angel shines just as bright in a brilliant sprint division; Lucinda Russell's One For Arthur wins the Grand National for Scotland; Padraig Beggy scores an unexpected Derby win on Wings Of Eagles; Willie Mullins fights off the challenge of Gordon Elliott in a compelling title showdown in Ireland

KEY EXCERPT 'To watch the three-year-old filly power to Arc victory was to witness the seemingly preordained' *Julian Muscat on Enable*

COVER STARS Native River and Might Bite go head to head from start to finish in a gripping private battle for the Cheltenham Gold Cup. 'Epic duel' is the headline on the inside story of the race of the year, relived in vivid detail by winning jockey Richard Johnson and the beaten Nico de Boinville

OTHER HEADLINERS
Nicky Henderson misses out with Might Bite but still wins two of the big three at Cheltenham with Buveur D'Air in the Champion Hurdle and Altior in the Champion Chase; Enable scores her second Arc triumph in thrilling style after a troubled season; Tiger Roll adds Grand National glory to his lengthening Cheltenham roll of honour; Stradivarius starts his domination of the staying division; Mark Johnston becomes the most prolific winning trainer of all time in Britain

KEY EXCERPT 'At the last they rose together, the race between these two, as it had been since the beginning' *Steve Dennis on the Gold Cup*

COVER STARS A cast of 'Superheroes': Frankie Dettori enjoys an incredibly successful season with the likes of Enable, Stradivarius and Crystal Ocean; Ruby Walsh bows out with a Grade 1 winner on an emotional day at Punchestown; Bryony Frost stars with Frodon on a magical day at Cheltenham; Hayley Turner lands her first Royal Ascot victory; Khadijah Mellah produces an inspiring performance at Glorious Goodwood. Plus there are The People's Champions, Enable and Tiger Roll

OTHER HEADLINERS
Al Boum Photo ends Willie Mullins' hoodoo in the Cheltenham Gold Cup; Altior goes past Big Buck's with a world record of 19 straight wins over jumps; Paisley Park adds to the magical feeling at Cheltenham with his Stayers' Hurdle victory; Oisin Murphy is British champion Flat jockey for the first time

KEY EXCERPT 'Not since Leonardo da Vinci has an Italian enjoyed a finer renaissance' *Lee Mottershead on Frankie Dettori*

COVER STARS
Stradivarius, Al Boum Photo, Enable, Battaash and Magical all returned to land signature races they had won before, providing racing with some sense of normality in this different world after the arrival of coronavirus

OTHER HEADLINERS
You've read all about them: Flat stars including Love, Ghaiyyath, Mohaather and Serpentine and jumps favourites such as Epatante, Faugheen, Politologue, Envoi Allen, Champ, Samcro and Honeysuckle, plus so many jockeys and trainers who made their mark in the racing world including Jim Crowley, Hollie Doyle, Cieren Fallon, Shane Foley, Barry Geraghty, Brian Hughes, Ger Lyons, Tom Marquand, Johnny Murtagh, Aidan, Joseph and Donnacha O'Brien, Kevin Stott, Roger Teal and Paul Townend. The year will long be remembered by them – and by all of us for good and bad reasons

KEY EXCERPT 'Dettori and Enable will always have Paris but so much more besides' *Lee Mottershead*

ENABLE ALTIOR TIGER ROLL STRADIVARIUS AL BOUM PHOTO BATTAASH

IN THE PICTURE

He Knows No Fear scores record-priced success at 300-1

HE KNOWS NO FEAR became the biggest-priced winner in the history of racing in Ireland or Britain when scoring at 300-1 for trainer-owner Luke Comer and jockey Chris Hayes at Leopardstown on August 13. The previous Irish/British record-holder was Equinoctial (250-1) over jumps at Kelso in November 1990.

In what was effectively He Knows No Fear's first proper race, after the three-year-old had missed the kick on his debut at Limerick the previous month, he was sent off as one of two 300-1 shots in a mile maiden at Leopardstown. The 15-runner line-up also included a 250-1 chance and two more at 200-1. Their long starting prices were a consequence of a big chunk of the market being taken up by the Group-placed maiden Agitare, the even-money favourite.

Agitare looked set for a comfortable first success when he took a clear lead inside the final furlong but He Knows No Fear came flying down the outside in pursuit. While the best of the other longshots finished ninth, beaten more than 11 lengths, the 300-1 shot (*pictured nearside*) made rapid headway and snared Agitare on the line to win by a head.

Comer is one of the richest men in Ireland and his operation is managed by Jim Gorman, who said: "We had a few quid on him each-way at Limerick but he broke so badly, so we didn't really know where we were with him. All of our horses for the past couple of weeks have been running well and they've been knocking on the door."

He Knows No Fear was bred by Comer from his own stallion Mourayan out of the mare Tripudium, who was bought for €5,000 at the sales in 2015. Gorman added: "We knew going to Limerick he was a nice horse and it's great for Luke as it's his own stallion and his own mare – that gives him the biggest thrill."

It was a remarkable year for big-priced winners. Just 18 days before He Knows No Fear's win, Chocquinto (150-1) had set the previous Irish-only Flat record at the Curragh on July 26, while on June 13 Intercessor (200-1) had equalled the previous Irish/British Flat record at Newbury.

Nando Parrado (150-1) set two records when winning the Coventry Stakes at Royal Ascot on June 20. The Clive Cox-trained juvenile became the longest-priced Pattern winner in Britain or Ireland since the Pattern was created in 1971 (Miss Therese, Hittite Glory, Hotbee, Sole Power and Ramone started at 100-1) and also the longest-priced winner ever at Royal Ascot (Fox Chapel and Flashmans Papers were 100-1 shots).

Picture: PATRICK McCANN (RACINGPOST.COM/PHOTOS)

START
FLAT
ABOUT
1 MILE
6 FURLONGS
ALBASTI
EQUIWORLD
9
LEOPARDSTOWN

Nick Pulford and Jonathan Harding with our selection of the horses and people likely to be making headlines in 2021, starting with three top Classic prospects

PRETTY GORGEOUS

MANY signs have pointed to the relentless march of Joseph O'Brien's stable and another appeared on Newmarket's Future Champions card in early October, when he saddled both favourites for the Group 1 juvenile races despite his father Aidan having Ballydoyle runners in opposition.

While Thunder Moon was beaten into third in the Dewhurst Stakes, finishing behind the Ballydoyle pair St Mark's Basilica and Wembley, the younger O'Brien was successful in the Fillies' Mile with the highly promising Pretty Gorgeous.

Having landed his first British Classic with Galileo Chrome in the St Leger the previous month, O'Brien looks well set to go for more in 2021 and Pretty Gorgeous could lead the way. Her half-length victory over Indigo Girl in the Fillies' Mile took her to favouritism for the 1,000 Guineas and she looks the type to train on.

The daughter of Lawman arrived at Newmarket by the traditional route through the Irish fillies' races but France rather than Britain had been the intended destination. She was diverted to the Fillies' Mile only after being withdrawn from the Prix Marcel Boussac the previous weekend owing to the contaminated feed scare.

There was more controversy in the Fillies' Mile with a mix-up over the numbers for the two Ballydoyle runners, but no doubt over the merit of Pretty Gorgeous's success. Having travelled supremely well, she was in front before the furlong pole and kept on strongly to hold off the fast-finishing Indigo Girl.

Back in sixth was Shale, trained by Joseph's younger brother Donnacha, and this result seemed to settle a private battle for supremacy that had gone on for a couple of months. Shale won their first meeting in the Group 3 Silver Flash Stakes at Leopardstown, with Pretty Gorgeous a length and a half behind in second, but then the positions were reversed at the Curragh a fortnight later when Pretty Gorgeous took the Group 2 Debutante Stakes by two and a half lengths.

Their final clash in Ireland came in the Group 1 Moyglare Stud Stakes, again at the Curragh, when Shale got back in front by three-quarters of a length, but at Newmarket there was no sign of a challenge to Pretty Gorgeous from her old rival.

It was an important marker for the 2021 Classics and not least for winning jockey Shane Crosse, who had been forced to miss the St Leger ride on Galileo Chrome after testing positive for Covid-19. The Fillies' Mile was the teenager's first Group 1 success and he can dream of more with Pretty Gorgeous over the winter.

O'Brien's previous Fillies' Mile winner was Iridessa in 2018 and she went on to further top-level

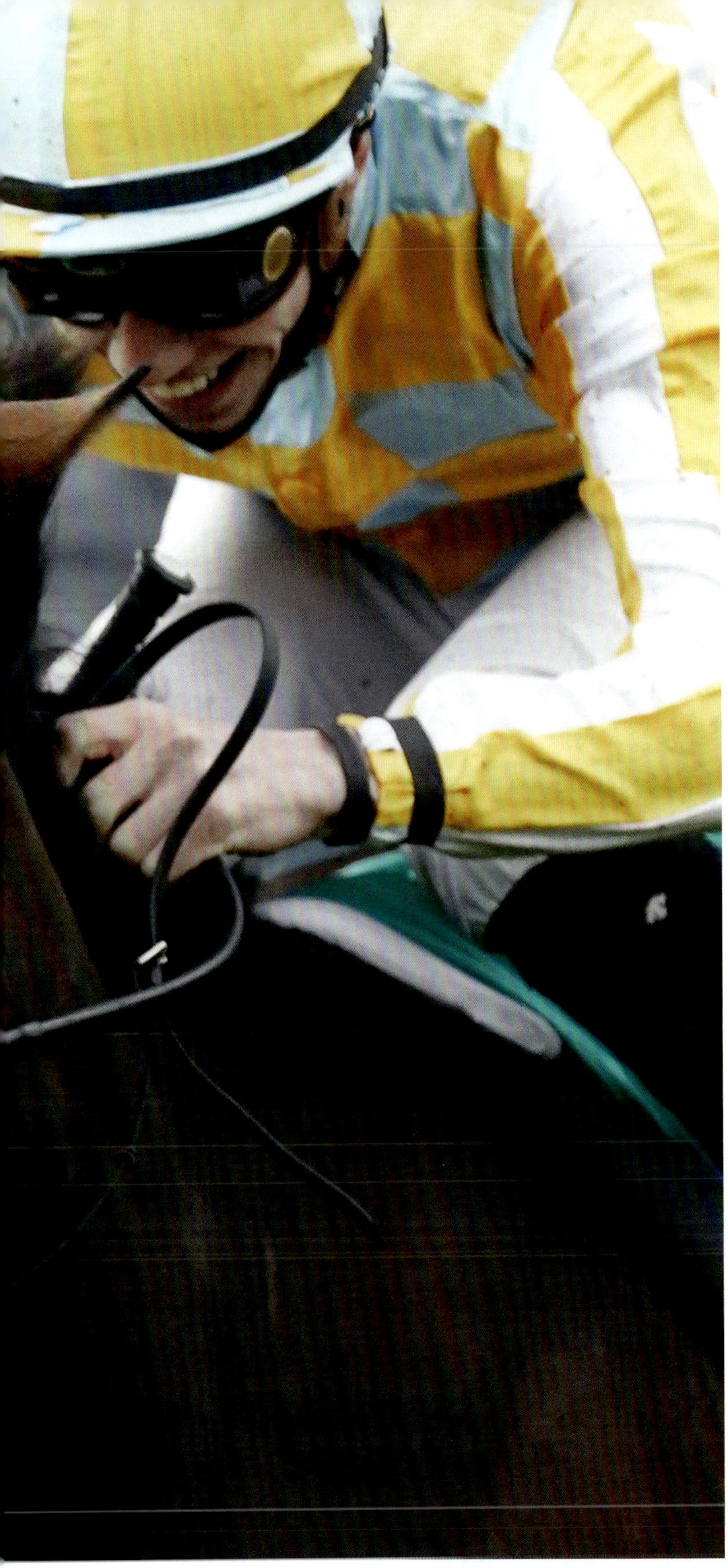

ST MARK'S BASILICA

THE Dewhurst Stakes, as so often, looks likely to be a key form pointer to the Classics and so much so that the first two from the strong 2020 edition are both included in this list.

St Mark's Basilica (*below right*) ran out the winner by three-quarters of a length under Frankie Dettori, making a rare appearance for Aidan O'Brien, with stablemate Wembley second and the favourite Thunder Moon another length and three-quarters back in third.

That was a turnaround from the previous month's Group 1 National Stakes at the Curragh, where Thunder Moon won by a length and a half with Wembley and St Mark's Basilica close together in second and third. Clearly all three have established strong credentials as juveniles.

St Mark's Basilica stepped up his game in the Dewhurst, registering a Racing Post Rating of 121. The draw played a part on the soft ground at Newmarket and Dettori felt the race had fallen right for him, but he was also impressed by the way St Mark's Basilica went about his job.

"They went fast," he said. "I was in the middle of the group and I got all the splits. In fairness, when I asked him to go he went and he never stopped. He didn't put a foot wrong. He would get a mile no problem."

As a half-brother to the 2019 2,000 Guineas winner Magna Grecia, and having cost 1.3 million guineas as a yearling, St Mark's Basilica started his racing career with high expectations of him. His first season has only raised them.

WEMBLEY

WEMBLEY was caught in the middle of the battles for the Group 1 National and Dewhurst Stakes, finishing second to Thunder Moon and then to St Mark's Basilica, but no-one would be surprised if he emerged on top as a three-year-old.

Ryan Moore rode the Aidan O'Brien-trained son of Galileo in the Dewhurst, with Frankie Dettori called up to partner St Mark's Basilica, and he cannot have been disappointed by the performance even if he was beaten three-quarters of a length.

Wembley (*below left*), drawn two, had to challenge widest of all on a day favouring the stands' rail and could not quite peg back his stablemate, who had the advantage of coming from stall 12. Many felt Moore's mount had emerged with plenty of credit, as did third-placed Thunder Moon from his tricky draw in five, and O'Brien was among those who reckoned the form was strong.

"The first three look like they're proper Guineas horses, don't they?" he said. "They have speed and were getting seven furlongs well."

Wembley's sign of stamina reserves was not surprising given that he is a brother to Johannes Vermeer, a Group 1 winner at two and later runner-up in the Melbourne Cup, but there is no lack of speed. Wembley would have been O'Brien's sole Dewhurst contender but for the contaminated feed problems that caused St Mark's Basilica to be rerouted from Longchamp to Newmarket.

Wembley could still turn out to be the best of Ballydoyle.

victories in the Pretty Polly Stakes, Matron Stakes and Breeders' Cup Filly & Mare Turf. The trainer left no doubt he has always expected the aptly named Pretty Gorgeous to take high rank.

"She's an outstanding physical specimen and from the first day she worked she's been impressive at home," he said after the Fillies' Mile. "She's very good, top class."

Her looks came with a 525,000gns price tag at Tattersalls as a yearling, when she was bought by powerful US owner John Oxley, and they have been backed up by racecourse performance. She looks pretty good.

JAMES FERGUSON

THERE can hardly have been a more challenging year to develop a new training business than 2020. Yet despite the severe ramifications of the coronavirus pandemic, a handful of intrepid souls weathered the storm.

James Ferguson, Joseph Parr, Terry Kent and George Boughey had barely got started as trainers before Covid-19 struck and, after surviving the uncertainty of the cessation of racing, they should make more progress next season.

Ferguson began his upward trajectory in 2020 with his first winner in January and he then struck with all three of his runners in February. In June and July, following the resumption, the Newmarket trainer had seven winners from just 27 runners.

"Lockdown was a challenge but I've got a good team and everyone's worked hard to get us through it," said Ferguson, 31, who is the son of former jumps trainer and Godolphin chief executive John Ferguson. "We made sure when we came out of lockdown the horses were ready to go."

Chief among them was the two-year-old Zoetic, who gave Ferguson his first Listed success when winning the St Hugh's Fillies' Stakes at Newbury, before being pitched into the Group 1 Cheveley Park Stakes. "She's turned out to be an absolute superstar who has progressed with every run," said Ferguson, who can map out further ambitious plans for her.

During a period when many were questioning the viability of training, Ferguson, along with his fellow neophyte trainers, managed not only to survive but to thrive in the face of huge adversity.

FLINTEUR SACRE

FLINTEUR SACRE had only one bumper win from two starts before hopes of further progress last season were scuppered by the lockdown, but he had already attracted great interest. The reason is simple: he is a brother to the great Sprinter Sacre and trained, like his illustrious sibling, by Nicky Henderson.

The younger model did not start quite as well as Sprinter Sacre, who won both his bumpers in 2010, but he followed a promising debut second at Newbury in January with an impressive success next time at Kempton. Henderson had raised the possibility of sending him for the Grade 2 bumper at Aintree's Grand National meeting before it was cancelled.

After the Kempton win, he said: "We brought him out quite quickly after his first run as he's been crazy wild at home. He had a nice time at Newbury, he wasn't allowed to have too hard a race there, so all in all it's a good start."

Speaking before his debut, Henderson said: "He's a slightly smaller version of his brother, but he's a quality horse, very good looking. We like him a lot, but I would be nervous about him in very soft ground. He's a very active horse, so it might not suit him."

There is a long way to go before Flinteur Sacre can even approach the heights scaled by Sprinter Sacre, whose nine Grade 1 wins included two Queen Mother Champion Chases and took him to a Racing Post Rating of 190, but his promising start has only added to the interest in his progress.

DYLAN BROWNE McMONAGLE

DYLAN BROWNE McMONAGLE came to prominence as a rider before he even entered his teens and lockdown did nothing to halt his rapid rise through the Irish jockey ranks. Shortly after the resumption of racing he scored the biggest win of his career when striking with Tonkinese in the Apprentice Derby at the Curragh and he continued to impress through the rest of the season.

The pony-riding sensation was the subject of a documentary following his success in the Dingle Derby at the age of 12, which led to him riding out with legendary jockey Sir Anthony McCoy. Now 17, he has been under the watchful eye of another champion rider, Joseph O'Brien, since September 2019 and is clearly learning well.

He really caught fire in August, racking up 11 winners from 61 rides at a strike-rate of 18 per cent, and he added another seven the following month as he reached his first anniversary in the job.

McMonagle was aware of the challenge he faced stepping into the professional game. "I know I'm at the bottom of the barrel now and I have to work my way up again," he said shortly after joining O'Brien. "Hopefully I can do that and keep getting a few winners. Ryan Moore is my favourite jockey. You have Shane Foley, Martin Harley, AP McCoy and Ruby Walsh, who have all given me advice. I just try to take it all on board."

Given the wealth of support around him, McMonagle has a strong base to build on.

UHTRED

UHTRED was ready for a hurdling campaign last season but Joseph O'Brien opted to take his time after one start over obstacles and he could be rewarded for his patient approach this term.

The five-year-old, who runs in the Gigginstown colours, won the big sales bumper at Fairyhouse on his debut in April 2019 and in November he was second to his stablemate Front View in a maiden hurdle at Cork. That was a fair effort as the winner ended the season with a rating of 135.

Uhtred then contested Navan's "Future Champions" bumper, which has an impressive roll of honour including Don Cossack, Samcro and Envoi Allen, and justified favouritism when storming clear by four and a half lengths.

As he did not qualify for the champion bumpers at Cheltenham or Punchestown, he looked set to go back over hurdles, but instead O'Brien chose to give him a lengthy break. Hopes are high that Uhtred can end up at one or more of the major festivals this season.

PRESENTING PERCY

GORDON ELLIOTT put one star of the 2018 Cheltenham Festival back on track with Samcro's revival and in the summer he was handed the chance to do the same with another, when Presenting Percy was transferred to his yard by owner Philip Reynolds.

On the same day Samcro won the Ballymore Novices' Hurdle at the 2018 festival, Presenting Percy took the RSA Insurance Novices' Chase in such convincing style that many felt sure he was a future Gold Cup winner. However, it is Al Boum Photo, a well-held third when falling two out that day, who has gone on to Gold Cup glory on two occasions while Presenting Percy's career has stalled. He was only eighth when favourite for the 2019 Gold Cup and fell two out in last season's race.

That proved to be the nine-year-old's last start for trainer Pat Kelly, who also won the 2017 Pertemps Handicap Hurdle with him at the festival. "It has been a very difficult decision but now is the right time for a change," said Reynolds, announcing the switch to Elliott.

With a Racing Post Rating of 172, achieved in the RSA and again in the Gold Cup despite his fall, Presenting Percy can be aimed high. Speaking on a Betfair podcast in the autumn, Elliott said: "He's being trained for the Gold Cup but I definitely have the English Grand National in the back of my mind. I think he's the type of horse who would suit the race. He's got a lot of class. He travels. He jumps."

Sounds exciting.

MINELLA INDO

CHAMP stole the race and the headlines with his phenomenal finish in the RSA Insurance Novices' Chase, leaving runner-up Minella Indo's connections to rue what might have been with a better jump at the final fence.

The Henry de Bromhead-trained challenger led from Allaho going to the last, with Champ still some way adrift, but he lost vital momentum with an awkward jump and that might have cost him in the end as Champ burst past near the line to win by a length. "He did everything right until the last but just missed that one unfortunately," De Bromhead said. "That may have cost us but who knows? He ran brilliantly."

At least the seven-year-old's fine performance confirmed his liking for Cheltenham, following his 2019 victory in the Albert Bartlett Novices' Hurdle. If there was a shock element to that 50-1 win, he dispelled the notion it was a fluke by following up in the Grade 1 novice hurdle at Punchestown and then with his smooth transition to top-level competition over fences.

The RSA was only the eighth run under rules for Minella Indo, who earned a Racing Post Rating of 166 in defeat and looks capable of climbing higher in his second season over fences.

RAY DAWSON

RAY DAWSON was one of the best claiming riders of the 2020 Flat season in Britain but his name did not appear on the list of leading apprentices. That is because an apprentice has to be aged 16 to 26; at 27, Dawson is classed as a claiming professional until he has ridden enough winners to lose his weight claim.

He seemed in a hurry to do that in 2020, which was easily the most productive year of a career that has taken a long time to get going, and he was in the spotlight with big handicap successes at the Ebor and St Leger meetings.

As Dawson revealed in a frank Racing Post interview in September, the reason for his late arrival on the scene was his long battle with alcoholism and substance abuse.

"My addiction kept taking everything away," he said. "I ended up without a job. I was basically homeless, living in my car and sleeping at people's houses. I was basically waiting to die – I had given up. That's the mindset when you're in the depths of addiction. I wouldn't want to think about where I'd be if I hadn't asked for help two years ago."

Dawson had failed to hold down jobs in Britain and his native Ireland but following an incident in April 2019 he came to a life-saving realisation and finally decided to reach out for help.

"I was drinking quite heavily in the house and I blacked out," he recalled. "I woke up in a police cell, which has happened a number of times, and was informed I had crashed my car. I really thought I might have killed somebody and it was unbelievably scary.

"I was in a lot of trouble but I felt a sense of relief. I knew it was going to be the beginning of me turning my life around. Something clicked. I got out two days later and went to my first AA meeting. I'd just had enough of that life and things have been better since."

Dawson has been sober since then and, after scoring aboard Tranchee at Doncaster in September in front of the ITV cameras, he used his new platform to encourage others to reach out for help. The jockey also discussed his experiences in a powerful video alongside his weighing-room colleague Kieran Shoemark.

"My advice for others is not to be scared and to trust people, especially in racing," Dawson said. Having taken that brave step, he has his life and his riding career back on track.

THE BIG BREAKAWAY

COLIN TIZZARD sent a promising team to the Cheltenham Festival, including several fancied novices, but came away empty-handed and then had no opportunity to seek better fortune at Aintree or any other of the big spring meetings.

The Dorset trainer later had a possible explanation for the festival disappointments – "From Christmas onwards we had a few of our horses not running too well. We had a few dirty noses" – and said he was worried after Fiddlerontheroof, joint-third favourite for the Supreme Novices' Hurdle, was only 11th in the curtain-raiser.

In the circumstances The Big Breakaway performed with credit to finish fourth in a strong-looking Ballymore Novices' Hurdle, beaten by Envoi Allen, Easywork and The Big Getaway. He went there with only two hurdles starts, having missed Trials Day at Cheltenham after banging a hock, and was inconvenienced by the leisurely gallop, which did not pick up until the final half-mile.

Considering the Albert Bartlett over three miles had been a serious option, the sedate pace was against The Big Breakaway, who at the age of five still has plenty of improvement to come, especially over fences and a longer trip.

"We're spoiled with novice hurdlers, they're the best we've had," was Tizzard's view going into the 2020 festival, and he added: "It's good for the next few seasons too." The Big Breakaway may well be one who really starts to show what his trainer meant.

SAINT ROI

SAINT ROI is a County Handicap Hurdle winner and the answer to a racing trivia question – who was the last of Barry Geraghty's 43 Cheltenham Festival winners? – but he might well be more than that.

The five-year-old had run just twice over hurdles for Willie Mullins before Cheltenham, winning only a maiden hurdle at Tramore in January, but he looked much better than a handicapper with his dominant victory in a strongly run County.

Eased into the race by Geraghty, he was going best of the four horses in a line over the last and powered up the hill to score by a convincing four and a half lengths.

Thousand Stars, Wicklow Brave and Arctic Fire – three of Mullins' previous four County winners – were Grade 1 scorers before or after the event and Saint Roi has the potential to compete at that level.

Geraghty said after the County: "There was a good vibe for this horse, who was unexposed. Willie was sweet and he's not a bad judge. I rode him at Willie's in the autumn and he was a lovely, sweet-travelling type, but to jump as well as he did when so inexperienced and going at pace was impressive. He was electric."

The County form was franked in no uncertain terms when runner-up Aramon, also trained by Mullins, took the Galway Hurdle in dominant style under top weight in July. Saint Roi's reputation went up another notch even in his absence and he looks set to rise much higher still.

INDIGO GIRL

FOUR of the last five Fillies' Mile winners have gone on to further Group 1 success in later life but the record of placed runners is also impressive and Indigo Girl, this year's runner-up, is one to note.

The John Gosden-trained daughter of Dubawi could not quite catch Pretty Gorgeous up the hill at Newmarket but her powerful finish indicated she would be suited by a strongly run 1,000 Guineas as well as by a step up in distance as a three-year-old.

Bred and owned by George Strawbridge, she is a sister to Journey, who was more of a late developer but ended up as a Group 1 winner over a mile and a half.

Indigo Girl is rated highly by Gosden. "I see her more as a mile to a mile-and-a-quarter filly," he said after she won the Group 2 May Hill Stakes at Doncaster in September. "She travels strongly and has a great turn of foot."

Indigo Girl showed that again in the Fillies' Mile and, even though she came up short then, Gosden looks to have another winner in the long game.

TOPOFTHEGAME

PAUL NICHOLLS erred on the side of caution and gave Topofthegame a season on the sidelines following a tendon injury but, a year later than planned, the aim now is the Cheltenham Gold Cup.

Last season ended before it began for Topofthegame, who had belied his inexperience and jumped beautifully to land the 2019 RSA Chase from Santini and Delta Work. His first target as a second-season chaser was the Ladbrokes Trophy, for which he was favourite, but he picked up a minor injury and Nicholls put the brakes on. This season he hopes to reap the reward of his careful handling.

While Topofthegame was away, his novice form looked ever stronger. Delta Work won Ireland's big two Grade 1 chases over three miles last season and Santini was runner-up to Al Boum Photo in the Gold Cup, with Delta Work fifth.

In addition, Lostintranslation, who had beaten Topofthegame into second in the Mildmay Novices' Chase at Aintree, stepped up to win the Betfair Chase and finish third in the Gold Cup.

Those formlines put Topofthegame in the mix to throw down a strong challenge to the established order and, before injury intervened, Nicholls said the towering son of Flemensfirth had a "serious chance" of making it to the top.

"He strikes me as an ideal Gold Cup horse," said Nicholls, who has won the race four times. "He travels beautifully, jumps and stays, and those are the qualities you need. He beat Santini fair and square, and the third horse boosted the form, so the first three at Cheltenham all look top class.

"Look at his early form. Any horse capable of giving Defi Du Seuil the best part of 25 lengths start, as Topofthegame did at Exeter [as a novice in December 2018], and then get within four lengths of him, must be a serious horse."

Following the eight-year-old's return to training, Nicholls said: "He's been so big and backward that a bit of time off won't have done him any harm – it was only a minor injury. He's not the easiest to train but a lot of the good ones aren't. When you get him right, he's obviously very good."

For a second opinion, there is Henrietta Knight's view when asked to pick the most exciting chasers for the new season. "The dark horse could be Topofthegame, who looked exciting when beating Santini in the RSA Chase," said the three-time Gold Cup-winning former trainer. "He's had a year off, but if 100 per cent he could be anything."

ONE RULER

THE Autumn Stakes at Newmarket's Future Champions meeting may be only a Group 3 but there is no doubting the high regard in which it is held by Godolphin.

The blue brigade have won four of the last five runnings – most notably in 2017 with Ghaiyyath – and the one winner they did not own was quickly switched to their colours. He was Persian King, the 2018 scorer, who went on to win the French 2,000 Guineas and finish third in the 2020 Prix de l'Arc de Triomphe.

Much interest, then, will surround One Ruler, their latest Autumn winner. Trained, like Ghaiyyath, by Charlie Appleby, he scored an impressive victory on soft ground in the mile contest by a length and three-quarters from Ballydoyle runner Van Gogh.

Jockey William Buick found plenty to like in One Ruler's display, saying: "Stepping up to a mile in this ground was a bit of a worry as he shows plenty of speed. That was a real good performance as he was last off the bridle and we know he likes better ground. I think he'll get further, maybe a mile and a quarter next year."

The Autumn was good; next spring and summer could be even better.

SHISHKIN

AL BOUM PHOTO is not the only star in Joe and Marie Donnelly's yellow and black checked colours, which have become increasingly prominent in big jump races over the last four years. Shishkin was their other winner at the 2020 Cheltenham Festival and he looks to be heading for the top too.

The six-year-old's narrow victory over Abacadabras in the Supreme Novices' Hurdle (*right*) confirmed his speed and courage, and plenty more besides. The Racing Post headline on the race report was "Against all odds" and that summed up Shishkin's performance perfectly.

Not only had overnight rain made the ground more testing than ideal, the Nicky Henderson-trained 6-1 shot made a mistake at the third hurdle and lost his place at the top of the hill. He was as big as 99-1 in running after coming mighty close to being brought down in a melee two out, where two rivals crashed out, but his electric turn of foot got him out of trouble. He quickened to catch Abacadabras 100 yards from home and gamely held his renewed challenge by a head.

The manner of victory marked him out as something special and so did the comments of his jockey Nico de Boinville. "That showed a bit of superstar quality," he said. "Everything conspired against him but he managed to find a way and that's what champions tend to do. He's so talented. He has tremendous gears and gets you out of an awful lot of trouble. It might be that we've found another really good one."

Shishkin, an Irish point-to-point winner in November 2018 who was bought for £170,000 the following month, is an exciting chasing prospect for the Donnellys, who have acquired an elite team of jump horses in recent years.

Joe Donnelly was an influential force in Irish bookmaking before selling his business in 2002, by which time he was already a wealthy man through shrewd investment in property and art. That portfolio has grown since the couple moved to France around 15 years ago and has now expanded into jump racing. Their other runners at the 2020 festival included Melon, beaten a nose by Samcro in the Grade 1 Marsh Novices' Chase, and Supreme fourth Asterion Forlonge.

A 'nothing but the best' strategy is also evident in their choice of champion trainers Willie Mullins and Henderson, who said of the latest star: "Only a good horse could get out of the trouble Shishkin did." He might be underplaying it; Shishkin could be very good indeed.

GAVIN RYAN

GAVIN RYAN was the go-to apprentice in Ireland, riding for many of the big stables in a winner-packed 2020, and the future looks bright for the 20-year-old even after his claim has gone.

His best moments included the leading rider award at the Galway festival with five winners for three different trainers, and a first Pattern win aboard Shale in the Group 3 Silver Flash Stakes at Leopardstown, where he was unable to use his 5lb claim for his boss Donnacha O'Brien but still came out on top by a length and a half.

Galway is arguably the trickiest track in Ireland to ride but Ryan lit up the festival. The pick of the bunch was his smash-and-grab raid on Saltonstall in the Colm Quinn BMW Mile Handicap on day two. That was one of three winners

during the week for Ado McGuinness and he also scored for O'Brien and Dermot Weld.

Ryan was a shrewd pick-up by O'Brien in his first season as a trainer and he has a high opinion of his young rider, who was previously with Jim Bolger.

"I think Gavin is very promising," O'Brien said. "He's clever, he's sharp, he's got a good brain, he's strong, he's good with both hands. Some lads just come through and you can see the way they think and you know they have a chance of being proper riders. I think he's one that everyone can see that in."

Ryan, having been under the tutelage of two masters, has learned well.

SUPREMACY

MEHMAS was the first-season sire sensation of 2020, having produced a crop rich in winners and promise, and Supremacy became his first Group 1 winner when he landed the Middle Park Stakes at Newmarket in September. The Clive Cox-trained speedball might well be a flagbearer for his sire as a three-year-old too.

Cox likes nothing better than a top sprinter and in 2020 he completed the hat-trick of Group 1 sprints at Royal Ascot when Golden Horde won the Commonwealth Cup, adding to the trainer's successes in the Diamond Jubilee Stakes with Lethal Force (2013) and King's Stand Stakes with Profitable (2016). Now he has Supremacy, who looks a natural for the Commonwealth Cup.

The son of Mehmas followed a similar path to Golden Horde as a two-year-old and came out better than his year-older stablemate on form. While both won the Richmond Stakes at Goodwood, a favourite target for Cox, Golden Horde was just beaten in the Middle Park whereas Supremacy made all at Newmarket and scored by half a length from Lucky Vega.

That earned Supremacy a Racing Post Rating of 118, 2lb better than Golden Horde at the same stage, and Cox left no doubt he expects him to rise higher. "He's a complete speedball," he said. "I'm really excited about him because I think he's got more developing and strengthening to do over the winter. He's pure class."

Words worth heeding from a sprint master.

JACK TUDOR

WHEN racing shut down in March, Jack Tudor was two chase winners short of the required number that would have allowed him to ride Potters Corner in the Grand National at Aintree. Christian Williams, Potters Corner's trainer, was confident his young conditional rider would have got there before the big day and Tudor is qualified now, having quickly built up his tally since the return of jump racing.

That raises the exciting prospect of teaming up again with Potters Corner, who gave Tudor – then claiming 7lb – a huge win at the age of 17 in the Welsh Grand National last December. "When you're Welsh, to win a Welsh National is one of the things you want to do," said Tudor, who is from Merthyr Mawr near Bridgend. "This is massive and for Christian and the owners to stick with me proves how good they are to me."

Williams had no hesitation in putting Tudor on board. "The safe option would have been to put a professional on but I knew Jack was capable and he was brilliant," he said.

Tudor's family is steeped in point-to-pointing – cousin James Tudor landed the Kim Muir aboard High Chimes at the 2008 Cheltenham Festival – and Williams reckons he could follow the path of James Bowen, another young Welsh National winner of recent times.

With Williams and Potters Corner on his side, Tudor could not have had a better start to his career.

STONEY MOUNTAIN

STONEY MOUNTAIN had been among the most promising young jumpers in Trevor Hemmings' famous emerald green and yellow quarters but he is now racing in new colours following the three-time Grand National-winning owner's decision to reduce his string to around 25 horses, a third of its previous size.

Hemmings, who lives on the Isle of Man, said the coronavirus pandemic was a driving factor in 56 of his horses going to a dispersal sale at Doncaster in September. "It has been a difficult decision but the reality is that I'm 85 years of age and a diabetic on insulin. Covid-19 has severely restricted my movements as I'm classed as high-risk. Attending race meetings, even with limited attendance, would not be possible," he said.

The dispersal generated £1.1m and the most highly valued was Stoney Mountain, bought by bloodstock agent Tom Malone for £140,000. Malone said the seven-year-old would join Jamie Snowden's yard, having previously been trained by Henry Daly for Hemmings.

"The form is in the book," Malone said. "He's a Grade 3-winning and Grade 2-placed hurdler who's been bought to go novice chasing. He's just a lovely horse to go Saturday racing with."

After the sale, Hemmings said: "I wish the new owners the very best of luck with the horses. I will watch their progress with interest and cheer every win."

One who looks set to raise plenty of cheers is Stoney Mountain.

A-Z of 2020

The year digested into 26 bite-size chunks

J

W

A is for ampersand, as in fathers and sons Simon & Ed Crisford and Paul & Oliver Cole, after training partnerships were allowed in Britain for the first time. The Coles created a slice of British racing history when Valpolicella's win at Newmarket on June 4 made them the first partnership to strike.

B is for better late than never. The 2,000 Guineas (June 6) and 1,000 Guineas (June 7) were run on their latest dates ever, five weeks after their intended slots, and the Derby was delayed by four weeks until July 4. Even tardier, the Kentucky Derby took place four months behind schedule in September.

C is for contamination. After the prohibited substance Zilpaterol was found in batches of feed supplied by Gain Equine Nutrition, several horses were sensationally withdrawn as a precautionary step on Arc weekend, most notably Aidan O'Brien's declared quartet for the big race – Mogul, Japan, Sovereign and Serpentine.

D is for dominance. Stradivarius ruled the staying division again as he became the first four-time winner of the Goodwood Cup, equalling the record for the most wins in a European Group 1, and took a third Gold Cup at Royal Ascot.

G

E is for eggs. Trainers, jockeys and owners all joined in the 'fun' of the raw egg challenge as part of the Do It For Dan campaign to raise money for one-year-old Dan Donoher, who suffers from a rare neuromuscular disease. Robert Cowell downed his egg from the Prix de l'Abbaye winning trainer's trophy, while Grand National-winning trainer Oliver Sherwood mixed his with vodka.

F is for Furlong Factor. Eighty people from all areas of the sport took part in racing's most tuneful response to the pandemic. Cheltenham racecourse regional manager Lara Telfer was crowned the winner of the singing competition, which passed its target of raising £50,000 for Racing Welfare's Covid-19 Emergency Appeal.

G is for gone too soon. Grand National-winning rider Liam Treadwell (*left, on Mon Mome*), 34, and James Banks, 36, another former jump jockey, both died tragically young, starkly highlighting the issue of mental health in racing.

H is for hairdressing. Saleem Golam, joint champion apprentice in 2005 with Hayley Turner, swapped boots and saddle for comb and scissors to become a barber. "Being a jockey is a great thing but it was time to start thinking outside the box to move on," said the 37-year-old after passing a course at the London School of Barbering in August.

I is for incroyable, used in the Racing Post headline after Princess Zoe's wonderful win in the Prix du Cadran. Incroyable, incredible, it was amazing in any language.

J is for June, the month British and Irish racing came out of their 11-week shutdowns. Let's not talk about April and May.

K is for kids' stuff. Aidan O'Brien's sons Joseph and Donnacha both won Classics thanks to Galileo Chrome and Fancy Blue.

L is for lost. Many big races were moved in a reshaped racing calendar following lockdown but some never made it to the 2020 record books, including the Grand National at Aintree, the Scottish version at Ayr, and the Group 1 Lockinge Stakes on the Flat.

M is for mum's the word. Jessica Marcialis, who returned to race-riding after having her son Leo, now 3, made French racing history with her Group 1 win on Tiger Tanaka in the Prix Marcel Boussac.

N is for new deal. Following a marathon period of negotiations, ITV finally agreed an extension of its partnership with racing until at least the end of 2023. The deal with Racecourse Media Group, Ascot and Arena Racing Company values racing's terrestrial rights in the region of £8-9 million per year, an increase on the £7.5m under the previous agreement.

O is for outsiders. In a bumper year for big-priced winners, records were set by He Knows No Fear at 300-1 and Nando Parrado, a 150-1 shot at Royal Ascot.

P is for prize-money. There was much less of it as racecourses faced up to a world in which a major chunk of their income was cut off by Covid. Not all 'horsemen' were happy, but without paying customers, hospitality and non-raceday activities, tracks were forced to cut purses. The Levy Board rode to racing's rescue but stressed it could not do so indefinitely.

Q is for quitting. Newmarket trainer Ed Vaughan cited British racing's prize-money crisis as the driving factor when he announced in July he would be wrapping up his 16-year career at the end of the Flat season. "I wouldn't rule out training elsewhere, but I just don't see a future for doing that in the UK," he said. Only a week earlier he had recorded the biggest success of his career when Dame Malliot won the Group 2 Princess of Wales's Stakes at Newmarket.

R is for Racing League. The long-mooted team competition got the go-ahead for 2021 – one year later than originally planned – when six meetings will be run on consecutive Thursdays starting in late July, offering total prize-money of £1.8 million. There will be 12 teams, each consisting of two to four trainers, three jockeys and 30 horses. Each of the 36 races, all 12-runner 0-90 handicaps over varying distances, will be worth £50,000.

S is for Slade. The glam rock band's Get Down And Get With It was revealed to be Mark Johnston's ringtone when he became the latest racing celebrity to appear on Desert Island Discs in June. Billy Joel, Dire Straits and Fleetwood Mac also featured, while his book was The Count of Monte Cristo by Alexandre Dumas and his luxury item was binoculars.

T is for three-peat. Enable in the King George and One Master in the Prix de la Foret completed historic hat-tricks, but Tiger Roll was denied his opportunity in the Grand National.

U is for unholy row. Having been in the job for less than a year, group chief executive Delia Bushell left the Jockey Club in the most explosive and acrimonious fashion. An independent barrister's report upheld extremely serious allegations about her conduct, while Bushell, in turn, ripped the Jockey Club to shreds in her response. Even by the standards of racing politics this was extraordinary.

V is for virtual. The CGI version of the Grand National took the place of the real thing on April 4 and secured by a huge margin the sport's biggest television audience of the year, with 4.8m watching on ITV, while the betting profits raised £2.6m for NHS Charities Together.

W is for Windsor, scene of another record-breaking feat by Hollie Doyle when she rode an 899-1 five-timer in August. W is also for wow!

X is for ex-race. The novice handicap chase was axed from the Cheltenham Festival, to be replaced in 2021 by the Mrs Paddy Power Mares' Chase, a Grade 2 event over two and a half miles.

Y is for youthful exuberance. A number of young jockeys shot to prominence on the Flat and chief among them were 22-year-old Tom Marquand, who landed his first Classic aboard Galileo Chrome in the St Leger, and Cieren Fallon, a Group 1 winner for the first time in the July Cup.

Z is for Zoom. The video conferencing technology was one of the big winners of lockdown, keeping families and workers connected, and in racing it became a vital tool for ownership groups, press conferences and ITV Racing's coverage.

RACING POST ANNUAL AWARDS

Our pick of the best of 2020

HORSE OF THE YEAR (FLAT)
Ghaiyyath
The glory to go with the power as he put together a string of world-class performances

HORSE OF THE YEAR (JUMPS)
Al Boum Photo
Doubled down on his Gold Cup mastery by fighting off a pack of new challengers

RACE OF THE YEAR (FLAT)
Irish Champion Stakes
Simply Magical as Ghaiyyath was beaten

RACE OF THE YEAR (JUMPS)
Marsh Novices' Chase
A rip-roaring battle between Samcro and Melon, with Faugheen snapping at their heels

RIDE OF THE YEAR (FLAT)
Emmet McNamara, Serpentine, Derby
Carpe diem: the ride of his life with a brilliant piece of front-running that took social distancing to extremes

RIDE OF THE YEAR (JUMPS)
Barry Geraghty, Champ, RSA Chase
One of Geraghty's final rides and one of his finest with a dramatic late power grab

RISING STAR
Hollie Doyle
Winning friends and influencing people with another barrier-breaking year

COMEBACK OF THE YEAR
Samcro
Doubted even by his own team, he rose again with a thrilling Cheltenham triumph

SURPRISE OF THE YEAR
He Knows No Fear, the 300-1 shot who doused a hot favourite and made history

UNLUCKIEST HORSE
Tiger Roll
History beckoned until his shot at a Grand National hat-trick was shut down

MOST IMPROVED HORSE
Princess Zoe
From 64-rated beaten handicapper to Group 1 winner in less than four months

DISAPPOINTMENT OF THE YEAR
Only two horses turning up to take on Enable in the King George

BEST 'I WAS THERE' MOMENT
There's nothing quite like the Cheltenham roar, even if we knew what was around the corner

BEST 'I WISH I COULD HAVE BEEN THERE' MOMENT
Take your pick. Ours is Royal Ascot, especially with the extra six races this year

▲ Memorable moments: clockwise from top left, Ghaiyyath, Al Boum Photo, Magical v Ghaiyyath in the Irish Champion Stakes, Champ on his way to victory in the RSA Chase, the roar of the Cheltenham Festival, Princess Zoe, Samcro and Hollie Doyle